T0297698

Wired for Speech

Wired for Speech

How Voice Activates and Advances the Human-Computer Relationship

Clifford Nass and Scott Brave

The MIT Press
Cambridge, Massachusetts
London, England

First MIT Press paperback edition, 2007

This book was set in Stone Serif and Stone Sans by SNP Best-set Typesetter Ltd., Hong Kong.

Library of Congress Cataloging-in-Publication Data

Nass, Clifford Ivar.
Wired for speech : how voice activates and advances the human-computer relationship / Clifford Nass, Scott Brave.
p. cm.
Includes bibliographical references and index.
ISBN-13 978-0-262-14092-8 (hc. : alk. paper)—978-0-262-64065-7 (pbk. : alk. paper)
1. Automatic speech recognition. 2. Human-computer interaction. 3. User interfaces (Computer systems) I. Brave, Scott. II. Title.

TK7895.S65N367 2005
004'.01'9—dc22

2004065645

The MIT Press is pleased to keep this title available in print by manufacturing single copies, on demand, via digital printing technology.

To my mentors:
Florence Nass, Jules Nass, and Michael Jay Nass
James Beniger and Steven Chaffee
Barbara Levitt and Matthew Levitt Nass
—Clifford Nass

To my family:
Ron, Patti, and Jamie Brave. Their love and support make every dream possible.
—Scott Brave

Contents

Preface

Wired for Speech: How Voice Activates and Advances the Human-Computer Relationship represents the culmination of ten years of research into the psychology and design of voice interfaces by Clifford Nass and his coworkers at Stanford University. Scott Brave joined the laboratory as a Ph.D. student in 1999 and, since graduating in June 2003, has continued as a postdoctoral scholar and integral member of the team.

Until 1996—when Cliff's first book (coauthored with Byron Reeves), *The Media Equation: How People Treat Computers, Television, and New Media Like Real People and Places*, appeared—the laboratory focused on textual and graphical user interfaces. Soon after, many companies and researchers turned their attention to interfaces that talked and listened. Voice-interface technology was not quite ready for prime time, but most agreed that it was "worth watching." Computers were routinely shipping with speakers; using interactive voice systems was proving to be more cost-effective than hiring additional workers for call centers; and efficient and inexpensive technologies for digital signal processing enabled voice interfaces to appear in cars, toys, and appliances.

Unfortunately, because little theoretical research or practical guidance was available on creating successful voice interfaces, most voice interactions with technology were frustrating and ineffective. The juxtaposition of the clear need for better interfaces and the opportunity for fundamental research in an intriguing and unexplored area was irresistible to our lab. Furthermore, the lab was in a unique position to make significant contributions: its focus has always been the *social* aspects of human-technology interactions, and nothing is more social than speech.

Unfortunately, building voice interfaces with which to test our theories was difficult. For the most part, technologies that could talk and listen required a tremendous amount of nurturance from engineers and were expensive and difficult to use. Even if we could assemble the requisite staff and funding, we could not craft new experiments with the necessary speed. The impediments seemed insurmountable until 2000, when the CSLU Toolkit appeared on the scene. This remarkable and free piece of software—available when voice extensible mark-up language (VXML) didn't yet exist—enabled virtually anyone to create synthetic speech files, perform voice recognition, produce lip-synch with a synthetic face, and even build a telephone call center.

Because we wanted to answer as many questions and train as many voice-interface researchers as quickly as we could, Cliff created an intensive, ten-week course that focused on design and execution of voice-interface experiments (Scott was a researcher in the class). The course was divided into nine research groups of three students each. Based on research concerning successful teams, we opted for maximum diversity: each group included at least one student from engineering, one student from the social sciences, one Ph.D. student, one undergraduate student, one male student, and one female student. At the start of the course, the groups were shown approximately thirty open questions in the research on voice interfaces that involved psychological as well as design issues. Students were told, "Meet early and often with your group, pick a question, design a relevant experiment, run it, analyze the results, and create a presentation that summarizes your findings. You have ten weeks." Cliff forgot to tell the groups and the teaching assistant, Eva Jettmar, that this was an impossible task, but (as Stanford students tend to do) they went beyond meeting the requirements of the course and produced research that was worthy of scientific and industry attention.

The abundance of compelling results prompted Cliff to invite industry and academic leaders to a two-hour presentation by the student groups, which was attended by seventy-five people from forty companies and universities from throughout the world. The significant and exciting discoveries concerning how people behave with and think about voice technology (many of which were subsequently published) coupled with the enthusiastic responses from industry encouraged researchers at the lab to continue with additional experiments that investigated human interactions with voice technologies.

At the same time that the laboratory was producing its insights, Cliff was independently pursuing the design of a number of voice interfaces for Microsoft (its AutoPC and CD-ROM products), BMW (a voice interface for the Five Series in the United States, Germany, and Japan), IBM (a corporate training system), Philips (a movie-selection system, Voices in Your Hand), Fidelity (a stock-ordering system in Japan), US West (a voice-mail system), Verizon (call centers), General Magic (the Portico Virtual Assistant), and OMRON (a factory automation system). This activity provided inspiration for basic research questions and sensitized the lab to the day-to-day issues that designers face.

Wired for Speech describes and synthesizes our research on voice interfaces in terms of how the human brain is activated by voice and how computers can best relate to us. This book is filled with general principles, specific examples, rigorous experiments, and "fascinating facts to know and tell." *Wired for Speech* should enable anyone who is interested in the present and future of voice products and services to understand their promise and pitfalls, scientists to refine their research on the psychology of voices and voice-based technology, and designers and marketers to produce interfaces that engage and support users rather than frustrate them.

Acknowledgments

Although we are responsible for the contents of this book, we have enlisted the members of our lab in reviewing every chapter for accuracy, utility, and readability. Their comments were invaluable, and it is hard to imagine a more talented, engaged, or helpful group of students (in alphabetical order): Elizabette Amaral, Brent Bannon, Stephen Boxwell, David Danielson, Hernan Gouet, Laura Granka, John Hu, Wendy Ju, Jong-Eun Roselyn Lee, Heidy Maldonado, Shailo Rao, Erica Robles, Leila Takayama, and QianYing Wang. In addition to these students, we were also fortunate to have six scholars (Ron Brave in engineering, Howie Giles in communication, Eve Clark in linguistics, Randy Harris in English, Barbara Levitt in sociology, and Teenie Matlock in psychology of language) thoroughly review the content and form of the entire manuscript and share their advice and insights with us. Particular thanks go to Randy Harris, who, although we had never met or even communicated, did a brilliant line-edit on the manuscript and provided numerous substantive ideas. Finally, we are thankful to the many scholars and friends who have commented on some or all of the manuscript: Jeremy Bailenson, Courtney Bennett, Celeste Biever, Cynthia Breazeal, Herb Clark, Ron Cole, Victoria Groom, Jim Hieronymous, Ronit Kampf, Jennifer Lai, Benjamin Levitt, Debbie Lieberman, Henry Lieberman, Kathy Lung, Dominic Massaro, John McIntosh, John Mullennix, Matthew Levitt Nass, Sung-Gwan Park, Barney Pell, Rosalind Picard, Jo Sanders, Syed Shariq, Ron Shipper, Mark Thompson, Gerald Watanabe, George White, and Kip Williams.

We also want to thank the people who worked on the experiments described in detail in this book: Courtney Bennett, Armen Berjikly, Hilary Bienenstock, Paul Carney, D. Christopher Dryer, Jack Endo, Ulla Foehr, B. J. Fogg, Li Gong, Nancy Green, Helen Harris, Charles Heenan, John Hu, Amy Huang, Katherine Isbister, Kimi Iwamura, Eva Jettmar, Ing-Marie Jonsson, Hadyn Kernal, Eun-Ju Lee, Francis Lee, Kwan-Min Lee, Youngme Moon, Yasunori Morishima, John Morkes, Sheba Najmi, Young Paik, Ben Reaves, Byron Reeves, Erica Robles, Caroline Simard, Michael Somoza,

Jonathan Steuer, Luke Swartz, Janice Ta, Leila Takayama, Yuri Takhteyev, Marissa Treinen, David Voelker, QianYing Wang, and Corrine Yates.

The research in this book has benefited from a successful model of university-industry collaboration that is grounded in no-strings-attached gifts rather than formal contracts. We appreciate the many companies that have trusted that bold, unfettered exploration would provide a better return on investment than university contracts. In response to this trust and support, everyone in our lab has devoted significant time and energy to thinking about how our discoveries and other social science and human-technology-interaction discoveries could be applied to the companies' particular information products and services. For example, companies have come to us and said, "We're really not sure about the following aspect of this product. What do you think?" While sometimes we have simply turned to the literature and rattled off the answer, in other cases, we have said, "Your question is actually an example of a larger, basic question in the social sciences that is extremely interesting and not well understood. We'll do the basic research, answering not only your initial question but also some other questions that you are likely to be interested in." This university-industry relationship has been a key source of ideas for many of the studies that are reported in *Wired for Speech*. We gratefully acknowledge the following companies that have taken part in this approach: Analog Devices, Inc., BMW, Boeing, Charles Schwab, Cisco, Deutsche Telecom, Fuji Xerox, General Magic, GlaxoSmithKline, IBM, Iizuka City, Intel, Intuit, Macromedia, Mattel/Fisher-Price, Motorola, NHK, Nokia, NTT, OMRON, PARC, Philips, Reuters, SABRE, SAP Labs, Scottish Enterprise, Sesame Workshop, Steelcase, SRI, Toyota, US Bank, US West, and Yamatake.

We have also benefited from the support of various university-based and public entities: the Center for Integrated Systems, Stanford University; the Center for Spoken Language Research, University of Colorado at Boulder; the Center for Spoken Language Understanding, Oregon Graduate Institute; the European Union Sixth Programme; and the National Science Foundation. Three entities at Stanford have provided us with a supportive environment for interdisciplinary research that has included intellectual stimulation, space, and financial support: the Department of Communication, the Center for the Study of Language and Information (CSLI), and MediaX.

A few individuals outside of Stanford played crucial roles in support of this research. Ron Cole and Jacques de Villiers provided tremendous support for the CSLU Toolkit. Dom Massaro similarly provided tremendous support for the Baldi face. Jack Endo (Toyota), Karen Fries (Microsoft), Eric Horvitz (Microsoft), Kimi Iwamura (OMRON), and Dale Stolizka (Analog Devices) have solved numerous problems.

We have been blessed with an extraordinary administrative staff. Joan Ferguson, our current administrator, enables us to give no thought whatsoever to managing research, money, students, or calendar: it just magically happens. Kathy Lung did a brilliant job as our prior administrator and organized the seminal industry get-together as well as many other events. The department manager, Barbara Kataoka, has managed the chaos of the diverse funding sources with remarkable inventiveness and aplomb: her motto has always been, "Let's figure out how to make this work." Susie Ementon, student services administrator, coped with the lab's rapidly changing deployment of Ph.D. students with creativity and patience. Kathleen Magner somehow made sure that all of our equipment was where it was supposed to be. Mark Urbanek and Norman Porticella provided technical support with skill and cheerfulness well beyond the call of duty. Adelaide Dawes, Keith Devlin, Christina Doering, Junco Norton, Roy Pea, Emma Pease, Najwa Salame, and Bob Smith have played key supporting roles via MediaX.

A number of people played key roles in the process of turning a manuscript into a book. Drue Kataoka create the Sumi-e creation *Ancient Spiral Anew*, which does a marvelous job of capturing the themes and spirit of *Wired for Speech*. The staff at MIT Press have been extraordinarily helpful and a delight to work with. Doug Sery was committed to this book from inception to sale, patiently addressing all of our questions and requests and facilitating the process at every step of the way; we can't imagine a better editor. Deborah Cantor-Adams was the production editor of the book, ensuring excellence, speed, and continuity. Rosemary Winfield was a ferocious and rigorous copy editor, leaving virtually no sentence untouched. Yasuyo Iguchi patiently and artfully dealt with all of our ideas for the cover, inspiring and laying out the final version. Tobiah Waldron created a thorough and detailed subject index. Finally, Susan Clark did a fabulous job on the marketing content.

Cliff initially brought in a postdoctoral scholar, Courtney Bennett, to move the book forward. Courtney did a wonderful job laying down the basic structure of the book, establishing the writing style, drafting chapter 1, and providing material for many other chapters. Unfortunately, running the laboratory proved extremely time-consuming for Cliff, and Courtney's superb foundation lay dormant for over a year. In one week in 2003, three events occurred that dramatically altered the course of the book. First, Robert (Robin) McNeil invited Cliff to feature the lab's research in an upcoming PBS series, *Do You Speak American?* Second, Doug Sery offered to facilitate publication of the book in any way possible. Third, and most important, Scott Brave decided not to take a faculty position and instead to stay with the laboratory as a postdoctoral scholar. The omens were clear: the book's time had come.

Cliff's Personal Acknowledgments

Although I have a tremendous number of wonderful colleagues at Stanford, a few deserve special mention in this book. Byron Reeves is a dear friend and a continuing influence on my research as well as on my fundamental understanding of how people interact with media. He has also played a key role as the director of both CSLI and Media-X. George White was the amazingly prescient scholar who continually urged me to study voice interfaces and provided valuable insights. Larry Leifer not only convinced me that running a course with small teams of students could be successful; he also taught me the tricks of the trade. Although we have chatted only once, Mark Lepper changed the direction of my research by urging me to pursue the study of behaviors as well as attitudes. Dikran Karaguezian initiated this book project; his love of books and authors provided me with the courage to pursue this book when all looked hopeless. Syed Shariq has been a great friend and wonderful colleague who picked up the slack as codirector of the Kozmetsky Global Collaboratory (KGC); Ade Mabogunje also played a key role keeping the KGC going. Beyond the influences of these individuals, I am grateful for the insights provided and the high standards set by the extraordinary faculty at Stanford.

Although Scott did not focus on voice interfaces during his time in graduate school, he was an amazingly fast study (as demonstrated by his brilliant work on the emotion chapter in the *Handbook of Human-Computer Interaction*), a talented writer, and a broad and creative thinker. We also have similar working styles and complimentary temperaments.

During the writing of this book, I lost my mother to liver cancer, which was a devastating blow. The days before and after her death were made bearable only by the loving support of my families: the Gellmans, the Leeds, the Nasses, the Natkins, and the Weltes.

Barbara Levitt, my wife, provided the understanding, patience, and support that allowed me to work day and night on this manuscript. Matthew Levitt Nass, my son, also provided continuing inspiration and support and proposed a number of the ideas that appear in the book. He is a fabulous son, a wonderful colleague, and my best buddy.

There is an adage that "To have a successful life, find a friend and find a mentor." For writing a book, friends are valuable but mentors are gold. My family of origin—Jules Nass, Florence Nass, and Michael Jay Nass—taught me the basic principles that guide my life. Barbara Levitt guided my creating of a new family. Matthew Levitt Nass has taught me that with confidence, one can always discover something new. James

Beniger was my Ph.D. advisor and remains a dear friend; he took an engineer and turned him into a social scientist. Steven Chaffee was my department chair, my colleague, and a wonderful friend; he took a social scientist and turned him into a professor.

Scott's Personal Acknowledgments

First, I want to thank Cliff for inviting me to coauthor this book with him. The thought of embarking on this adventure, immediately after completing my dissertation, brought mixed emotions. But working with Cliff on this project truly has been a pleasure. As a mentor, Cliff continues to amaze and inspire me more than I could have ever imagined.

I feel lucky to be surrounded by many supportive colleagues and friends. My fellow students and postdocs at Stanford are insightful and kind people. I especially want to thank two friends, Zephyr and Desiree, for keeping me grounded throughout this process, and my girlfriend, Lauren, for keeping me both sane and happy.

To my dad, Ron, whose success at life inspires and who never lets me give up or doubt myself; to my mom, Patti, whose understanding and compassion are unparalleled in this world; and to my sister, Jamie, who, with her incredible wisdom, always helps me to find the perspective I most need, I dedicate this book.

Final Words

A book of this kind draws on the insights and ideas of an enormous number of people. If we have unintentionally (but perhaps inevitably) omitted even one person who should be listed above, we apologize. The references acknowledge many of those not acknowledged above. We truly appreciate these scholars' contributions to our understanding of how humans are wired for speech and how computers will speak with us.

A Note to Readers

We have written *Wired for Speech: How Voice Activates and Advances the Human-Computer Relationship* so that readers can ignore its footnotes:

- If something is worth saying, we say it in the text. There is no new content in the footnotes.
- Most of the footnotes simply acknowledge the original source of the information that we present without any additional explanation.
- The remaining footnotes provide questionnaire items, data tables, and statistical analyses. The inclusion of this material is a convention when research is presented, especially when studies have not been previously published. Readers can skip these footnotes because descriptions, interpretations, and implications of the results are included in the text.

Wired for Speech

1 Wired for Speech: Activating the Human-Computer Relationship

Speech is the fundamental means of human communication. Even when other forms of communication—such as writing, facial expressions, or sign language—would be equally expressive, (hearing) people in all cultures persuade, inform, and build relationships primarily through speech.[1]

Perhaps the greatest proof of the importance of speech comes from the deep and broad ways that humans have evolved to process and understand speech. Speech is such an integral part of being human that people with IQ scores as low as 50 or brains as small as 400 grams (one-third the size of a normal human brain) can speak.[2] Although scientists debate whether the brain contains a "speech organ,"[3] there is no question that speech implicates more parts of the brain than any other function.[4] Humans are so tuned to speech production and processing that from about the age of eighteen months, children on average learn eight to ten new words a day and typically retain that rate until adolescence.[5]

Humans are also the only species that is wired to understand speech fully. It has long been known that the left side of the brain (which corresponds to the right ear) shows a clear advantage in processing the hearer's native language, nonsense syllables, speech in foreign languages, and even speech played backwards, while the left ear attends to all other sounds.[6] New research suggests that even the ears themselves are different. In the right outer ear, hair cells, which amplify sounds that are transmitted to the acoustic nerve in the brain, react more to sounds that reflect speech than do hairs in the left outer ear.[7]

This specialization appears very early in human development. One-day-old infants respond differently to speech-like sounds than they do to any other sounds.[8] By four days after birth, babies' brains automatically distinguish and prefer the sounds of their native language over the sounds of other languages.[9] By the teens, humans can perceive speech at the phenomenally fast rate of up to forty to fifty phonemes (the smallest distinguishable speech sound) per second, while other sounds become indistinguishable at twenty phonemes per second.[10]

Brains Are Voice Experts

Speech does more than simply transmit words from a speaker to a listener.[11] Humans have evolved voices and listening apparatuses that convey a wide range of socially relevant cues that human brains are wired to analyze and respond to.[12] Indeed, some scholars argue that language evolved primarily to exchange social information rather than information about the environment.[13] For example, because information concerning gender[14] is of great evolutionary importance, people rapidly categorize voices as male or female based on pitch, cadence, and other factors.[15] Even if people change their minds about whether they are listening to a male or a female, the gender they assign to the voice influences their interpretation of everything that is said.[16] Other parameters, such as speech rate and volume, convey more subtle human characteristics, such as personality, emotion, and hometown: extroverts,[17] excited people,[18] and people from New York City[19] speak much more rapidly and more loudly than average.

Humans are so attuned to vocal characteristics that they quickly and accurately distinguish one person's voice from another.[20] Even before birth, a fetus in the womb can distinguish its mother's voice from all other voices (demonstrated via increased heart rate for the mother's voice and decreased heart rate for strangers' voices).[21] Within a few days after birth, a newborn prefers his or her mother's voice over that of a stranger's[22] and can distinguish one unfamiliar voice from another.[23] By eight months, infants can tune in to a particular voice even when another voice is speaking.[24]

The words that people select also carry social information. Sentences that use the first person (such as "I made a mistake" or "I would like the following information") evoke different meanings and feelings than sentences that avoid the use of "I" (such as "Mistakes were made" or "The following information should be provided").[25] Similarly, a person can address a misunderstood comment by taking responsibility ("I'm sorry. I didn't understand that"), blaming the speaker ("Be more articulate"), or scapegoating ("The transmission tower is having problems. Could you please repeat that?"). These differing approaches have dramatic consequences.[26]

Of course, voices and spoken words are not independent.[27] Consider how odd it would seem if a deep, booming voice asked, "Could I possibly ask you if you wouldn't mind doing a tiny favor?" or a high-pitched, soft voice announced, "You had better help me right now!"[28]

As a result of human evolution, humans are automatic experts at extracting the social aspects of speech.[29] People do not receive formal training to discern social cues from voice. Even distinguishing between subtle wording differences[30] and deciphering words with multiple meanings[31] seem to be in-born human abilities.

The ability to extract social meaning from speech is not a parlor trick or the accidental outgrowth of the ability to process sound waves. Every society provides rules about *how* to use categories of voices and words to guide attitudes, thoughts, and behaviors.[32] These rules, whether evolved or culturally selected, provide systematic guidance for determining gender-, personality-, and emotion-specific actions. These rules also advise people whom to like, whom to trust, and with whom to do business.

Sensitivity to voice and language cues has played a critical role in interactions with other people for as long as humans have lived in social groups. Those in the past whose brains automatically and easily responded to social cues in voices had an enormous evolutionary advantage. People with social intelligence were better judges of whom to trust and with whom to mate and were better able to convince others to trust them and mate with them.[33] By contrast, those who spent time struggling with the identification of social cues could not maximize opportunities. The ability to quickly classify others and use those judgments to guide behavior predicts success in all aspects of life. The ancestors of current humans—those who won the evolutionary battle—were equipped to learn and apply the social rules of voice.

In sum, over the course of 200,000 years of evolution, humans have become *voice-activated* with brains that are wired to equate voices with people and to act quickly on that identification.[34] Talking, listening, and human society have elegantly coevolved into a remarkably interwoven, effective, and stable system.

New Media, New Rules?

Evolution resolved many of the complex problems of voice communication among humans. Recently, however, tricky new technologies have emerged that can produce and understand voices. People now routinely use voice-input and voice-output systems to check airline reservations, order stocks, control cars, navigate the Web, dictate memos into a word processor, entertain children, and perform a host of other tasks. Voice user interfaces complement and at times replace graphical user interfaces, freeing people from the constraints of "WIMP" (windows, icons, menus and pointers).[35] Handheld and mobile devices, televisions, and household appliances can be controlled by spoken commands. Ubiquitous computing[36]—access to all information for anyone, anywhere, at any time—relies on speech for those whose eyes or hands are directed to other tasks (such as driving, holding, or building) or for those who cannot read or type (such as children, the blind, or the disabled).

At the same time, however, these interfaces create an interesting problem. Suddenly people's successful and stable perception of voices as intrinsically part of the social world is misguided because they are conversing with technologies as well as with people. *How will a voice-activated brain that associates voice with social relationships react when confronted with technologies that talk or listen?*

This book demonstrates that the conscious knowledge that speech can have a non-human origin is not enough for the brain to overcome the historically appropriate activation of social relationships by voice. As a number of experiments will show, the human brain rarely makes distinctions between speaking to a machine—even those machines with very poor speech understanding and low-quality speech production—and speaking to a person. In fact, humans use the same parts of the brain to interact with machines as they do to interact with humans.

Listeners and talkers cannot suppress their natural responses to speech, regardless of source. People draw conclusions about technology-based voices and determine appropriate behavior by applying the same rules and shortcuts that they use when interacting with people. These technologies, like the speech of other people, *activate* all parts of the brain that are associated with social interaction.

As a result of these automatic and unconscious social responses to voice technologies, the psychology of interface speech is the psychology of human speech: voice interfaces are intrinsically social interfaces. Designers must create voice interfaces for brains that are obsessed with extracting as much social information as possible from speech and with using that information to guide attitudes and behaviors.

Because humans will respond socially to voice interfaces, designers can tap into the automatic and powerful responses elicited by all voices, whether of human or machine origin, to increase liking, trust, efficiency, learning, and even buying.[37] Using insights from both traditional social science and new research on how people interact with technology, this book answers critical questions concerning the future of voice interfaces. For example, how will people respond to an e-commerce application with a female voice? (Learn from the research on human females who sell products; see chapter 3.) Should an automated call center apologize when it can't understand a spoken request? (Leverage the finding that modest people are interpreted to be likeable but unintelligent; see chapter 14.) Should a car's voice sound enthusiastic or subdued? (Voices, like people, are more effective when they match the emotion of the listener; see chapter 7.) And when would an interface benefit from multiple voices?

(People who are distinguished as specialists are perceived to be more knowledgeable than generalists; see chapter 9.)

How Dare You Claim That?

If people respond to technology-based voices in the same way that they respond to people, then prediction and design might seem to be trivial. Theoretical issues and design questions could be resolved in the social science section of the library: simply find a description of a similar situation among humans, and apply the results. Unfortunately, this approach has four limitations.

The first limitation of this approach is that psychological theories and design prescriptions compete sometimes. For example, will people like voice interfaces with personalities similar to their own (the "birds of a feather flock together" principle[38]), or will they prefer voice personalities that complement their own (the "opposites attract" principle[39])?[40] Experimentation provides a rigorous way to resolve such contradictory principles.

A second limitation of relying on previous research is that the scientific literature may be silent on important design or theory questions. For example, would a voice interface be more persuasive when using the first person ("I have a beautiful lamp for sale") or the third person ("There is a beautiful lamp for sale")? The previous research literature ignores this question (for the answer, see chapter 10). Furthermore, new technologies suggest questions that could not previously be addressed or even asked. For example, no humans exhibit the bizarre speech patterns that are ssociated with synthetic speech (chapter 2), nor would any normal humans consistently exhibit a mismatch between the emotions that are in their voice and the words that they are saying (chapter 8), problems that are uniquely associated with voice interfaces. The systematic experimentation described in this book addresses these questions.

A third reason for reaching conclusions from experiments rather than merely relying on previous research is that all theories have boundaries and limitations. Even if a theory is essentially correct, it will not apply in every situation. For example, accents that match the listener's accent lead to greater trust.[41] However, in some cases, using an accent that matches the user is the wrong strategy (chapter 6). Experimental evidence and interpretation of the evidence allows definitive statements to be made that specify when and why particular theories and designs work or fail.

The final reason for performing experiments is that they provide the necessary resistance to the temptations of anecdote. When watching a usability test, everyone notices and remembers the "cute" remark or the "ideal" behavior. These are seductive and rhetorically convincing but can frequently mislead. To ensure that an idea is valid or a design is effective, results from numerous experimental participants must be systematically and rigorously analyzed.

In this book, common theories and assumptions are thoroughly tested via twenty experiments with thousands of participants. The results are frequently surprising and often turn common understandings and design practices on their heads. To ensure that the theories were rigorously tested and could be applied confidently across a range of products and services, the research included a wide variety of contexts and technologies. The participants in the research learned, bid in auctions, disclosed personal information, listened to news, creatively answered questions, received advice, and heard jokes. Some people worked directly with a computer; others used the telephone, the Web, a wireless array microphone, or a driving simulator. The interfaces sometimes only talked, sometimes only listened, and sometimes did both.

Moving Forward

By communicating via the method that humans have evolved to use, voice interfaces should represent an extraordinarily pleasant and effective way to interact with technology. They conveniently fit in with the user's environment, providing access to information products and services through ubiquitous technologies such as telephones. Interaction through voice also frees up users' hands, eyes, and legs, enabling them to concurrently perform other tasks, such as driving. Finally, voice interfaces provide significant ergonomic advantages over traditional interfaces, as they do not require users to sit in fixed positions or repeatedly perform unnatural physical actions, such as typing or mouse clicking.

Given the elegant ways that voice interfaces could fit into people's lives, how is it possible that they have become notorious for fostering frustration and failure rather than encouraging effectiveness and enjoyment? Designers often blame limitations of technology as the underlying cause: "Yes, speech recognition can be frustrating," they say, "but that's because it's just not good enough yet," or "People have such unrealistic expectations about voice user interfaces that they're doomed to be frustrated," or "Advanced interfaces are intrinsically complicated; people have to accept a learning curve before they become proficient." While there is certainly validity to these arguments, people are remarkably willing and able to interact with nonnative speakers or young children, chat via a noisy phone line, or listen to poor-quality audio speakers—situations that have the same, if not more, limitations than computer technologies present.

As this book demonstrates, voice interfaces can be significantly improved by a careful understanding and application of how people are built for speech. Each of the following chapters first describes in detail how an understanding of the wiring of the human brain from birth (and even before!) informs how people think, feel, and behave. The chapter then describes, via a participant's view, one or more experiments that provide grounding and nuance for the way people respond to speaking technology. (For the detail-oriented, all of the measures, data tables, and statistical analysis can be found in the notes for each chapter.) The results of the experiments are discussed in terms of both human psychology and their application to the creation of more likeable, effective, and engaging products and services, including automated call centers, personal computer software, e-commerce Web sites, vehicles, home appliances, and toys.

The fundamental insights obtained from the theories, experiments, and applications discussed in this book will help designers build better interfaces, scientists construct better theories, and everyone gain better understandings of the future of machines that speak with us.

2 Gender of Voices: Making Interfaces Male or Female

If you say to someone, "Please write a description of yourself for someone who knows nothing about you," the first sentence will likely be "I am female" or "I am male."[1] Information theorists might argue that this is not a wise choice: the responder would be most informative by mentioning his or her most unusual characteristic.[2] However, for biological, psychological, and cultural reasons, the definition of self begins with gender.[3] Indeed, in many languages, including English, it is almost impossible to talk about a person without indicating gender through the use of pronouns (such as *he* or *she*) or other gender markers.

From the age of two or three years old, children identify themselves and others as exclusively belonging to a group called "female" or a group called "male."[4] In all cultures, the majority of people spend the majority of their time with people of the same gender,[5] and even very young children show a striking tendency to segregate by gender when choosing with whom to play.[6] This sense of membership provides the lens through which every perception, of both observer and observed, is filtered.[7]

Generally, people have to know each other's gender before they can interact comfortably.[8] Individuals with unclear gender, such as "Pat" on the television show *Saturday Night Live*, become "evocative objects"[9] that create inner turmoil and disturb and fascinate through their ambiguity.

Given the prominence of gender and voice in everyday life, it is not surprising that voice plays a key role in identifying gender.[10] Six-month-old infants are able to categorize voices into female and male,[11] and between the ages of eleven and fourteen months, infants learn to recognize the association between the gender of voices (women have "higher voices")[12] and people shown in photographs, suggesting that gender rapidly crosses sensory modalities.

Gender is one of the first attributes that people identify in a human voice; it is generally discernible within seconds.[13] Although people might simply think of females as the "higher-pitched gender,"[14] the assignment of gender is based on a number of voice characteristics,[15] all of which are analyzed in language-related areas of the brain.[16] Indeed, the brain is so cued to gender categorization that when people are asked how similar voices are, the most important criterion is whether the voice is male or female.[17] Remarkably, even when pitch (fundamental frequency) and the range of the natural voice spectra (characteristics of the sound waves) are equalized, people can nevertheless identify gender.[18]

A further combination of biology and culture (the relative extent of each is hotly debated) may then prescribe other gender characteristics that distinguish the speaking of females and males. For example, in the United States, women's voices tend to exhibit wider pitch range, more expressiveness, and more sentences with rising pitch than do men's voices.[19] In addition, female speech tends to include more questions and a greater proportion of social and relational information than male speech.[20]

The unrelenting identification of and prescriptions for gender in one's own life, in others' lives, and in the larger social structure make the determination of whether another person's gender is the same as or different than one's own the most powerful and basic judgment a person can make. *Social identification*—the decision of whether someone is "like me" or "not like me"[21]—is critical to a fundamental human principle: the more similar two people are, the more positively they will be disposed toward each other. Thus, social identification leads to greater trust, liking, perceived intelligence, and other positive judgments:[22] "socially identified with" means "socially favored by." The mere awareness of categories is sufficient to encourage people to "choose sides" and exhibit in-group bias.[23]

Because of its fundamental role in understanding human behavior, various social scientists have provided explanations for the link between social identification and positive attitudes and behaviors. Social psychologists point to predictability:[24] the more similar people are to you, the more easily you can predict their behavior, and hence the safer you feel with them.[25] Cognitive psychologists argue from human preferences for "cognitive economy":[26] the more similar people are to you, the more readily you can understand their thoughts and behaviors without contemplation. Anthropologists claim that throughout most of human evolution, humans lived in highly interdependent, homogeneous small groups that shared shelter, food, rituals, and language:[27] similarity meant social support. Sociologists note that societies tend to encourage interactions between those who are similar:[28] similarity implies familiarity, and familiarity leads to liking.[29] Although mating certainly requires opposite sexes, even evolutionary psychology can explain the general rule of "similar is positive." Reproductive success can be defined as the presence of one's genes in the next generation. Because similarity is associated with similar genes, a similar other's reproductive success is almost as valuable as an individual's own reproductive success.[30]

The desirability and simplicity of same-gender interactions is one of the most consistent findings in the social science literature. Indeed, research demonstrates that children as young as three years of age like their own gender more than the other[31] and attribute more positive attributes to their own gender than the opposite gender.[32]

How can these discoveries transfer from the world of human-human interactions to human-technology interactions? People do not spend a majority of their time with *technologies* that are male or female, and use of most technologies does not involve any requirement to consider gender. Technologies do not have biology of male and female, although people sometimes refer to certain machines with gender labels (for example, boats as "she"). Technologies also do not think differently based on their "genders" and have not been socialized as female or male by spending time with others of that gender.

Gender and Technology-Generated Voices

Because of limitations of storage space (digital recordings are large), processing speed (finding and combining arbitrary utterances can be slow), bandwidth speed (sound files do not transmit gracefully over a 33 kilobyte phone line), dynamism of content (all of the Web's content cannot be spoken and recorded in real time), and other technical constraints, much of the speech that is and will be produced by computers, the Web, telephone interfaces, and wireless devices will be "synthesized" speech, also known as text to speech (TTS).[33] Thus, more and more interfaces will not simply present fully recorded words and phrases but will produce speech artificially.

While synthesized-voice systems effectively communicate content, even the best synthesized-speech systems do not yet match the quality and structure of natural human speech.[34] Speech systems tend to have inexplicable pauses, misplaced accents and word emphases, discontinuities across phonemes, and inconsistent structures that make them sound nonhuman. All of these cues remind users that they are not interacting with something that has an intrinsic gender, just as a broken film during a screening reminds people that "It's only a movie." In other words, synthetic-speech systems should make apparent that the vocal cues that suggest gender are artificial and therefore not worthy of interpretation.

On the other hand, the human brain evolved with a very liberal definition of *speech*.[35] People even process nonsense syllables and speech played backward as if they were normal speech.[36] All speech is regarded as a communicative act,[37] and people will struggle through assigning meaning to sounds even when they are garbled or unclear. Thus, the wiring of the human brain suggests that despite the many reminders that gender has nothing to do with synthetic speech, people might forget that they are working with a machine. This could lead people to take seriously cues, such as pitch, that lead them to socially identify with the voice.

The question is whether, given all the ways in which a computer (or other technology) indicates gender neutrality—a clearly mechanical voice and a box instead of a body—can the automatic activation of gender assignment by voice, combined with a cultural emphasis on gender differentiation, overcome the clear reminders that a user is working with a technology rather than a person?

Confronting People with "Machine" Gender

To answer this question, a variant of a traditional social psychology experiment was conducted.[38] Of the forty-eight adults who participated in the study, half were female and half were male.

For this study, participants read descriptions of situations in which a person had to choose between two courses of action: the classic dilemma. Psychologists study choice dilemmas[39] because situations with two options are the easiest to analyze statistically.[40] The dilemmas for this experiment were written so that they would not have an obvious (that is, a clearly more desirable or socially appropriate) choice. This design made it possible for the voice to influence people to accept one option or the other.

Here is an example of a typical choice dilemma, which was presented in text for the participant to read:

> Amy and John are college students who have been living together in an apartment near campus. John's allowance buys food, and they are sharing the rent. Amy has told her parents that she is rooming with another girl, and now her parents are coming to visit their daughter. They have never seen the apartment. Should Amy ask John to move out for the time that her parents are in town?

The dilemma in this case is whether Amy should or should not ask John to move out. After reading the dilemma, the participant clicked on a button, which caused an obviously computer-synthesized voice to provide a recommendation about which course of action should be taken. The computer always made a forceful argument for one of the two possible options. For example, here is the computer voice's argument, presented to all participants, for the moving-out dilemma:

> She should ask him to leave for a while. If she tells the truth to her parents, it would cause a lot of unnecessary trouble. She can always confess her situation to her parents later when she feels that it is the right time.

Half of the male and half of the female participants heard a voice that was computer-generated but "female"; the other half heard a voice that was computer-generated but "male."[41] The primary distinction between the voices was fundamental frequency (pitch): the "female" voice had the average fundamental frequency of human females (210 Hz), and the "male" voice had the average fundamental frequency of human males (110 Hz).[42] The voices had similar characteristics (such as their volumes and frequency ranges) to control for the possibility of effects from personality, accents, and emotion.[43] The voices gave the identical advice for each scenario. The voices were selected to be clearly artificial and sounded nothing like actual people. They had bizarre accents, phrasings, and mispronunciations, expressed no emotion or understanding of the content, and had a "mechanical" sound. Nonetheless, all participants indicated that they could fully understand what the voice said.

The research strategy was to give half of the males and half of the females an opportunity to "socially identify" with the voice whose gender "matched" their own. If people do not socially identify with machine voices, then the gender of the voice would prove irrelevant. If, however, the gender of a voice—even a clearly machine-like voice—activates the brain's obsessive focus on gender, then a synthetic voice would elicit the same social identification effects that a human voice does. Thus, for females, a synthetic female voice should be perceived as more credible and likeable than a synthetic male voice, while the opposite should be true for males.

After listening to the computer's argument in support of one of the two possible positions, participants indicated their opinion about what the person confronted with the dilemma should do. Users' recommendations were given on an eight-point scale from "Definitely do option A" ("Ask John to leave") to "Definitely do option B" ("Not ask John to leave"). The scales displayed an even number of points so that people had to take a stand: there was no middle point. If people identified socially with these bizarre voices, then people would agree more with what the voice suggested when it "matched" their gender than when it did not match.

One way to study this phenomenon would be to ask people their opinion before hearing the voice and then ask again after they heard the voice. This would seem to be a more precise measure than assuming that prior to the experiment, all people had the same average opinion. Unfortunately, psychologists have discovered that this strategy is ineffective, perhaps because people often are reluctant to change their answers once they are "on record."[44] Hence, the average responses of people who heard a similarly gendered voice were compared to the average of those who heard a differently gendered voice.

Focusing on a single scenario is risky. A given scenario might be one for which women always opt for option A while men always opt for option B, thereby masking the effects of voice. More generally, the scenario might be one that triggers strong personal reactions that would make people immune to persuasion. Conversely, researchers might be "lucky" and find the only scenario that elicits a particular phenomenon; basing their conclusions on that single scenario would be misleading. Thus, the norm in research is to choose a range of choice dilemmas (or any type of scenario) to make sure that none is problematic and then to average across the scenarios.[45] (In the current research, six different scenarios were averaged.)

When participants finished going through all six decisions—first hearing the computer's opinion and then making their own decision—they completed a questionnaire.[46] The questionnaire was designed to provide further evidence for social identification and to answer the most basic question of whether people noticed that the voice was "female" or "male." First, participants were asked to rate the trustworthiness of the voice that they heard.[47] If people social identify with synthetic voices, the participants would indicate more trust in the "matched" voice than the "mismatched" voice. Second, participants were asked to rate the likeability of the voice that they heard.[48] This was important both because social identification predicts liking and because likeability is often found to be highly correlated with user satisfaction and with likelihood of purchase and reuse. Finally, participants were asked to rate the masculinity or femininity of the computer voice that they heard.[49]

Does Machine Gender Equal Human Gender?

We found that users clearly distinguished voices based on gender cues,[50] rating the male synthesized voice as significantly more masculine than the female synthesized voice.[51] This demonstrates that the voices activated a categorization that is profoundly associated with living things: sex. The automatic assignment of gender to voices thus extends beyond the realm of humans to the technological world.

Despite all of the signals that indicated to the participants that the processes that underlie social identification are not applicable to the voices they heard, participants' choices conformed more to the suggestions made by the voices that "matched" their gender than did the choices of participants who heard voices that did not "match."[52] Female participants found the female voice to be more trustworthy than the male voice, while males felt the opposite,[53] another indicator that social identification can lead to persuasion.

The liking measure also revealed effects indicating social identification. Males liked the male voice better than the female voice, while female users liked the female voice better than the male.[54]

When we were presenting these results at a conference, a woman in the audience raised her hand and asked, "Women often have the experience that when they say something a meeting, people don't seem to listen to them, but when men say the same things, people seem to pay attention. Did that happen in your research?"[55] We *did* pay attention to her and rushed back to the data to see if her experience was corroborated. Sure enough, in addition to the social identification effects, we also found a simple effect from the gender of the voice: people conformed much more with the male voice than the female voice, even though the male and female voices made identical statements.[56] Listeners also found the male voice to be more trustworthy.[57] This meant that males listening to the male voice were the most convinced by the voice, and males listening to a female voice were the least convinced. Sadly, this tendency for people, especially males, to take males more seriously than females extended to the obviously synthetic world of technology. This was not a result of simple liking of one voice over another (the male voice was not more likable overall than the female voice) but was a reflection of learned social behaviors and assumptions.

Extending Gender in Voice Interfaces

Gender of voice is as prominent and definitive in the technological world as it is in the social world: users treat synthetic voices as if they reflected the biological and sociocultural realities of sex and gender. Just as any voice that sounds even remotely like human speech is processed as human speech, any voice that sounds remotely male or female is likely to be automatically classified as such. Even a hint of gender, as manifested through the pitch of a synthetic voice, is enough to activate the social-identification processes that bias people positively toward others of the same gender. This activation led people to be more conforming, trusting, and positively oriented toward synthetic voices whose "gender" matched their own.

Male and Female versus Masculine and Feminine

Although the roots of the words *feminine* and *masculine* come from *female* and *male*, respectively, the concepts of masculine and feminine are not grounded purely in biology. Each culture defines canonical behaviors for females and males,[58] and individuals of both genders can adhere to those prescriptions to varying degrees. Thus, unlike the concepts of female and male, feminine and masculine are personality traits and follow all the rules of personality design discussed in later chapters.[59] For example, feminine people tend to like feminine voices, while masculine people like masculine voices.

Many psychologists do not view femininity and masculinity as opposite sides of the same dimension.[60] Instead, they argue that a person can be *high* on *both* masculinity and femininity (androgynous), *low* on *both* masculinity and femininity (undifferentiated), or high on one and low on the other (clearly feminine or clearly masculine). In the United States, there are strong similarities between masculinity and the *dominance/submissiveness* aspect of personality and between femininity and the *friendly/unfriendly* dimension of personality.[61]

A voice—whether male or female, synthetic or recorded—can be made to sound more feminine and less masculine by cutting off the low frequencies and increasing the volume of the high frequencies.[62] Conversely, a voice can be made to sound more masculine and less feminine—regardless of perceived gender—by cutting off the high frequencies and increasing the volume of the low frequencies. The more feminine-sounding the voice is (regardless of whether it is a male or a female voice), the more female gender stereotypes will be attributed to and expected from it, and conversely, the more masculine-sounding the voice is, the more male stereotypes will be attributed to and expected from it.

Confusion in Gender of Voices: Is It Desirable?

If female voices sound too masculine or male voices sound too feminine, the listener may become puzzled as to which gender is speaking. This does not mean that people will view a gender-ambiguous synthetic or recorded voice as neither male nor female. There is clear evidence that although people can be uncertain about ambiguous voices and can even go back and forth between the determination that "It's a female" or "It's a male," people's brains are committed to assigning one and only one gender at any one moment.[63] Thus, an ambiguous voice is like a Necker cube,[64] the optical illusion in which people always perceive one orientation at a time but frequently switch from one orientation to the other.

Although people will assign a gender, a tremendous amount of evidence has been accumulated over the past thirty years that people strongly prefer clarity in classifying and categorizing people.[65] Anyone or anything with an ambiguous voice is classified as strange, dislikable, dishonest, and unintelligent.[66] Therefore, whether using a recorded or a computer-synthesized voice, clarity of gender (and other characteristics) is critical.

Coping with Gendered Interfaces

When the "gender" of a synthesized computer voice "matches" the gender of a user, people exhibit social-identification effects. Specifically, people conform more to synthetic voices whose gender matches their own and find matching voices more trustworthy. Furthermore, females like female voices more than male voices, even when they know that they are machine-generated, while males like male voices. These results suggest that people automatically assign gender, determine whether it matches their own, and follow the basic principle of "similar is better."

It is impossible to live in or even contemplate the social world without gender. These biological, social, and cultural constructs are automatically manifested by voices, both real and artificial, and automatically recognized by listeners' brains. A careful leveraging of gender identification can make users feel positive and supported, while ignorance of gender identification can unintentionally drive users away. No matter how unnatural or unclear the voice, voice gender is at the heart of interfaces that speak.

3 Gender Stereotyping of Voices: Sex Is Everywhere

The previous chapter demonstrates that people respond to machine-based voices as if they were "male" or "female." Furthermore, people see so much similarity between machine gender and their own gender that females identify with "females" and males identify with "males."

Since the work of Lawrence Kohlberg,[1] psychologists have understood that from childhood onward, people must figure out not only what gender identity they possess but also how that gender identity should guide their behavior. From a very young age, children are "gender detectives" who search for cues about which gender should or should not engage in a particular behavior,[2] primarily by spending time with and modeling others of the same gender.[3]

Children strive to come up with clear and unambiguous decision rules as to how females and males should and do act.[4] By the time children are five years old and continuing until the age of seven, they have extremely rigid rules about appropriate female and male behaviors.[5] For example, if a boy as young as three is told that a toy is "usually used by females,"[6] he will pay less attention to it and remember less about it than will girls; girls will pay less attention to and remember less about a "boyish toy."[7] Toys that have a hint of a female gender marker, such as a pink color, will be labeled as female, and therefore welcomed by girls and rejected by boys.[8] Toys with male indicators elicit the opposite reaction.

Although the absolutist notions of gender that are exhibited by five- to seven-year-olds tend to become less rigid as they grow older, the number and elaboration of social rules concerning gender only grow over time.[9] Adults have absorbed literally thousands of stereotypes about how gender should guide what to expect of each person, how to behave toward each person, and how each person is expected to behave in return.[10]

Even with the startling breadth and depth of guidelines, there seems to be an insatiable demand for further explanations of how women and men think and behave differently. Best-sellers such as *You Just Don't Understand: Women and Men in Conversation*[11] and *Men Are from Mars, Women Are from Venus*[12] give specific guidelines for understanding how females and males behave differently, and two of the one hundred best American movies of all time (according to the American Film Institute)[13]—*Some Like It Hot* and *Tootsie*—focus on what can be learned when individuals from one gender try to behave like the other. Much of modern literature has at least one character struggling with "Who should I be?" with exploration of gender identity as the point of departure.

Of course, gender stereotypes, like all stereotypes, are misleading when applied to a particular individual. Nonetheless, virtually all people apply gender stereotypes frequently, even if those stereotypes are unfavorable to their own gender.[14] One reason for this stereotyping is that humans have limited processing capabilities.[15] People would find it extremely taxing if they could not filter decisions through a simple dichotomy whose two options provided wide-ranging guidance. For example, when people don't know what to do, they can simply think, "Let's see. I can be only one of two categories: female or male. It's easy to remember which. Knowing that, I can consult my 'rule book' to determine what to do without thinking very hard." The fewer the categories and the greater the homogeneity that are within each category, the smaller the burden of information gathering and analysis that is required to obtain a given level of certainty and the lower the likelihood of error.[16] In sum, there is a great deal of evolutionary pressure to rely on gender stereotypes.

Gender Stereotypes and Technology

The study described in the previous chapter gives the first hint that people might apply gender stereotypes as well as social identification to synthetic voices. Specifically, people seemed to follow the (regrettable) stereotype that females are less worthy of serious attention than males are.[17] Regardless of their own gender, participants found the male voice to be more trustworthy than the female voice. They also generally conformed more to the suggestions that were made by the male voice than those made by the female voice.[18]

Although stereotyping was not a focus of that study, the results suggest an approach that researchers could take to determine whether people routinely gender-stereotype technologies:

1. Select a situation in which one or more gender stereotypes provide misleading guidance about what a person should think or how a person should behave. That is, the

gender stereotype should suggest a different approach or conclusion than would a purely rational and objective response.

2. Confront people with technologies that have male or female voices, and measure their responses with respect to the stereotypes. The simplest approach is to have some people use female-voiced technologies and other people use male-voiced technologies and compare the responses of the two groups. This "between-participants" approach[19] to research is the model that is used in chapter 2 and in the first experiment described below. A more subtle but sometimes more powerful approach, called the "within-participants approach,"[20] is to have people interact with *both* female and male voices doing the same task and determine whether the *same* person evaluates, feels, or acts differently depending on the voice they heard. The second study that is described in this chapter is a within-participants experiment.

Gender Stereotyping and Recorded Speech

The first study was inspired by a close friend. She was one of the first female professors at a well-known university's business school. A few (male) faculty members told her that she was likely to be evaluated more harshly by the students because she was a female teaching in a traditionally male discipline (a claim confirmed by the research literature).[21] Their advice was that she "dress and sound more like a man." There were two implications of this. The first—that any pernicious gender stereotyping was *her* problem to address—seemed beyond the realm of experimental research (although it did reveal how accepting her colleagues were of gender stereotyping in the first place). However, the second implication—that if she behaved "correctly," she would not suffer from gender stereotypes—led us to ask the following: *if a female removed all visual indicators of gender, said the same things that a male did, and clearly was not socialized as female, would she then be able to avoid being stereotyped?* Because this study would be impossible to do with an actual person, we used computers[22] with female or male voices.

This first experiment[23] employed computers with recorded female and male voices in a college teaching context. There has long been a concern about the effect of gender on teacher assessment in educational institutions. For example, professors are expected to perform according to gender stereotypes and are penalized when they do not.[24] Students expect female professors to be much more nurturing and supportive than male professors:[25] Female professors are evaluated more harshly when they make jokes about students' performance as compared to self-deprecating jokes, while male professors are not penalized for making students look foolish.[26] Furthermore, female professors get less credit for making positive comments about students than do male professors, as the former are "doing what they are supposed to be doing"[27] while the latter are being unusually likeable and kind.[28]

Another important finding is that professors are evaluated differently depending on whether they are stereotypically knowledgeable about their disciplines.[29] For example, females who teach in technical areas are evaluated more harshly than females who teach in more stereotypically feminine areas, such as literature or women's studies.[30]

To determine whether these stereotypes would affect people's perceptions of voices on computers, forty college students—half men and half women—worked with a tutoring, testing, and tutor-evaluation system that a university was ostensibly considering for possible deployment. Specifically, the participants were told that they would use three networked computers. The first computer would provide an interactive tutoring session; the second computer would determine how much the student had learned from the tutoring computer; and the third computer would evaluate both the student's performance and the tutoring computer's performance. All three computers were physically identical and were located in three different corners of the room.

First, the "tutor" computer orally presented the participant with ten facts about a stereotypically male topic, technology (for example, "The more wires a computer has, the more slowly it runs"), and ten facts about a stereotypically female topic, love and relationships (for example, "More flowers are ordered for Mother's Day than for any other holiday"). Half of the participants (randomly selected) heard these facts spoken by a prerecorded female voice, and half heard the facts spoken by a prerecorded male voice. After receiving each fact, the participant indicated on a three-point scale ("Very familiar, Somewhat familiar, Not at all familiar") how much he or she knew about that fact. Although participants were told that the computer used this information to choose the next fact to present, thus making the participant feel that the computer was interactive, all participants actually received the same twenty facts.

Next, the participant was directed to the second computer to determine what he or she had learned from the tutoring session. The twelve-item, *text-based*, multiple-choice test[31] included questions that were relevant to but not directly answered by the tutoring session.

After completing this testing session, the participant was directed to a third, "evaluator" computer. The voice used by the evaluator computer was different than that used by the tutoring computer and was either female or male.[32] Thus, some people had a "female" tutor and a (different) "female" evaluator, some had a "male" tutor and a (different) "male" evaluator, and some had a tutor with a voice of one gender and an evaluator of the opposite gender. Equal numbers of male and female participants were randomly assigned to each of the four conditions (two genders of tutor by two genders of evaluator).

For each question on the test, the evaluator computer began by indicating whether the person gave the wrong or right answer. The evaluator computer then evaluated the tutor computer's preparation of the participant. The evaluator's assessment of the tutor computer's performance was almost always positive (for example, "Your answer to this question was correct. The tutor computer chose useful facts for answering this question. Therefore, the tutor computer performed well") regardless of the participant's actual performance; two negative comments were included to make the evaluation plausible.

After the evaluation session, participants were asked to fill out a paper-and-pencil questionnaire. There were two sets of questions.[33] The first set asked participants for their assessment of the *tutoring* computer's overall competence,[34] the computer tutor's likeability,[35] and the informativeness of each round of the tutoring session.[36] If participants were more influenced by the male-voiced evaluator than the female-voice evaluator, then participants who heard a "male" evaluator praise the tutor would think that the tutor was more competent and likeable in general. Beyond this general effect, if gender stereotyping was applied to the tutoring computer, then the female-voiced computer would be perceived as a better teacher of love and relationships and a worse teacher of computing than would a male-voiced computer, even though they performed identically.

The second set of questions asked participants about the likeability of the evaluator computer.[37] If participants were influenced by gender stereotypes, then the male-voiced evaluator would be perceived as more likeable than the female-voiced evaluator, even though the two computers said the same thing.

Even Computers Are Gender Stereotyped

Participants treated the computer tutors with the same stereotypes as actual professors.[38] Consistent with the stereotype that praise from male professors is more credible than praise from female professors,[39] the tutor was perceived as significantly more competent when praised by the "male" computer,[40] even though the tutor computer's performance and the evaluator's comments were identical in all cases. The tutor was also perceived as significantly more likeable when praised by the "male" computer.[41] The female computer that praised benefited itself less than the male computer that praised: consistent with the stereotype, the male evaluator was perceived as significantly more likable than the female evaluator.[42]

Gender stereotyping was so powerful that it led people to assess the *same computer* differently depending on the topic.[43] Thus, the female-voiced computer was seen as a better teacher of love and relationships and a worse teacher of technical subjects than was the male-voiced computer.[44]

As with the previous studies, individuals vehemently denied that they were influenced by the gender of the computer voices. They said that the voices were "arbitrary" and that it is obvious that computers are not "male" or "female." They denied that they harbored gender stereotypes with respect to people, let alone computers. The results of the study belie all of these claims.

What about social-identification effects? That is, did females feel more positively toward the female-voiced computers than the male-voiced computers (and conversely for males), as we found in the previous chapter? Unfortunately, the study did not have enough participants to allow us to do the statistical analysis that would address the question.[45] To remedy this deficiency and to explore a new context and additional stereotypes, a second study was run.

Stereotyping in E-Commerce

The second study[46] expanded on the findings of the first. This study used synthetic voices (similar to the ones used in chapter 2) to determine whether users would gender-stereotype even when the voices sounded distinctly machinelike and nonhuman. Instead of education, the experiment was grounded in e-commerce—specifically, an auction site that provided products that are stereotypically female (such as an encyclopedia of sewing) and stereotypically male (such as an encyclopedia of guns). This context invited different stereotypes to come into play. Finally, enough participants were included to determine whether social-identification effects *as well as* gender-stereotyping effects could be identified.

The first stereotype explored was whether some products would be consistently labeled as "feminine" while other products would be consistently labeled as "masculine." Identifying products as male or female does not terminate at childhood: adults tend to identify colors, clothes, food (*Real Men Don't Eat Quiche*[47]), entertainment ("chick flick"), and virtually every other product or service based on its appropriateness for a particular sex.

A second stereotype is that females (female voices) are believed to be more credible in their descriptions of female products, while males (male voices) are believed to be more credible in their description of male products.[48] In marketing, this is called the "match-up" hypothesis:[49] consistency between spokesperson and product characteristics is believed to create more effective, persuasive messages. Thus, because of stereotyping, a male spokesperson may more effectively and appropriately promote power tools (a stereotypically male product) than a woman, while a female spokesperson may more effectively and appropriately promote lingerie (a stereotypically female product) than a man,[50] even when consumers know that the spokesperson is simply reading a script that could be delivered by anyone.

Another stereotype is that whether more knowledgeable or not, females tend to talk more about female products while males tend to talk more about male products.[51] Thus, a voice (and the speaker) that discusses stereotypically female products will be perceived as more feminine than a voice that describes male products, regardless of the gender of the voice. This influence also works in the opposite direction: products that are described by a female voice will be perceived as more feminine than products described by a male voice, regardless of the gender stereotypically associated with the product.

Gender Stereotyping and Synthetic Speech

A total of eighty (forty male and forty female) adults participated in the experiment. Participants were directed to an online auction site that presented products from four different product categories—encyclopedias, matchbooks, watches, and cowboy boots. Each product category included a stereotypically male and stereotypically female instantiation, with all descriptions derived from eBay. Here is the description for the stereotypically female encyclopedia:

The Encyclopedia of Sewing. Doubleday, New York, 1987, 1st edition. 538 pages, hard cover in good condition, some edge/corner wear and shelf wear, corners bumped. All your sewing questions answered quickly and easily. Over 1,000 how-to entries arranged in alphabetical order with detailed step-by-step illustrations ranging from pillow to curtain making. A one-of-a-kind sewing guide you will not want to be without.

Here is the description of the stereotypically male encyclopedia:

The Complete Illustrated Encyclopedia of the World's Firearms by Ian V. Hogg. A. & W. Publishers, Incorporated, New York. 1978. 320 pages, hard cover, with over 500 illustrations, including 50 in color. An A to Z directory of 750 firearm makes and makers from 1830 to present. From Colt revolvers to Winchester rifles and shotguns, this volume is an indispensable reference for firearm owners and enthusiasts alike.

For the matchbook product categories, the examples were "Women's Rights: Susan B. Anthony" and "1934 Roy Parmelee" (a member of the New York Giants baseball team);

for the watches, a woman's classic and a man's retro pilot; and for the cowboy boots, MIU MIU outrageous and Men's Frye All Leather Western.[52]

Each participant heard a description of two randomly selected female products and two randomly selected male products, each from different product categories. A female synthesized voice (randomly) described one of the stereotypically female products and one of the stereotypically male products; a male synthesized voice did the same. The gender of the synthesized voice was created by manipulating vocal markers of gender (pitch and pitch range).

After listening to each product description, participants answered questions regarding the item itself, the item description, and the voice that read the description.[53] Participants were asked to judge both the femininity or masculinity of the voice[54] and the femininity or masculinity of the product.[55] This rating enabled the determination of whether the gender of the voice affected participants' perception of the gender of the product and conversely, whether the gender of the product affected participants' perception of the voice's gender. To test the stereotype that females are more knowledgeable about female products and males are more knowledgeable about male products, participants were asked to rate the credibility of the description that they heard.[56] To test directly whether people thought that females should be talking about female products and males should be talking about male products, participants were asked about the appropriateness of each particular voice-product combination.[57] Finally, to test social identification, we examined whether the match between the gender of the user and the gender of the voice would affect the perceived credibility of the descriptions.

Even Synthetic Voices Activate a Wide Range of Stereotypes

Participants knew which products were "female" or "male"[58]: the stereotypically female products were ranked as significantly more feminine than the stereotypically male products.[59]

The gender of the technology-based spokespersons was as influential as the gender of human spokespersons has been shown to be. Product descriptions were seen as more credible when the gender of the voice matched the gender of the product described.[60] Thus, even though participants knew that the voices were arbitrary and had no unique knowledge of any products, let alone gendered products, the participants were as swayed by synthetic voices as they are by a human spokesperson. Similarly, voices that matched the product gender were seen as more appropriate for describing the products than were mismatched voices.[61]

The gender of voice affected users' perceptions of the masculinity or femininity of the product. Female voices made products seem more feminine, and male voices made products seem more masculine.[62] Conversely, female voices were perceived as less feminine when describing a male product, and male voices were perceived as less masculine when describing a female product.[63] In other words, voice gender and product gender exerted a mutual influence on one another, consistent with stereotyping.

In addition to gender stereotyping, participants also relied on social identification. Females found the descriptions to be more credible when the female voice described the products as compared to the male voice, while the opposite was true for males.[64] This effect was in addition to the effect of the match between voice gender and product gender.

Manifesting Gender in Language

Gender is marked in speech by more than just the sound of a voice. Even within the confines of a given topic, men and women speak and write very differently.[65] In general, women's writing and speaking tend to be more "involved," while men's writing tends to be more "informational."[66] "Involved language" focuses on the interaction: It highlights interpersonal aspects and personal feelings more than specific, detailed information.[67] "Informational language," conversely, focuses on details about the things being mentioned. Thus, females tend to talk more about relationships than males, employing much greater use of "I" and "you," among other markers.[68] Females also express more concern for the listener than do males.[69] Thus, it is not surprising that females tend to use more compliments[70] and apologies[71] than men. Conversely, men tend to focus on objects and their characteristics and more frequently use the word "its."[72] Men also provide more details about place and time.[73]

Even the simplest words reflect differences between females and males. Females tend to use more personal pronouns—for example, *I, you, she, her, their, myself, herself*—than males, while males use a much larger number of determiners—*a, the, that, these*—and quantifiers—*one, two, some more*—than do females.[74] Thus, women's language tends to be about how things relate to each other, while men's language tends to focus on the object under scrutiny. Even the same simple word is used differently by females and males: Females strongly use "they" to refer to living things, while males more frequently use "they" for inanimate things.[75]

The above findings have been validated via a careful analysis of spoken and written dialogues. The ability of these small differences to very effectively (over 80%)[76] predict whether a particular piece of dialogue or text was produced by a male or a female suggests that individuals could benefit from using these differences when determination of gender through language is important. Unfortunately, there is no research to determine whether individuals do in fact look for these cues. Nonetheless, given the negative consequences of consistency violation and the societal consequences of reinforcing stereotypes, producers of content should be very mindful of these differences and ensure that: (1) the content associated with a particular speaker should have a uniform style with respect to these differences, and (2) the style selected, especially when it involves gendered products, should be carefully considered.

Living and Designing in a World of Gender Stereotypes

The experiments that are described in this chapter suggest that gender stereotyping dominates people's views of the world. Gender stereotypes run so deep that people are often unaware that they harbor them. They are so readily elicited that even a newspaper article that provides biological explanations for gender differences can significantly increase people's endorsements of gender stereotypes.[77]

It was ironic that in both of the studies, participants insisted (when chatting with the experimenters after the experiment was completed) that applying gender stereotypes to computers or synthetic voices would be ludicrous. They also insisted that they were not guided by gender stereotypes in real life. According to the people in our study, they viewed male and female teachers equally and "knew" that the characteristics of spokespersons had nothing to do with their credibility assessments.

Gender stereotypes are pernicious because they discourage the treatment of each person as a unique and important individual and prevent people from realizing their full potential. Relevant morphological differences between the sexes are important for evolutionary success, but modern societies would benefit from a virtual elimination of dangerous overgeneralizations based on gender.

But stereotypes do not exist simply for their evolutionary convenience. Human brains are much too small and slow to process every fact about every individual. Regardless of mating, the simplicity of gender as a variable (only two categories) and its (generally) easy determinability make it a natural locus for limiting the efforts of a brain that is overmatched by a complex world. If the human brain fully eliminated gender stereotypes, it would need many more stereotypes, likely just as pernicious, to replace them.

We advocate a two-pronged approach to the issue of gender stereotypes in voice user interfaces, although it is not an optimal solution. At the macro (social) level, people need to be made more aware that *everyone* harbors significant and limiting gender stereotypes, regardless of how enlightened they feel, and that such beliefs limit individuals and society by preventing everyone from realizing their potentials. At the micro (individual) level, designers should operate within the limitations of individuals' cognitive system while remaining respectful of all people. The following shows how this might play out in a few domains.

Gender in Teaching and Learning Software

Learners bring role expectations to the education context: teachers are perceived as better when they operate within disciplines in which they are stereotypically expert. For example, in the United States, hunting and fishing are stereotypically male, while cooking and sewing are stereotypically female. This tendency to stereotype then leads to a vicious cycle. As students perceive that certain disciplines are appropriate for one gender or the other, they use these expectations to guide their selections of disciplines. This selection process increasingly skews the gender distribution of those disciplines, thereby reinforcing the initial belief about appropriateness and reinforcing the pattern.[78]

Attempts to break the cycle run into the "pipeline problem." Because very few individuals of a particular gender go into fields that are stereotyped for the other gender, remedying the gender distribution that causes the perception in the first place is difficult. Because decisions about fields of interest often start in middle school, overturning stereotypes takes a very long time.

Technology provides a wonderful opportunity to overcome the "pipeline problem." Rapidly increasing the number of female teachers in stereotypically male disciplines (or vice versa) might be difficult, but it is easy to give female *voices* to all of the educational software for stereotypically male disciplines by simply hiring voice talents of the desired gender or manipulating the parameters of the synthetic voice. Just as people bring gender expectations *to* technology, they can draw gender expectations *from* technology. By "staffing" educational software with male or female voices that counter stereotypes, people are likely to draw the conclusion that people of both genders "belong" in all disciplines.[79] An even stronger strategy would be to have multiple voices in the software, with the vast majority of the voices reflecting the "atypical" gender. By having a limited number of exemplars from the dominant group and the majority from the less dominant group, the presence of the atypical gender will become even more salient.[80]

If these "unusual" assignments of gender might harm the initial credibility of the software, designers could make the female voices "masculine" and the male voices "feminine," whether recorded or synthetic, by using the technique discussed in chapter 2.[81] This transitional step could be used until disciplinary stereotypes are weakened and voice gender can be selected based on other factors.

Gender in E-Commerce Software

In contexts where the credibility of the description is critical or the stereotype is unambiguous and not detrimental, designers should ensure that the voice matches the "gender" of the product or service. For example, a Web site that sells linen, cosmetics, or romance novels would benefit from a female voice, all other things being equal, while a site that sells hammers, oscilloscopes, or war novels would benefit from a male voice. Gender of voice can also distinguish a product category: a site that sells Barbie dolls would be more credible with a female voice, but a site that sells "action figures" would be more credible with a male voice.

When the product or service is not "gendered," a male voice tends to be perceived as more credible. But designers should also take social identification into account: females tend to believe female voices more than male voices, while males tend to believe male voices.

Credibility is not the only criterion in e-commerce, however. For example, when attention is the key consideration, there are two strategies. First, female voices that suggest that they are physiologically aroused (by using breathy speech, for example) will attract male (heterosexual) listeners, and vice versa. Second, people feel uncomfortable in situations where they are the only person of a particular gender.[82] Thus, a set of uniformly female voices will draw attention from female listeners and discourage male listeners, while the converse would attract males and discourage females.

In some cases, the particular task to be completed by the listener (and not the product or service category) is the most relevant factor in voice selection. For example, imagine a telephone-based call center that sells a stereotypically male product, such as football gear. While a male voice would be a logical choice for the initial sales function, the complaint line might be "staffed" by a female voice because women are perceived as more sensitive, emotionally responsive, people-oriented, understanding, cooperative, and kind.[83] However, if the call center has a rigid policy of "no refunds, no returns," the interface would benefit from a male voice, as females are harshly evaluated when they adopt a position of dominance.[84]

Gender in International Interfaces

All cultures have a wide range of gender stereotypes, but the specifics of the stereotypes differ from culture to culture. In the United States, there are not strong norms about who can provide directions to someone who is lost (although males stereotypically should not *ask* for directions). Thus, both female-voiced and male-voiced navigation systems can be found in cars. However, BMW in Germany had to have a product recall for a car navigation system that had a female voice: German male drivers (the vast majority of BMW drivers) do not take directions from females.[85] Cross-cultural gender stereotyping thus applies to voice systems as well. As another example, in the United States, all aspects of stock transactions are stereotypically handled by males. In Japan, conversely, females are considered more suited to researching and communicating stock information, while males are more suited to handling stock purchases. Hence, the design of a telephone-based stock brokerage system in Japan switched the user from listening to a female recorded voice (when the user obtained information) to a male recorded voice when the user made a purchase. Thus, internationalization involves not simply translating words from one language to another but also being aware of the gender stereotypes that are prevalent in that particular culture.

Gender Stereotypes: Friend or Foe?

Regardless of their appropriateness or accuracy, stereotypes serve a powerful and consequential role in all aspects of life, whether one interacts with people or with technologies. On the one hand, conforming to stereotypes seems to create more natural and effective interfaces—doing so simply acknowledges and leverages users' expectations. But at the same time, mindlessly designing interfaces to conform to every stereotype is often unjustified and even detrimental to society at large.[86] There are no easy answers to this dilemma, but designers must make conscious and considered decisions when choosing to follow, counter, or ignore gender stereotypes as they build computers that talk and listen.

4 Personality of Voices: Similars Attract

If gender is the most basic means for classifying people, personality is the richest. Such descriptions as extroverted or introverted, judging or intuiting, kind or unkind, and a host of other traits provide a powerful framework for understanding how other people think, feel, and behave.

People assign personality rapidly and automatically.[1] They make personality judgments in the first minutes of an encounter,[2] and those judgments strongly influence all subsequent interactions. The ability to rapidly assign personality is very useful: because it broadly predicts a wide range of attitudes and behaviors,[3] personality allows people to know how to behave toward others and what to expect in return.

What signals do people send that let others quickly make judgments about their personality? And how do people's personalities affect others' feelings about them?

Markers of Personality

People use a variety of cues to interpret personality.[4] For example, individuals observe that extroverts charge into situations, while introverts proceed cautiously.[5] Similarly, extroverts talk more than they listen and tend to use strong terms like *definitely* and *absolutely*, while introverts listen more than they talk and favor more neutral words like *perhaps* and *maybe*.[6] Other clues come from posture, with extroverts using many broad gestures, opening their arms wide, and holding their head erect.[7] Introverts, in contrast, use fewer, tighter gestures and hold their arms close to the side and their heads down. People even rely on body shape to guide their judgments:[8] tall and muscular people are perceived as more extroverted than short and frail people.

The sound of someone's voice also provides many important personality cues, which humans have evolved to identify and analyze.[9] Indeed, the term *personality* comes from the Latin *personare*, to "sound through," referring to the mouth opening in an actor's mask.[10] Assessing personality from voice is an evolved skill.[11] Because you can often hear people before you see them, voice analysis allows a quick prediction of the speaker's attitudes and behaviors.

Four fundamental aspects of voices indicate personality.[12] The first is volume: compare the booming voice of a person who loves socializing to the soft voice of someone who prefers to read books.[13] Another is pitch, or how high or low a voice is:[14] the hyperactive comedian with a high voice suggests a different personality than the deep voiced news anchor.[15] A third is pitch range, or how much the voice ranges between highs and lows:[16] everyone has experienced the rich ups and downs of an animated story teller and the monotone delivery of a technical presenter. Similarly, rising intonation at the end of a statement is associated with a tentative stance, while falling intonation at the end of a statement is associated with confidence.[17] Finally, there is speech rate—the exuberant fast talker versus the calm articulator.[18] These four vocal indicators exert such a powerful influence on human attitudes that people may rely more on voice characteristics to make judgments about people's personalities than on the actual *content* of their speech.[19]

Each of these voice characteristics tells us something about a person, but in combination they become particularly influential.[20] For example, when people meet someone who speaks loudly and rapidly, in a high pitch, and with a wide voice range, they feel confident that they are dealing with the life of the party. Conversely, when people hear a soft, deep, monotone voice speaking slowly, they feel equally confident that this person is shy.

People do not use voice characteristics simply to identify a speaker's personality. They further use their decisions about voice personality to guide their feelings and behaviors toward the speaker.

Similars Attract

One of the most powerful and consistent behavioral patterns with respect to personality is "similarity attraction":[21] people are attracted to other people who are similar to themselves. When people encounter someone who seems to have a personality like their own, they tend to have positive feelings toward the person. People usually like the person and think that the person is intelligent, trustworthy, and friendly. In fact, people will attribute almost any positive characteristic to people who are similar to them.

Similarity attraction can best be thought of as an *overgeneralization* of social identification.[22] People who share similar genes or similar socialization experiences are likely to share the same evolutionary goals—that is, survival of their community.[23] Thus, people are more positively oriented to family and clan members than to others. There are, then, evolutionary advantages in rapidly associating "like me" with "positive orientation." At the same time, however, people seem to overuse this heuristic and base it on attributes, such as personality, that very possibly have no relevant genetic or shared cultural basis.

What about the saying "Opposites attract"? Oddly enough, opposites who eventually like each other do so *because* of similarity attraction. Research shows that people like others whose personality mismatches them initially and then changes to be more similar to their own more than they like people who consistently match them from the beginning.[24] A third adage ties these seemingly conflicting proverbs together: "Imitation is flattery."[25]

Similarity Attraction and Technology

Will people further overgeneralize the notion of "similar is good" and apply it to voices on the Web, the telephone, and wireless devices? Although one of the ultimate goals of artificial intelligence researchers is to create technologies with a "personality," this goal has not seemed likely to happen in the foreseeable future. First, technologies do not seem to *have* personalities. Indeed, it is not a coincidence that the word *person* is imbedded in the word *personality*. (When people say that the Macintosh and Windows operating systems have different "personalities," they are referring to characteristics of appearance and design philosophy that are important but distinct from the psychological notions presented here.) Even if a computer could project the same vocal personality cues that a person can, and even if a listener would say, "That sounds like an extrovert," most people would draw a distinction between a computer "sounding like an extrovert" and a computer actually being extroverted.

Another reason to expect that similarity attraction would not carry over into human-computer voice interactions is that most speech that is presented via technologies is not and does not sound like human speech.[26] These incessant reminders that computer-generated voices are not human should logically discourage the assignment of personality.

On the other hand, as discussed in previous chapters, the human brain can detect paralinguistic cues in synthetic speech just as it does when listening to true human speech. As with gender,[27] determining another's personality may be so important that when people hear any voice, no matter how clearly not human, they automatically and unconsciously use their voice-analysis skills to assign a personality to the voice. Once they make this judgment, they may go even further and use the seeming similarity or difference between their perception of the voice's personality and their own to draw conclusions about the system's intelligence, likeability, and trustworthiness, exactly as if they were interacting with another person. Essentially, although people know that synthetic speech systems do not really have personalities, the evolution-derived tendencies to assume that voices are social and respond accordingly may overwhelm that knowledge.

If the evolution-oriented view is correct, then designers should be able to manipulate the speech characteristics of any technology that can produce speech and thereby give it a "personality." For example, designers of Web sites, voice portals, or handheld devices could suggest an extroverted personality by creating a synthesized voice with a fast speech rate, loud volume level, high pitch, and wide pitch range, and "introverted" devices could be given the opposite type of voice. If these cues are successful, people will identify, perhaps subconsciously, the personality in the voice and will be influenced by their perceptions of the system and its content. And because artificial speech can be manipulated in real time, it provides opportunities for adapting to users that would not be available to recorded speech systems.

Do People Feel Like They Are Similar to Machine Voices?

To explore the relationship between synthesized voices and personality, an experiment[28] was conducted to determine whether varying the four key vocal cues (volume, pitch, pitch range, and speed rate) while presenting the same content will lead people to respond as if they encountered different personalities and whether matching users' personalities to the personalities of synthetic voices leads to similarity attraction.

The context for this study was a book-selling Web site.[29] The Web site presented five different books on the same screen, using a visual display similar to the one used by the online book retailer Amazon.com.[30] The screen displayed the title, author, and cover of each book but no text description. Instead, participants had to click on a link to an audio file to hear a description of the book.

For each book, participants heard the audio description and responded to Web-based questions[31] about the quality of the book, the likeability and quality of the description, and their likelihood of buying the book. Then participants answered Web-based questions that assessed their judgments of the Web site's voice, the descriptions of the books, and the reviewer.[32] Finally, because each participant's voice needed to be categorized as extroverted or introverted, all participants were recorded saying their name and describing their experiences in the experiment.

This study required some participants who were clearly extroverted and other participants who were clearly introverted. Using two Web-based standard personality tests,[33] we chose people who had the most extreme and consistent scores[34]—thirty-six extroverts and thirty-six introverts. To ensure that all combinations of participant personality and voice personality were included, half of the extroverts and half of the introverts heard the extroverted voice, while the other half heard the introverted voice.[35] To safeguard the results from the effects of the gender of the participants (some studies have found levels of extroversion to differ between men and women), every combination of participant personality and voice personality had approximately equal numbers of men and women.

Except for voice personality, all participants saw and heard the same visual layouts, instructions, book content descriptions, and questions. The synthesized voices were made to sound as realistic and compelling as possible[36] by simultaneously making all four fundamental voice features (volume, pitch, pitch range, and speech rate) extroverted or introverted.[37] To ensure that only the personality of the voices was manipulated, the voices were checked to ensure that they received similar ratings in categories such as gender, age, informativeness, and persuasiveness independent of personality.

We combined people's answers to the Web-based questions into eight concepts:[38] voice personality,[39] liking of the voice,[40] quality of the review,[41] credibility of the review,[42] whether users would purchase the book,[43] liking of the reviewer,[44] credibility of the reviewer,[45] and personality of the reviewer.[46] Because the book reviews were relatively similar, answers were combined across the reviews.[47]

Synthetic Personality Equals Human Personality

The participants in the book-description study had no problem indicating whether the voice they heard was extroverted or introverted:[48] the extrovert voice was rated as clearly more extroverted than the introvert voice.[49] This confirms that individuals will classify even synthesized voices by their personality.

A more important question is whether the personality of the voice influenced how people *liked* aspects of the Web-based book-selling system. Showing the power of similarity attraction, extroverts liked the extroverted voice more than the introverted voice, while introverts liked the introverted voice more than the extroverted voice.[50] The effects of the voice personality extended to user's feelings about the book descriptions, with extroverts liking the book reviews more when they were read by the extrovert voice, and introverts liking the reviews more when they were read by the introvert voice, even though the content was identical.[51] Similarly, people found the book descriptions more credible when the voice speaking the descriptions matched their own personalities.[52]

The perceptions of the book descriptions even influenced people's intention to buy. Extroverted participants were more likely to buy the books when the descriptions were presented with an extroverted voice, while introverted participants were more likely to buy when the descriptions were read by an introverted voice,[53] showing the tremendous power of the brain's automatic assignment of personality.

Even though it was clear that the person who wrote the review was not actually speaking, participants liked the reviewer more when the reader's voice matched their own personality.[54] The reviewer also was perceived to be more credible when the reader's and participant's personalities matched.[55]

Even though all book reviews had identical content, the synthesized voice's personality influenced people's perceptions of the human reviewer's personality. People thought the human review writer was more extroverted when the extrovert computer voice narrated the review as compared to the introvert narrator.[56] This result reflects people's well-established tendency to gather personality cues from the closest source and apply that information to judgments about seemingly unrelated people and things.[57] Put another way, the messenger strongly influences people's perception of the message.

There was no instance in which the personality of the voice, *independent* of the user's personality, had a direct effect.[58]

Did You Think about This?

A compelling alternative explanation to the results that were obtained from this experiment is that people like *voices* that sound like their own voices; personality is irrelevant. That is, similarity is not grounded in comparison of the participant's personality and the voice's personality; it is instead based on volume, pitch, pitch range, and speech rate. This distinction is critical. If similarity refers to voice parameters rather than personality, then designers and researchers should be using pitch meters and vocal-analysis tools rather than personality questionnaires. In other words, should designers measure people's personalities via questionnaires (or other attitudinal and behavioral manifestations) and adapt voice interfaces to their personality? Or should they instead derive numeric assessments of people's four major voice characteristics and set the synthetic speech to have identical values?

Of course, if peoples' voices always mirror their personalities, then the question is moot: designers can measure people in whatever way is most convenient. To determine whether this was the case, two trained raters classified the tape recordings of each participant's voice as either extroverted or introverted.[59] Of the seventy-two participants, forty-one participants were classified as having an extroverted voice, and thirty were classified as having an introverted voice (one person declined to have her voice recorded).

The relationship between people's personalities as measured by the written personality tests and by the classification of their voices was remarkably low (although statistically significant).[60] This finding tells us that clear and possibly consequential differences exist between a person's personality and a person's voice. This somewhat puzzling and unexpected result may mean that while people *perceive* voices to be good indicators of personality and respond accordingly, voice characteristics may be deceptive.

We also tested whether the similarity between participants' voices and the computer's voice affected people's perceptions of the computer's voice. All of the statistical analyses were repeated using the participants' voice ratings rather than questionnaire ratings. The analyses showed *no* evidence that people liked voices that were similar to their own voices;[61,62] this effect, if it exists, must be very small or overwhelmed by the assignment of personality. Thus, the best approach to integrating personality and design seems to be to measure personality via a questionnaire (or other reliable methods) and then adapt voice interfaces to the user's responses.

Leveraging the Power of Synthetic Personality

People in the study interacted with obviously nonhuman voices that, because of their artificiality, constantly reminded participants of the nonsocial nature of the interaction. Surprisingly, people nonetheless assigned a fundamental, complex human property—personality—to the synthesized voice. In turn, that personality strongly influenced participants' attitudes, feelings, and intentions.

To date, designers have focused on making synthesized voices easier to understand. This effort has met with considerable success: current systems that use synthetic speech are generally quite comprehensible, even for nonnative speakers. Systems continue to progress in this regard, although the work is technically complex, labor- and computing-intensive, and accessible only to the coders of speech-synthesis systems.[63]

Tremendous opportunities also exist for rapid progress in the *social* aspects of design. Synthesized speech can be made to evoke different personalities quickly and easily simply by modifying a few parameters in real time. Thus, in contrast to the computer scientists who thought that personality would require high levels of artificial intelligence, graphics, and a host of other complex, if even attainable, technologies,[64] the creation of personality is immediately available to everyone.[65] This is particularly true because all of the principles, findings, and design ideas that are discussed in this chapter and throughout the book (with a few exceptions[66]) apply uniformly to both recorded and synthetic voices.

Overall, this experiment shows that the similarity-attraction principle applies to synthesized voices: people like voices that manifest personalities that are similar to their own. The positive feelings about the voice go beyond the voice itself to influence perceptions of the content and willingness to buy.

How can designers leverage these findings to build better interfaces? In traditional media, one of the key concerns is "casting"—the selection of a person for a particular role.[67] Clarity of speech is not a crucial quality. If it were, performers with nonstandard American accents (such as Sylvester Stallone, Arnold Schwarzenegger, Benicio del Toro, and Carol Channing) would not be stars. The producer's goal is to identify actors who can connect with the audience, regardless of paralinguistic characteristics.

When selecting a synthesized voice, the same idea applies: designers should select the voice that serves their goals for the product. Because virtually all voice interfaces want to increase some combination of liking, trust, perceived intelligence, and buying behavior, designers who discriminate among synthetic voices solely on the basis of minimal differences in comprehensibility are missing an enormous opportunity, especially now that virtually all synthetic voices have acceptable clarity. Because text-to-speech systems produce sounds instantaneously and can immediately conform to settings of volume, pitch, pitch range, and speech rate, it is inexpensive to make people feel that the system is "just like them" and hence worthy of affection, trust, and a range of other attributes.[68]

Learning about Users' Personalities: Some Strategies

Imagine that an interface were to say, "Before you can use this system, you must answer the following fifty personality questions about yourself. Once you do that, the system will select the voice that is right for you." This approach would be a mistake. First of all, most business models rightfully preclude any barriers between the system and the user: requiring people to fill out a form before buying, seeing advertisements, or performing other tasks desired by the company is a poor strategy. Additionally, questions that ask about a person's personality and come from faceless companies or Web sites justifiably elicit feelings of suspicion and resistance because that information is personal. Finally, requiring answers rather than making them optional implies a level of presumptive control that can be disturbing.

Designers might argue that while these concerns are valid, users should be willing to do virtually anything that will make them happy in the long run. But the argument that designers are trying to "make" people happy reminds users that although the system can produce many different voices, the choice is *completely out of their hands.* Instead of presenting users with a series of voices and asking them which one they would like, the system paternalistically (and annoyingly) forces them to give answers and removes them from all decision making. Furthermore, the system doesn't say *how* the answers will affect the selection, inviting users to suspect that the company or interface is selecting voices that serve interests other than the users'.

If designers decide that a direct personality assessment would not be appropriate but do want information about a user's personality, then they can use a number of strategies. First, many interfaces ask users to fill out profile information. The profile could potentially include "personality" questions that do not look like personality questions. For example, a travel site can ask, "While you're on vacation, do you prefer spending time with others or taking time to read or walk alone?" and "Do you prefer visiting famous landmarks or spending time in museums and quieter places?" both of which are good measures of extroversion versus introversion.

There are even more indirect measures of personality. For example, certain occupations are associated with certain personality types; indeed, one of the standard measures for helping people determine the appropriate occupation asks personality questions rather than skill questions.[69] A more creative and whimsical example of personality assessment comes from a Web site that had a picture of a dog and asked, "Which would you give this dog for its birthday: a choke collar [controlling person] or a chewy toy [less controlling person]?" The system could then assign a voice personality based on the person's response.

Designers can also assess personality from user behavior. People who rapidly make choices, especially in new situations, are likely to be more impulsive than those who carefully ponder each option. In addition, sometimes users' personalities can be predicted from their presence at a particular Web site. For example, a site that sells party supplies is likely to be frequented by extroverts, while introverts may frequent a site that sells hobby items. Thus, the former site could confidently deploy only an extroverted voice, while the latter could use only an introverted voice (this would also conform with the consistency principle discussed in the next chapter).

If the User's Personality Remains Unknown, Use an Extroverted Voice

What if the user's personality cannot be discovered? When the brand and role of the voice do not dictate the selection of a particular personality,[70] use an extroverted voice. Designers of traditional media have long understood this principle: the stars of virtually every situation comedy, the evening news anchors, spokespeople, and the most popular cartoon characters (including Bugs Bunny, Fred Flintstone, and Scooby-Doo) have extroverted personalities and voices.[71] These people and characters speak quickly, loudly, and with significant frequency range. The only exception to the extroversion rule is that when designers want to stress a system's competence, voices with deeper-than-average pitch are perceived as more effective.[72]

Why is extroversion more popular than introversion? The basic reason is that people like others who are expressive.[73] The evolutionary basis for this is that expressiveness is associated with predictability, and predictability reduces cognitive load and increases comfort. Extroverts are also friendlier and more attention getting.[74] Thus, while this selection will not prove optimal for all users, if only one voice can be deployed, an extroverted voice would be better than any other choice.

Attempting to placate all users by having one voice exhibit a variety of personality cues (that is, some cues consistent with one personality and other cues consistent with a conflicting personality) is not an effective solution. People do not respond to these voices as "somewhat like me." Instead, voices with mixed cues (such as faster than average speech, louder volume, higher frequency, but low frequency range), much like voices with ambiguous gender,[75] seem aberrant and therefore less intelligent and trustworthy.[76] People also report high levels of discomfort as they try to draw conclusions about a mixed voice's underlying personality.[77] Like the comic strip character Charlie Brown, hybrid voices get classified as "wishy-washy" rather than "half extroverted and half introverted" and thereby satisfy no one.

Changing the Voice's Personality

In some cases, the personality of the user emerges over time. Can a system significantly change its voice once it learns the user's personality? While gradual adaptation to the user is effective,[78] if a Web site, phone system, or wireless device drastically changes its voice, people will respond as if they are interacting with a different person.[79] This behavior creates a number of problems. First, wondering why a new voice was introduced will distract people and prevent them from processing the content.[80] That is why the standard in radio is either to make an explicit transition from one voice to the next (for example, "I am now turning you over to Pamela Smith in Washington") or to introduce all of the speakers at the beginning ("With us today is Fred Jones." "Good to be here"). Designers should apply these same standards when using multiple voices (see chapter 9 for a further discussion).

A second problem with this transition from one voice to another is that all aspects of the relationship with the first voice will now have to be reestablished for the second voice: the sense of trust and loyalty built up with the initial voice will not automatically carry over. Indeed, the fact that the person was handed over to a new "person" may lead to psychological resistance. An explicit transition that provides an explanation of the consequences and *reasons* for the change is critical. A system could say, for example, "Because you have been such a wise investor [flattery is an effective strategy[81]], you will now work with our Tier 1 system." As was noted earlier, people do not respond well to the idea that systems are trying to match the voice to their personality. Hence, users should be presented with a different rationale for the change (although the ethics of this alternative explanation are questionable).

Other Personality Traits and Voice

Although voices do not convey all personality characteristics (for example, voices do not indicate whether a person is intuitive, relies on facts, plans ahead, or is spontaneous), there is a model that allows designers to make a more nuanced selection of voice personality than simply extroversion or introversion. This model, developed by the psychologist Jerry S. Wiggins, has two basic dimensions: friendly to unfriendly and dominant to submissive.[82]

The friendly to unfriendly dimension distinguishes people who are warm and sympathetic from people who are unpleasant and hard-hearted. Friendly voices are marked by high pitch (both male and female), wide frequency range, and rapid speech.[83] Classic TV moms of the 1950s are examples of extreme friendliness: they tended to have high, expressive voices and to speak rapidly. Conversely, TV hermits and misanthropes, who have contempt for others but don't actively attack or defend, tend to have deeper voices with little modulation and with measured speed.

The dominant to submissive dimension separates the assertive from the timid. Dominant voices are marked by low pitch, limited frequency range, and loudness.[84] Actors like James Earl Jones, John Wayne, and Clint Eastwood have the classic dominant voice, and they tend to play characters that control or overcome their environments without being particularly kind or unkind. Submissives are buffeted by events and people and are essentially actionless: they usually don't have starring roles in media because they tend to reflect the plot rather than move the plot forward. Most Woody Allen roles and William Hurt in the title role in *The Accidental Tourist* are exceptions that are marked by relatively high and soft voices.

An added benefit of this dimensional scheme is that it allows the designer to mix these pure types in various ways without creating diffuse and unclear voices or personalities. For example, the mix of dominance with extreme unfriendliness creates the deep, slow, stolid voice of evil characters like Darth Vader in *Star Wars*. Superheroes, in contrast, combine the deepness of a dominant voice with wider frequency range and greater speed than evil doers, showing that they are the "good guys." Classic sidekicks—from Sancho Panza to Lou Costello to Robin the Boy Wonder—have submissive and friendly voices: soft, quick, high, and highly varying. Henchmen (submissive and unfriendly) also have varying voices, but they have deeper and slower voices than their friendly counterparts.

Casting Studies Are Quick and Valuable

The rules outlined above for manifesting personality in voice provide basic guidance for creating personality-rich voices. Nonetheless, the only way to ensure that designers have succeeded is to determine the feelings of a sample of prospective users of the system—that is, to do a casting study. In these studies, designers gather participants and have them listen to each voice in turn (ideally, different users hear the voices in different orders). The content should be relatively neutral. If each voice says something different or says something that strongly marks a personality, the content will influence perception of the voice.[85] The presentation need be only two or three minutes long because people rapidly and reliably assign personality. After hearing each voice, the user is presented with a questionnaire (paper-and-pencil or Web-based) and asked, "How well does each of these adjectives (or sentences) describe the voice?" Research with respect to casting suggests that the Wiggins adjectives are particularly useful for this assessment.

How many participants would a study like this require? The good news is that because assignment of personality is determined by the wiring of the brain, people tend to agree on the personality manifested by a particular voice. Hence, fifteen to twenty people are usually sufficient. Because human speech tends to be more rich and complex than its synthetic counterpart, verifying the selection of a voice or voices with a casting study is critical for recorded voices.

Personality Is Powerful

Voices are not merely a handy means to transmit information to the user. All voices—natural, recorded, or synthetic—activate automatic judgments about personality. These judgments influence people's expectations about the system and its behavior and determine whether they will like the system, trust it, and be willing to buy from it. Rarely does a change as inexpensive and simple as creating the appropriate volume, pitch, pitch rate, and speech rate initiate such large differences in how users will think, feel, and behave.

5 Personality of Voices and Words: Multiple Personalities Are Dangerous

For newborn infants, voice is the alpha and omega of social life. As noted in chapter 1, within days after birth, infants can distinguish their mother's voices from all other voices[1] and can use the sound of voices to distinguish people from other animals,[2] one person from another,[3] and people of their own culture from people of other cultures.[4] Hearing voices is also the first way in which babies identify other people's gender[5] and emotions.[6]

The extreme focus on the sounds of human speech has an even more important benefit: attending to speech is how children learn language.[7] The acquisition of language requires some deep insights:[8] speech sounds are tied to things (nouns), actions (verbs), and descriptions (adjectives and adverbs); words are the building blocks of sentences (all languages have sentences); the same sounds can have different meanings (homophones are present in almost every language); and the order of words is not arbitrary ("The man walked to the woman" conveys a different action than "The woman walked to the man").

It is remarkable that children can learn language in the way they do:[9] There is little systematic repetition in language learning.[10] Complex grammatical forms are introduced before simple ones are mastered, and people use different terms to refer to the same thing.[11] Speakers omit key words via a gesture or a glance. Different teachers (speakers) have different pronunciations and proclivities, people insert nonlinguistic sounds (such as "um" and "uh"), and many of the spoken sentences that the child hears are patently ungrammatical.[12] Some cultures do not even prescribe verbal interactions with babies until the infants demonstrate that they can understand.[13]

Children become fluent speakers in any one of an incredibly diverse set of languages by leveraging the voice activation of their brain and combining it with intensive, ingenious strategies for extracting syntax and semantics from the chaos of surrounding sounds. The key insight that justifies the child's brain's allocation of so much mental attention is that language is an *intentional* activity.[15] Thus, the brain is wired to view every aspect of every human utterance as *meaningful*.[16] Any sound emanating from a person's mouth is viewed as speech unless proven otherwise. Because language is an intentional activity, the *particular choice of words* describes more than objective content; it also tells the listener about the speaker. Even children as young as two years old understand that various descriptors of their pet—such as *dog, doggy, dawg* (if the speaker is from New Jersey), *puppy, Spot, Spotty, silly dog, funny dog,* or *little fuzz-ball*—reflect the orientation of the speaker as much as the situation, as does the descriptiveness of language—"The woman throws the ball" conveys a different image than "The gray-haired, seventy-year-old woman throws the green, ovoid ball at blisteringly high speed."[17] More sophisticated listeners know that even subtle grammatical differences—such as "I broke the computer" and "The computer was broken by me"—can inform the listener about the speaker.[18] In sum, just as the voice of the speaker enables the brain to extract information that is socially relevant, so does the surface structure of every sentence.[19]

Personality is a primary predictor of how people will speak.[20] Extroverts, for example, tend to use highly expressive language, filling their speech with adjectives, adverbs, and more words overall.[21] Extroverts also tend to talk about objects and situations with extreme phrases such as "the most" and "the worst" and to describe the world in absolute terms.[22] They also tend to use facilitative tags (questions at the end of sentences that seem to invite the listener to respond), such as "I like this movie; don't you?"[23] Introverts, on the other hand, tend to state things more moderately, tentatively, and succinctly, and tend not to refer to the speaker.[24]

Personality in Textual Interfaces

An important transition in the world of technology occurred when computers and computer-based technologies shifted from producing only numbers to displaying, initially on teletypes and eventually on screens, actual words and sentences.[25] This was a tiny step compared to the leap envisioned by Alan Turing when he described a technology that used speech so effectively that it would be indistinguishable from a person,[26] but moving from zeros and ones to outputting something as simple as "Hello World"[27] dramatically changed the accessibility of computers.[28]

Just as every voice, no matter how "neutral," carries paralinguistic cues that can be potentially used to identify personality, every instance of content, no matter how "neutral," carries linguistic cues that can be potentially used to identify personality.[29] All e-mails, Web sites, teaching software, and other text-based materials present content that is influenced by the personality of the writer. Attempts to eradicate personality by implementing numerous guidelines for the creation of content simply replace writer personality with brand personality or the personality of the rule maker. Although cues are available, will people attribute personality to content in an interface, just as they attribute personality to computer voices? If the analogy between content and oral cues is carried one step further, it also makes sense to inquire about similarity attraction: Will people prefer content whose "personality" matches their own, just as they prefer voice personalities that match their own?

When there is *only* textual content (that is, no voices), an extensive literature on textual personality on computers answers both of these questions with an unequivocal yes.[30] In these studies, the researcher keeps the core content identical while making the following changes: (1) the extroverted computer uses strong, assertive language during the task (such as "You should definitely do this"), and the introverted computer uses more equivocal language (such as "Perhaps you should do this"), and (2) the extroverted computer expresses high confidence in its actions during the task, and the introverted computer expresses low confidence.[31] In the first study of its kind, extroverted or introverted participants were paired with a computer that either matched or mismatched their personality.[32] Consistent with the principle of "similarity attraction" described in the previous chapter, extroverted participants were found to be more attracted to, to assign greater intelligence to, and to conform more with the extroverted computer compared to the introvert computer. Introverted participants reacted the same way to the introverted computer compared to the extroverted computer, despite the essentially identical content.

These initial results have been extended and replicated numerous times, making it one of the most robust findings in the human-technology interaction literature. For example, when people use a "matching" text-based computer, they are more willing to purchase.[33] Textual personality similarity can overcome the "self-serving bias":[34] when a computer's "personality" matches that of the user, individuals are more likely to give the computer credit for success and less likely to blame the computer for failure, compared to when there is a personality mismatch.[35] Personality cues can even be influential when the personality-infused content is not the user's primary interest: the same music, humor, and health advice were perceived as significantly better when the personality of a Web-based "News and Entertainment Guide" matched the user than when the guide did not match.[36]

Mixing Linguistic and Paralinguistic Personalities

If the human brain analyzed speech as simply linguistic cues (the words that are spoken) plus paralinguistic cues (the sounds of the voice), drawing conclusions about the effects of manifesting personality through speech would be easy. The observer would (1) determine the effects of paralinguistic personality cues (voices) in isolation, (2) determine the effects of linguistic personality cues (content) in isolation, and (3) average the results of (1) and (2). However, the brain intimately links sounds and words from the moment the first syllable hits the ear.[37] The previous chapters provide suggestive evidence. For example, the personality of a synthetic voice influenced listeners' perceptions of book descriptions, as indicated by assessments of the reviewer.[38] Similarly, topics were perceived as more feminine when presented in a feminine rather than a masculine voice, and voices were perceived as more feminine when they were presenting feminine rather than masculine topics.[39] Voices and words are the warp and woof of speech; it is impossible to think about one without the other.

If words and sounds are intimately linked, then what happens when words and sounds manifest inconsistent personalities? Are people comfortable with an extroverted voice reading introverted content or with an introverted voice describing something using the expansive language of extroverts? In normal social interaction, this is rare: most extroverts both sound like extroverts and use words like extroverts, and similarly for introverts.[40] Even though creators of fiction can make anything happen, people expect the casting director to make sure that each character is portrayed by someone who manifests the matching personality. Personality matching is so ingrained that a reader probably would find it difficult to intone forcefully and rapidly with great verbal dynamics, "Perhaps you might like to do this?" or to whisper in a monotone, "This is absolutely the most important thing that you should do."[41]

Laboratory studies show that the brain struggles with inconsistency.[42] In J. Ridley Stroop's classic 1935 study, people were shown a word on a screen and asked to say the color of the ink in which the word was written.[43] People took much longer to identify red ink and say "red" when the word on the screen was *blue* than when the word on the screen was arbitrary, such as *ball* or *chair*. The inconsistent color word seemed to *interfere* with the processing of the ink color, an effect known as the "Stroop effect."[44] This discovery triggered hundreds of similar studies, most of which confirmed the Stroop effect.[45]

Similar studies have been conducted in the speech domain. In one 1972 study, the words *high* and *low* were spoken in either a high pitch (175 Hz) or a low pitch (110 Hz), and people were asked to repeat the word.[46] When the word was spoken with the inconsistent pitch, participants took much longer to say the word than when the word was consistent with the pitch. Similarly, it was more difficult to say which side of the room a word came from when the words *left* and *right* were spoken on the inconsistent rather than the consistent side of the room.[47] Finally, participants were slower to identify the speaker's gender when a male voice said the word *girl* and when a female voice said the word *boy* than when the voice said the word with the consistent gender.[48] Hence, inconsistency between the content of *what* is said, verbally, and *how* it is said, vocally, leads to difficulties in perception and processing.

Research has found that inconsistency in personality, in addition to requiring longer and more effortful processing,[49] leads to negative affect and dislike for the inconsistent person.[50] For the past twenty-five years, an enormous number of studies have demonstrated that participants report less liking of a hypothetical person when that person is described with inconsistent personality traits than when that person is described with consistent traits.[51] Without consistency of personality, people become confused, uncertain, and somewhat disturbed because they rely on a consistent personality to predict the future behaviors of another person.[52] In addition to similarity attraction, then, there is *consistency attraction*.[53]

Mixing Personalities in Interfaces: It Happens All the Time

Unfortunately, using words associated with one personality type and a voice associated with a different personality type in interfaces is a common occurrence. First, interfaces that are designed to read content written by others must contend with a wide range of personalities. For example, an e-mail reader must read missives from a stereotypical cheerleader, librarian, military general, and shoe salesman: how could a single voice personality appropriately manifest them all? Amazon has millions of book descriptions written by people representing every conceivable personality type: what voice personality could be consistent with all of these books? Second, unlike synthetic voice personality, in which creating one personality rather than another is straightforward, there is no simple, automated method to reliably "translate" and "homogenize" content from one personality to another.

If the foregoing theoretical framework is applicable to computer-synthesized voices, then there should be strong negative effects for inconsistency. However, as noted in the first chapter, sometimes psychological theories make conflicting predictions. In this case, strong evidence suggests that people "are not content simply to note inconsistencies or to let them sit where they are. [Inconsistency] is puzzling, and prompts [them] to look more deeply."[54] The most common strategies to resolve seeming inconsistencies are to attribute the inconsistent behavior to a unique aspect of the situation[55] or to ignore the inconsistent information.[56] With technology, users could potentially say to themselves: "That voice just doesn't sound right. Voices like that shouldn't say things like that. Now I see what the problem is. I fell into the silly idea that computer voices have personality. I may have been lured into feeling that way when there was no inconsistency, such as when the content is neutral, but now that I think about it, I should simply ignore the personality of the voice." If this view is correct, then synthetic voice personality should have no effect at all. The critical question is whether people automatically integrate technology-based voice personality and content personality or whether they separate and possibly ignore the personalities.

Encounters with Confused Personalities: When the Voice Belies the Words

To address these questions, we needed a context in which it would be natural for the same core content to be presented with either an extroverted style or an introverted style.[57] Auction Web sites[58] seemed perfect: they are filled with content that manifests every imaginable personality because of the diversity of the people who submit objects for bids.

A few weeks before the experiment started, a personality test was given to approximately 120 people. Based on the results of that test, forty extroverts and forty introverts were selected to participate in the experiment (we did not tell them that the test was the basis for their selection). Gender was approximately balanced across conditions, and all participants were native English speakers.

Participants were directed to an online auction site, complete with an eBay-like interface. The site included the names and pictures of nine antique or collectible auction items: a 1963 stained-glass lamp, a 1995 limited-edition Marilyn Monroe watch, a 1920s radio, a 1968 Russian circus poster, an old (1910–1920s) church key, a 1916 map of the town of Oxford, a 1920 letter opener, a 1940s U.S. Treasury award medal, and a 1965 black rotary wall phone. The items were chosen so that they would not be of great interest to most participants: desire for a particular item could confuse the results.

For each item, two descriptions were created—one written by an extrovert and one written by an introvert. The descriptions were based on an actual description from eBay. The different personalities were created by modifying the length of the descriptions, word choice, and phrasing. The extroverted descriptions of the auction items were long, were filled with adjectives and adverbs, and used strong and descriptive language expressed in the form of confident assertions and exclamations. They also used self- and other references, such as "I am sure you will like this." In contrast, the introverted descriptions were relatively short, used fewer adjectives and adverbs, used more tentative and matter-of-fact language, and did not reference either the other person or themselves. For example, the extroverted description of the lamp read as follows:

> This is a reproduction of one of the most famous of the Tiffany stained-glass pieces. The colors are absolutely sensational! The first-class hand-made copper-foiled stained-glass shade is over six and one-half inches in diameter and over five inches tall. I am sure that this gorgeous lamp will accent any environment and bring a classic touch of the past to a stylish present. It is guaranteed to be in excellent condition! I would very highly recommend it.

Here is the introverted description of the lamp:

> This is a reproduction of a Tiffany stained-glass piece. The colors are quite rich. The hand-made copper-foiled stained-glass shade is about six and one-half inches in diameter and five inches tall.

The personality of the synthetic voice was created by using the four voice qualities discussed in the previous chapter—volume, pitch, pitch range, and speech rate. The introverted voice had a lower volume, lower pitch, smaller pitch range, and slow speech rate, and the extroverted voice had higher volume, higher pitch, wider pitch range, and rapid speed rate.

When participants clicked on a button next to each of the nine auction items, they heard either an extroverted or introverted description of the item via either an introverted or extroverted synthetic voice. That is, for all items, one-fourth of the participants heard extroverted descriptions spoken by an extroverted voice, one-fourth heard extroverted descriptions spoken by an introverted voice, one-fourth heard introverted descriptions spoken by an introverted voice, and one-fourth heard introverted descriptions spoken by an extroverted voice. Equal numbers of introverted and extroverted participants were randomly assigned to each of these four conditions.

After listening to the descriptions of all nine auction items, participants filled out a Web-based questionnaire.[59] These questions were asked to examine similarity attraction with respect to each of the modalities (voice and words) separately and to determine whether there was consistency attraction (preference for matching voices and words). Participants first indicated how much they liked the voice[60] and the content.[61] They were also asked how much they liked the description writers[62] and how much they trusted the description writers.[63]

To give further insights into whether people holistically process the content presented by synthetic voices, participants were also asked to assess the personality of the content[64] and the personality of the voice.[65] If the personality of one affects the perception of the other, this would provide evidence of a tight coupling.

Too Many Personalities Spoil the Auction

Despite the personality of the content, participants were significantly more positive about the auction when the voice's personality matched their own.[66] Users liked the voice more and liked the writers of the description more; there was no significant difference in how much they liked the descriptions or trusted the description writer, although the results were in the expected direction. In general, then, matching voice personality remains beneficial (although less powerful) even when the content being spoken exhibits a clear personality of its own.

With respect to the (spoken) content, similarity attraction was weaker than generally found with text, although the results paralleled the results for voice. Once again, participants liked the voice more and liked the writers of the descriptions significantly more when the content and user personalities were similar; there was no significant difference in how much participants liked the descriptions or trusted the description writer, although both were in the expected direction. Thus, voice personality and text personality were both seen as similarly diagnostic of the actual personality of the interface, even though the former was created by a computer and the latter by a person.

The most powerful effects, however, seemed to come from consistency. When the voice personality and content personality were consistent, people clearly liked the voice itself more and liked the content more. That is, consistency independently improved the perception of both modalities. People also clearly liked the writer more and found the writer to be more credible when the interface was consistent.

There was also strong evidence that voices and words are intimately linked. The personality of the voice affected users' perception of the personality of the content (as in the previous chapter): users who heard item descriptions spoken by an extroverted voice rated the descriptions as clearly more extroverted than the same descriptions spoken by an introverted voice.[67] This influence is particularly striking given that the personality of the text was unambiguously manifested in word choice, sentence length, ratio of nouns to adjectives, etc.

Consistency of Casting: The Case of Cars

Whenever possible, the best way to ensure consistency is to *start* with the personality of the interface and then have all of the content *emerge* from that personality. Ideally, an entire "back story" is created in which the designers describe the entire life story of the persona[68] of the interface, providing richness and nuance that can emerge over the course of the interaction. Even if the interface is a portal to content with a diverse set of personality markers, the interaction that provides access to the content must have a consistent personality.[69]

The design of the BMW car interface presents a wonderful example of this process. When BMW first introduced its in-car navigation system in Germany, it provided highly accurate information about the car's location and how to get to almost all city and street addresses. Unfortunately, a large number of drivers had a strong negative reaction to this model of engineering excellence and demanded a product recall. The German drivers felt uncomfortable with, and untrusting of, a "female" giving directions. In what has become known as the "gender fender bender,"[70] BMW acquiesced and agreed to provide a male voice. However, rather than simply exchanging the female voice for a male voice, the company used the same rigorous level of care in designing a voice interface as it did in every other aspect of its cars' design. A multidisciplinary team (which included the first author) was put together to decide on the voice interface's new persona.

In addition to providing driving directions, BMW's voice interface had to support a variety of other functions in the present and the future. Car computers have advanced from giving directions to providing mechanical warnings (such as "Your wiper fluid is low" and "Time to check your oil"), information ("There is an accident on Highway 280" and "You are driving 15 miles over the speed limit"), safety ("There is a pedestrian crossing in the middle of the road 0.5 miles ahead" and "There is black ice on the road"), and control ("Now playing the third song on your Beatles CD" and "This car is stopping for a school bus"). The BMW interface thus needed a voice whose personality and role was consistent with all of these potential functions.

BMW was also concerned with making sure that the personality of the voice was consistent with its branding, one of the greatest assets that a car company can have. Because cars are bought by both extroverts and introverts, the company was less concerned with matching the personality of the customer.

The first idea was to have the voice be the car itself; the model was KITT from the television series *Knight Rider*.[71] This idea was rejected because voice interfaces, especially in cars, make frequent mistakes,[72] which would undermine the car's perfect-design branding. This requirement of technical excellence also meant that the voice had to be recorded rather than synthetic.

The next thought was to use a loud, dominant, slightly unfriendly voice that suggested a German automotive engineer. Who could know more about cars? But the engineer was felt to be an overcompetent role that would lead drivers to feel under constant pressure to meet the expectations of the voice.

Another set of possibilities was to put the interface voice in charge of the car. For example, the voice could be that of a pilot (very dominant and neutral on friendliness) or a chauffeur (very submissive, neutral on friendliness, and a slightly British accent). These roles were rejected because people who buy this kind of car are "drivers" who like to control the machine (although luxury cars also appeal to elderly drivers who might benefit from a voice that suggests that the driver is being driven).

Roles such as "friend" or "golf buddy," which strongly implicate similarity attraction, would require the car to know the user's personality; this was beyond the capabilities of the system. Also, people are reluctant to issue commands to peers. "Sidekick" (very friendly and submissive) or the slightly crazy person who rides "shotgun" in the old Western (extreme friendliness, constant talking, enormous pitch variation) would highlight loyalty, which might lead to loyalty in return, but they were clearly problematic for manifesting competence. "Back-seat driver" and "in-law" were rejected immediately with roars of laughter.

A detailed analysis of the potential function of the voice interface and the car's branding suggested that the perfect voice would be a stereotypical copilot. Unlike a pilot, the copilot knows that the driver is in charge but is always ready to step in if the driver needs help. Copilots are extremely knowledgeable about the equipment but always defer to the judgment of the pilot (the driver). Copilots can also have a variety of responsibilities, so that the same voice could adopt additional responsibilities over time.

After choosing this role for the computer navigation system, we decided that the voice had to suggest a male who was very slightly dominant, somewhat friendly, and highly competent. This led to a voice that was medium in volume (with little volume range), was relatively deep in pitch, had moderate pitch range, and had a slightly faster than average speech rate. The interface's language was relatively terse and phrased as statements rather than commands (pilot) or questions (chauffeur). The voice did not say "I." Although our research demonstrates that is generally advisable for recorded voices to use "I,"[73] copilots try to place themselves in a subordinate role and thus avoid the use of "I."

But not every car voice interface should sound like a copilot. For example, a rounded, playful car such as the Volkswagen Beetle could have an extremely extroverted female voice. Cars driven by chauffeurs should have an extremely submissive voice, so that the drivers do not feel overwhelmed by too many directives. Companies that are not extremely concerned about branding of particular vehicles can consider installing the voices of famous people, thereby drawing orientation away from the car and toward the interface itself.

Making decisions about the persona of the voice is a critical part of the development of any product or service interface. Voices can be used to homogenize products within a brand (for example, by using the same type of voice across various product types) and to differentiate brands (for example, by choosing a different style of voice than those used by competitors). If the personality of the interface is selected in advance, each writer should be guided by a "manual of style" that dictates all of the characteristics that make up the personality. At the last stage, a writer should audit the content to ensure that *every sentence* and *every interaction* is consistent with the selected personality.

Consistency Versus Similarity: What Should Designers Choose?

This chapter's experiment has shown the importance of both the *similarity* between the personality of the voice and the personality of the user and the *consistency* between the personality of the voice and the words that it says. The similarity-attraction effects confirm the results of the previous chapter: people like voices whose personality matches their own. Similarity-attraction also extends to words: users respond positively to content that reflects their personality. The consistency-attraction results mirror the results for gender:[74] people like and trust interactions more when the voice "matches" the personality of the content. Finally, voice personality is so strong that it even shapes perceptions of the personality of the content.

In a perfect world, the personalities of the user, the voice, and the content would all match or be matchable—that is, voice or content could be easily changed when mismatches occurred. Unfortunately, in many cases, the designer does not have control over both voice personality and content personality. Sometimes a business has selected a particular voice (usually recorded) as the voice of the company: when that voice doesn't match the user, how should the content be sculpted? Conversely, an enormous amount of previously produced content must be presented by voice: when the content personality doesn't match the user, what voice should be adopted? The following sections address these questions.

Who Cares about Consistency? Who Cares about Similarity?

Everyone likes consistency, and everyone likes similarity, but different personality types place greater emphasis on one or the other. In general, people who are strongly oriented to social relationships and their place in the social world tend to be more concerned with similarity than consistency, while people who are inner-oriented focus on consistency more than similarity. In other words, extroverts tend to be more concerned about relationships between themselves and others than with the internal workings of the other person. Hence, extroverts would likely be more concerned with similarity than consistency.[75] Conversely, introverts are less concerned with how another person is reacting to them than with their ability to predict the other person's behavior; thus they desire the comfort of consistency over similarity. With respect to the three other Myers-Briggs dimensions (information processing, decision making, and organization styles)[76] people who are labeled intuitive, feeling, and perceiving are likely to be more concerned with similarity, and sensing, thinking, and judging people are likely to be more concerned with consistency. Similarly, people who are at the extremes of the friendliness dimension of the Wiggins interpersonal circumplex[77] (highly friendly or highly unfriendly) tend to be influenced by similarity, and people toward the middle tend to be influenced by consistency because they are less socially oriented.

Other personality differences may also guide the tradeoff between consistency and similarity. For example, people with a high need for cognition (that is, people who enjoy thinking hard)[78] tend to be more concerned with consistency than similarity. Conversely, people with a low need for cognition tend to be more concerned with a readily discernible match between their own personality and that of the voice and less concerned about the complex interrelationships between words and sounds. Similarly, people with an external locus of control[79] (that is, people who believe that their fate is determined by others) tend to be concerned with how others orient toward them (similarity), and people with an internal locus of control tend to be concerned with the predictability (consistency) of others.

Adapting to the User and the Content

Adapting the interface to the user and content during long-term interactions begins with users' psychological preference for the usual over the unusual.[80] People are accustomed to encountering others who have clear and unambiguous personalities that are unlike their own but not to encountering people who display inconsistencies between words and voice. Hence, if the user's personality and the content personality do not match (and the content is fixed), designers should implement interfaces that initially present a voice that is consistent with the content rather than similar to the user. Over time, however, the voice could change to be more like the user, increasing similarity attraction.[81]

The key to the voice-adaptation strategy is to keep the adaptation gradual and natural. For example, when people talk to each other, they often adapt their speech rate to match the other's. A voice interface could also gradually do this without causing major alarm. Similarly, a system could subtly alter its volume and frequency range to match the user's more closely because people naturally make these adjustments in everyday conversation. On the other hand, fundamental frequency (pitch) should never be changed because it is determined by biological or physical characteristics that people cannot easily or naturally change. In general, the principle is straightforward: if people can and do change a speech characteristic to match the person they are interacting with, then the system can as well.

Personality certainly can change over long periods of time. For example, in the various film versions of *A Christmas Carol*, the actor who plays Ebenezer Scrooge invariably starts the movie with a classic dominant, unfriendly voice—loud and deep with limited modulation. The content of his words is harsh and forceful. As Scrooge goes through his transformational experiences (meeting the ghosts of Christmas past, present, and future), his voice becomes friendly and warmer—softer and slightly higher, with much more lilt and pitch range—and his language indicates that while he is still dominant, he now believes in making people happy. This transitional strategy can be leveraged by product-recommendation software: begin with an authoritative voice and language that is purely dominant. As the customer moves from information gathering to purchase, the voice and language can become friendlier, although both linguistic and paralinguistic cues should retain an air of confidence.

If, on the other hand, the user personality and voice personality do not match (and the voice is fixed), the choice for content personality adaptation is simple: select content that matches the voice. Consistency is clearly a stronger effect than similarity attraction between the user and content, so very little is lost by changing the content to match the voice rather than the user.

Personality Is More Than Voice and Words

In a conversation, certain personality types can be diagnosed without information about the speaker's words *or* voice. For example, extroverts are much more likely to interrupt, occupy a larger percentage of "air time," and be less tolerant of silence in the conversation than are introverts. Thus, for example, the time that a voice-input system waits before it assumes that the user is done speaking should be shorter for an extroverted interface than for an introverted interface.

When the interface is embodied, for example, through an on-screen character, nonverbal cues are also important.[82] For example, extroverts tend to stand closer to other people, face them more directly, make larger and faster gestures, stand more upright, and make more eye contact with others than do introverts;[83] people prefer characters whose postures conform to their speech.[84]

Finally, according to the theory of somatotypes, body types are also associated with personality.[85] For example, mesomorphs are people with muscular bodies and erect posture (such as Superman) and are perceived as energetic and assertive. Ectomorphs are tall, thin, and small-shouldered (such as Ichabod Crane and Woody Allen) and are viewed as fearful and introverted. Finally, endomorphs are people with round physiques and soft bodies (such as Santa Claus) and are viewed as gregarious and fun-loving. Every manifestation of personality in an interface must be consistent for maximum user liking and comfort.

Personality Is Greater Than the Sum of Its Parts

The human brain likes a neat and orderly world. Inconsistencies are uncomfortable, require significant processing, and lead to dislike and mistrust of the source of the confusion. Dissimilarity between the user and the voice or content is also frustrating and makes interfaces seem less desirable. In sum, because words and voices both provide so many different and unrelenting dimensions with which personality can be indicated, consistency and similarity must be considerations from the moment that design begins to avoid the extraordinary design or writing burden of repairing an inconsistent and ineffective voice interface.

6 Accents, Race, and Ethnicity: It's Who You Are, Not What You Look Like

When two strangers meet, the question "Where are you from?" usually is asked early in the conversation. One reason for asking this question is that the answer provides the strangers with an opportunity to find "common ground"[1]—that is, shared knowledge and beliefs.[2] When two people cannot find a topic that they both know something about, conversation, which is intrinsically cooperative,[3] simply breaks down.[4] Places are particularly fruitful bases for shared knowledge because even if one speaker has never been to the place, a characteristic of the location (a famous landmark or a friend who lived there, for example) can often provide a starting point for shared understanding.

A second reason for inquiring about a person's geographic origins is that place of origin can be as powerful as gender and personality in allowing someone to predict a conversational partner's attitudes and behaviors. Throughout most of human history, place of birth predicted culture, language, and family ties because cultures appeared within regions and there was limited mobility from one region (and hence culture) to another.[5] Thus, people who describe themselves as "Easterners," "Texans," or "Laplanders" provide much more than simply knowledge about natal locale. Like gender and personality, place of origin is one of the most critical traits that define a person.[6] Indeed, place of origin can be a greater predictor of people's attitudes and behaviors than gender or personality because most of the people that the developing child encounters during his or her formative years come from the same place and culture as the child does.[7]

Accents are the voice's way of manifesting hometown.[8] Newborn infants have the ability to produce any speech sound in any language in the world. Accents appear because over time babies learn which sounds are relevant and useful (the ones used by the people they hear) and which sounds are not important.[9] Children who emigrate under the age of seven rapidly acquire the accent of their new country.[10] However, children who change countries between the ages of eight and fifteen usually retain some vocal remnants of their home country. By the age of seventeen, original accents seem to be fully solidified and unalterable.[11]

Because languages do not have an "official pronunciation," every speaker has an accent.[12] "Accent neutralization"[13]—an active topic of discussion today as telephone-based call centers move to countries with lower wages and different accents—is a misnomer. Although speakers can change their speech to reflect the most common paralinguistic cues in a particular locale, this simply replaces one accent with another.

Accents are manifested, for the most part, via different pronunciations of vowels. For example, in New York English, *Mary*, *marry*, and *merry* are pronounced differently. However, in parts of California and many other parts of the country, these words are pronounced in exactly the same way.[14] Less frequently, accents can also be marked by the inability to produce certain consonant sounds, as in the *shibboleth* example below.

Although it is unlikely that the brain evolved specifically for accent recognition, the brain's hyperattention to speech makes it easy for a person to distinguish whether someone else's speech patterns matches his or her own. For example, the word *shibboleth* (a password or marker of belonging) was a Hebrew word that could not be pronounced correctly by the fleeing Ephraimites. They pronounced it "sibboleth" and therefore were identified as enemies and killed by the Gileadites.[15] During World War II, Germans could not correctly pronounce the Dutch town name *Scheveningen*, which allowed the Dutch resistance to identify Nazi spies.

Dialects are differences in grammar and word choice that are associated with a region. Some parts of the United States refer to *soda*, while others refer to *pop*. New Yorkers use Yiddish phrases that are much less commonly used in the rest of the country, and Southerners use the phrase *you all* when they are talking to several people at once. Similarly, the differences between Australian (*G'day, mate*), British (*Cheerio*), and U.S. (*Goodbye*) English are often the basis of confusion and amusement. No speaker fails to use words that distinguish hometown: everyone sounds like they were brought up somewhere.[16]

Another socially relevant meaning of *place of origin* is where someone's ancestors came from and is usually referred to as *race*. Race is generally indicated by physical appearance,[17] and features like skin color and shape of the head frequently indicate that a person's progenitors once lived in a part of the world for which their body characteristics were optimized.[18] Hence, race is generally discernible by simply visually observing a person.

Because migration was very limited throughout most of human history, language and race were consistent. People who looked like a given race almost always belonged to the culture associated with people of that race and vice versa. Indeed, culture and race were so inextricably linked that the term *ethnicity* has come to be used interchangeably for both.[19] However, these two definitions of place of origin are not intrinsically related. Neither physical environments nor the genes that determine racial characteristics dictate speech or language characteristics (although speech characteristics are associated with geographic areas). All evidence suggests that any normal infant can learn any human language and will speak with the accent and words used in the geographic region in which he or she grows up. When children are raised in countries far from where their ancestors lived, their language and accent are almost wholly influenced by their adopted country. (Accents of family members are a limited constraint, as children's accents are determined much more by their peers than by their parents.)[20] Hence, race does not predict accents. Conversely, dialect has no effect on the appearance of a speaker or a speaker's children or grandchildren. Because evolution works slowly, multitudes of generations need to pass before the physical characteristics of immigrants come to match that of indigenous people[21] (although consistent intermarriage across ethnicities can result in physical changes much more rapidly). In sum, speech manifests cultural origins, and faces and skin manifest long-ago biological origins.[22]

One critical consequence of language and race independence is that people can "speak differently than they look." In one sense, this is a *non sequitur*: speech has nothing to do with physical appearance, so the word "differently" makes no sense. However, because most speakers of virtually any dialect tend to look like most other speakers of that dialect (mobility remains limited), people can be surprised and puzzled when an accent doesn't seem to "match" a voice. Although it is simple to explain how someone who looks Korean can speak with an Australian accent and use Australian phrases or vice versa, how someone who is racially South Indian can speak with a pure French accent, or how people with biological roots in Namibia can have an Irish brogue, encountering unexpected speech patterns is nonetheless surprising.

How do people socially identify with individuals who send these "mixed signals"—that is, how do people decide whether the individual is "similar to them" or "not similar to them"? This is a critical question because (as discussed in previous chapters) similarity is a strong predictor of a variety of positive responses, including liking, trust, and perception of intelligence.[23] One possible response to these mixed signals is to weigh the speech markers and the racial markers differently. That is, people might think, "I primarily care about speech, but race is not irrelevant to my assessments. Because speech counts 73 percent and race counts 27 percent, I will socially identify[24] with this person about three-quarters as much as I would if she or he were wholly like me." At the extremes, this would play out as, "This person exhibits the same linguistic and paralinguistic cues as I do. Therefore, regardless of her race, I will clearly socially identify with her." (Speech and race could be reversed in the previous two sentences.)

Another possible response to these mixed signals is to integrate faces and voices and voices and word choice[25] in the same way. That is, people might think, "I prefer people who 'look like they talk.' Although I can logically understand why this type of inconsistency could happen, the novelty of it makes me uncomfortable.[26] I don't like or trust people who seem to be inconsistent,[27] no matter how explicable that inconsistency is."

In previous chapters, the psychological literature provided insights into (although not direct predictions of) how people would think and feel about voice interfaces. In this case, unfortunately, the psychological literature is silent on people's reactions to voices derived from one part of the world and faces derived from another. By addressing this question in the context of voice user interfaces, the current experiment can produce research results that are relevant to other domains by starting with technology and allowing others to apply the results to interactions between actual people.[28]

Adding a Face to the Interface

Early voice interfaces were restricted to audio only because the limited adoption of videophones effectively restricted telephone call centers to voice output. The large size of picture files relative to voice files prevented the inclusion of faces in applications for the desktop (hard-disk limitations) and the Web (transmission-speed limitations), and screens were much more expensive and power-consuming than speakers. Even though faces draw attention[29] and can improve speech understanding,[30] the technological constraints meant that voice user interfaces were much more like radio than television.

Thanks to Moore's law[31] (which predicts that computer components and hence computers will become inexorably faster and cheaper, doubling capacity about every eighteen months) faces can now be readily added to voice user interfaces. Cell phones now routinely come with screens that allow the high-quality presentation of at least still pictures, and video output to cell phones will soon be widely available. Computer hard disks have become so large that they easily store pictures and even video. Full-motion video (via streaming video) and video conferencing are now available to any computer with a high-speed Internet connection, and limited moving pictures via the Web can even be received with dial-up telephone lines. Screens have become so inexpensive that some household appliances have visual output as well as voices.

In these new technologies, voice user interfaces present combinations of speech and body. These "embodied conversational agents" or "embodied computer characters"[32] might be a still picture of a (possibly mythical) call-center representative, a training video with voice input, an animated conversational facilitator[33] or a synthetic character to teach deaf children to speak[34] and are becoming an increasingly popular interaction technique.[35]

Embodied conversational agents have been shown to make interactions between people and technology more natural and social.[36] Some dimensions of cultural variability that have been explored with animated characters include appearance, content and manner of speech, manner of gesturing, emotional dynamics, social-interaction patterns, and role dynamics.[37] Designers have recently begun to consider the possibility of localizing characters to the cultures where they will be deployed,[38] but they have yet to explore interactions with a character whose voice and appearance characteristics are not culturally consistent. That is, when voices and faces are shown together, do people integrate the two, even when they know that the two can be assigned independently? This question is addressed by examining social identification[39] and consistency-attraction[40] effects in interfaces that have clearly accented voices and clearly marked races.

Mixing and Matching Accent, Race, and Ethnicity

To test the effects on users of an agent's regionally marked speech and race, an experiment with an online e-commerce site was conducted.[41] A total of ninety-six male college students participated in the experiment. The participants were either Caucasian Americans (forty-eight participants) or first-generation Koreans (forty-eight participants). Participants were directed to an e-commerce Web site that displayed photographs of four different products—a backpack, a bicycle, an inflatable couch, and a desk lamp.

Half of the Korean American participants and half of the Caucasian American participants heard four product descriptions read by a voice with a Korean accent that occasionally used distinctly Korean phrases (such as "Anyonghaseyo," which is Korean for "hello"). The other half of the participants heard four product descriptions read by a voice with an Australian accent that occasionally used phrases associated with Australians (such as "G'day, mate").[42]

For a given participant, each of the four product descriptions was read by the same voice, and each description was accompanied by one of four full-length photographs of the same person in different poses (to give users a sense of animacy).

To hear the description of an item, participants clicked on the person's photograph. For participants who heard the Korean-accented voice, half were shown a photograph of a racially Korean male, and half were shown a photograph of a racially Caucasian Australian male. Similarly, for participants who heard the Australian-accented voice, half were shown a photograph of a racially Caucasian Australian male, and half were shown a photograph of a Korean male. Half of the participants in each of the four conditions were culturally and racially Korean, and half were culturally and racially Caucasian Americans.

To ensure that any effects were not attributable to a particular voice or face, the study used two different Korean voices, two different Australian voices, two different ethnically Korean faces, and two different ethnically Australian faces. Participants were randomly provided with one voice and one face that represented a particular combination of accent and race. The descriptions of the four products were identical except for a few stereotypically Australian words in the Australian-accented descriptions and a few stereotypically Korean words in the Korean-accented descriptions.

After hearing each product description, participants were asked to respond to a questionnaire that asked about the product's likeability[43] and the description's credibility.[44] After listening to the descriptions of all four products, participants were also asked to rate the agent's overall quality.[45] These questions allowed the effects of social identification and consistency on perceptions of the product and credibility of the agent to be assessed.

Agent's Accent, Agent's Race, or Consistency: What Is Most Important to Users?

Consistent with the results that have been obtained from studies of voice and gender,[46] people socially identified with the paralinguistic cue of accents (at least when coupled with verbal markers of hometown), regardless of the race of the agent.[47] The agents were rated much more positively when they spoke in an accent that matched the user's ethnicity.[48] Participants also evaluated the products[49] and product descriptions[50] more positively when they were spoken by an agent whose accent allowed the participant to socially identify with it. Hence, shared accents, which mark similar childhood cultures, clearly encouraged social identification.

There were no social-identification effects found for the *race* of the agent, however.[51] In other words, the match between the race of the user and the race of the agent (as manifested by the four photographs of the same person in four different poses) did not affect users' ratings of the agent or the products. Thus, participants' ancestral history did not seem to be an independent point of reference when evaluating the agent.

Although the paralinguistic cues of the voice and race of the agent are not logically linked, participants were disturbed when the agent did not "look the way it sounded." The photographic agents that had "consistent" voices and faces were perceived to be higher quality than those that were inconsistent, regardless of the ethnicity of the user.[52] Participants also found the products to be better[53] and the product descriptions to be more credible[54] when the two places of origin seemed to be consistent. Thus, people integrate voices and faces, even when the voice is clearly independent of the nonmoving mouth of the still photograph.[55] This integration also leads the race of the face to influence people's perceptions of the accent.[56]

Accent-uating Speech in Interfaces

Interfaces and software applications often have many places of origin. Each implementation task—design, programming, voice recording, photography, testing, burning to disk, placement on a server, warehousing—can be performed in a different region of the world. While the producers of voice interfaces must worry about all of these steps along the supply chain, consumers can ignore these diverse locales and simply define place of origin in terms of what is apparent and socially relevant to them—the voice, the face, and the content. The current research suggests that of the two places of origin—hometown and ancestral homelands—accent, which reflects the culture in which the person grew up, is critical for responses to interfaces, even when knowledge of an agent's (or person's) ancestry is readily apparent.

Users socially identify with agents based on the cultural background that is evident in the agent's voice but not based on the racial background evident in the agent's appearance. Voice may therefore more effectively localize a Web site to a particular region than the appearance of pictorial agents does. Multinational companies that attempt to make their Web sites cater to specific countries or populations should realize that the culture of the country, rather than its race, should be their key focus. Designers should worry about the language of the Web site, the accent of the voice, and other cultural references on the site much more than whether the skin color of an agent matches the most common race of the user population.

Creating and Identifying Accents

Because accents are simply a reflection of the way that the vowels and consonants of a language are pronounced, all synthetic and recorded voices manifest accents. Thus, both machine-generated and recorded voices lead to determinations of place of origin that automatically elicit assumptions about the speaker. Place of origin and its accompanying assumptions can be further supported by having the voice use unique words that are associated with a dialect that matches the accent.[57]

There is currently no automated method for detecting accents in users. The most straightforward approach compares the phonemes of the speaker to phonemes derived from different accents, but the number of voices needed to represent each accent with a high degree of accuracy is currently prohibitively high, and a significant amount of speech is needed before an accent can be reliably discerned. The best available approach is to learn the location of the user (perhaps by using telephone caller ID or e-mail Internet protocol address) and then to select the dominant accent of that location. One elegant example of this comes from a Japanese company with an automated call center that determined the area code of the caller and automatically assigned the caller to a voice whose accent matched the region from which the call came. This strategy was particularly effective in Japan, where geographic mobility and hence accent dispersion is much lower than in the United States, but it should be effective anywhere in the world.

In addition to social identification, accents in voice interfaces are likely to elicit stereotypes, much as gender of voice does.[58] Particular accents are associated with particular characteristics, whether those stereotypes are grounded in socialization processes or not.[59] For example, in the United States, people with British accents are perceived as more intelligent than average, whereas people with Brooklyn accents are perceived as less intelligent than average, even though, as described by accent prestige theory,[60] there is no formal basis for these stereotypes. Similarly, people with Boston accents ("I pahked the cah in Hah-vahd Yahd" instead of "I parked the car in Harvard Yard") are perceived as elitist, while Southern U.S. accents are perceived as more egalitarian (although there are also racist stereotypes associated with Southern accents). As discussed earlier,[61] designers must decide when to conform to and thereby reinforce stereotypes (for example, by having history tutorials presented with a British accent) and when to challenge them (by using a person with a Brooklyn accent to explain brain surgery).[62]

Labels Are Powerful

All social identification and stereotyping is grounded in labels that make the labeled characteristic salient and blur other characteristics of the person.[63] Thus, once the brain is activated to focus on a personal category such as gender, place of origin, or personality, other attributes that might have been relevant, including whether a voice is synthetic or recorded, move to the background.

Labels serve a number of purposes. First, broad, sweeping generalizations about others based on labels allow the human brain to make quick assumptions and predictions about other people and help the brain cope with the complexities of social interactions.[64] Second, when a label is determined to be similar to the label that someone assigns to herself or himself, that person can apply the principle of similarity attraction and attribute a wide range of positive characteristics to the voice.[65] Finally, labels allow people to learn how to behave: when labels match, people can observe others to answer the question, "What would a person like me do in a case like this?"[66] Thus, labeling is a fundamental human process that dramatically decreases the need for decision making or information processing at the expense of nuance and accuracy.[67]

Age

Gender, accent, and personality are three of the strongest bases for labeling others. The most powerful category not yet discussed is age.[68] Individuals certainly define themselves by their age cohort, with people quickly announcing their age range in answer to the question "Who am I?" Although perceived age ranges differ as a function of culture and even age itself[69] (for example, an adult sees fewer age categories in children than children do),[70] age is almost as salient a characteristic as gender. Societies tend to be segregated by age:[71] individuals of an age group tend to have most of their interactions with others from the same age cohort. Age also enables people to make reasonable predictions about the physical and mental capabilities of people that they encounter.

As with gender, there are clear voice markers of age.[72] In general, voices of both males and females get deeper as they grow older. Very young children and the elderly both speak more slowly on average than people in their twenties.[73] Anecdotally, individuals have no problem in assigning an age range as well as a gender to machine-generated (as well as human) voices.

Race

Race has been intentionally left out of the list of important social categories, even though it is one of the best predictors of virtually any phenomenon in the sociological literature.[74] The current research suggests that race is not important as an independent effect, at least when an accompanying voice provides broader and deeper information than what can be determined from ancestral geography. The linguistic and paralinguistic cues are so informative that identifying a person's geographic progenitors is simply not valuable.

One caveat associated with the previous conclusion is that differences in responses to accent and race could be attributed to the contrast between a dynamic voice and a static face. This explanation seems dubious because participants are unlikely not to notice a face. First, whenever people see anything that looks even remotely like a face, they think of it as a face,[75] so it is highly improbable that people in our experiment were not drawn to the face. Second, we found large effects with respect to the mismatch between the face and the voice (if people ignored the face, there would be no effects for inconsistency). Nevertheless, the current study should be replicated with dynamic video or other moving images instead of still photographs of agents. This would likely produce an even tighter linkage between the agent's face and voice than still photographs did.

Other Social Categories

Other social categories that are manifested by speech—that is, by paralinguistic and language cues—include education and intelligence[76] (for example, educated people have greater fluency of speech, have larger vocabularies, and use more varied sentence structures) and class and status[77] (for example, in many cultures, certain accents and word selections are assigned as "high status"). In general, all categories that are associated with clear social and behavioral consequences tend to be recognizable through speech.[78]

Creating Social Identity When Users Are Unknown

What can designers do when they do not know the user's relevant social categories and hence cannot leverage social identification via those categories? The best method is to create *pseudocommunity*, an artificial bond between a diverse set of people.[79] For example, in all parts of the eBay Web site and in all its contacts with the customer, eBay refers to the "eBay community" and "eBay members like you." This is essentially the creation of a social category—eBay users—that had not been apparent previously. This category *a priori* matches the user and thereby encourages positive social identification. In a very different domain, an MP3 player oriented to the MTV audience could use a voice and a language that sound like a typical rock music lover; in that case, traditional categories of social identification would be almost invisible compared to this highly relevant category.

Children's television provides many examples of establishing social identity even when it might seem difficult to create. For example, Fred Rogers of *'Mister Rogers' Neighborhood* (a long-running children's U.S. public television series) has a famous line:

"Won't you be my neighbor?" Although Rogers eventually was old enough to be a grandfather to his fans, was Caucasian despite a diverse audience, and had a Pittsburgh accent, his invitation to children to join his community highlighted the similarities between him and his viewers. Similarly, Barney, the star of *Barney & Friends*, another popular children's public television series, is a six-foot-tall, purple dinosaur; nonetheless, he effectively reminds preschoolers that "We're a happy family."

Although social identification can be a powerful tool for designers, it can sometimes be a liability. For example, many voice interfaces use the term *we* to refer to the company ("We at XYZ company want you to be happy)" rather than to link the voice and the user. This implicitly tells the user that she or he should *not* identify with the voice, thereby increasing the probability that the user will become angry and frustrated during the interaction. Even more egregious are cases in which the user is given a choice of voices that represent the same social category, such as different female voices teaching cooking or nine-year-old voices teaching reading. Although these voices might conform to stereotypes or assumptions about the audience, respectively, the Hobson's choice[80] presented to people who do not match the relevant category (a man who is learning how to cook or an adult who is learning how to read) strongly reminds them how unusual they are.

Consistency in Agents

As discussed earlier, consistency is a fundamental human desire.[81] For example, a person who speaks in a happy voice while frowning is unlikely to inspire trust or liking.[82] Similarly, users would almost certainly prefer consistent visual and vocal cues of gender, age, and personality over inconsistent ones. Imagine the surprise of a person who discovers that a young, friendly looking female agent sounds like a surly old man. Inconsistency can make people feel uncomfortable well before this level of incompatibility.

Even though there was no logical or technological relationship between the voice and the body in the previous study, clear negative consequences were found when the two were mismatched. For social information in which the face and voice manifest redundant information, for example, emotion, consistency is even more important.

International companies have yet another dimension of consistency to consider—the country of origin of the product. For example, a Web site might sell Dresden glass, Chinese sculpture, or Iranian rugs. If the pictured spokesperson is of the race that is associated with the region of the product, the consistency of matching an accent with both the product and the spokesperson would likely overcome any benefits that might be associated with matching the user. Situations in which the race of the product spokesperson does not match the region of the product are more complicated. Yet more complicated are cases in which both knowledge of the region and an understanding of the user are valuable: the most obvious category is tourism. In these cases, the picture and voice combination might be more trouble than help unless all components can be aligned.

People Are More Than Social Categories, But . . .

At a fundamental psychological level, users generally do not distinguish between voices coming from an actual human and voices coming from a computer.[83] Even though talking about a computer as having a gender, hometown, or personality makes no logical sense, if it has a voice, users will attribute all of these social categories to it. For best effect, designers must therefore consider all of these cues and their impact on stereotyping and identification when choosing a voice for an interface.

Everyone wants to be appreciated as a rich and unique person that "contains multitudes."[84] People insist on being "a name, not a number."[85] Similarly, the best interface designers carefully cast and script every aspect of a voice user interface, whether or not it is accompanied by pictorial representations.[86] But every voice activates certain responses in listeners—a rapid determination of relevant categories[87] and blindness to subtle and difficult-to-process categories—thereby enabling rapid social identification and social stereotyping. By attending to a limited number of categories, designers have a tremendous opportunity to optimize how users will feel and behave.

7 User Emotion and Voice Emotion: Talking Cars Should Know Their Drivers

The previous chapters describe how users respond to voices, both computer-generated and recorded, as if they manifest gender, accents, and personality. Each of these characteristics is an unvarying aspect of a person, known as a *trait*: sex (barring surgery), childhood socialization, and personality[1] last a lifetime. These unwavering qualities allow observers to predict a wide range of behaviors and attitudes and the general orientation that speakers will have toward themselves, other people, and the world around them. If humans were defined only by traits, life (and design) would be simple: Listen to people briefly, classify them, and from then on worry only about those paralinguistic cues (such as the generally rising tone at the end of a question) that affect interpretation of what they meant.

For better and worse, however, people are dramatically affected by their environment. Indeed, traits give us a broad sense of what a person will think and do, but predicting a person's behavior at any given moment in time also requires attention to the user's *state*—that is, the particular feelings, knowledge, and physical situation of the person. Extroverts are generally talkative, but they might be as silent as introverts in a library or even quieter when they bump into their secret crush. The most "feminine" female will exhibit a range of masculine characteristics when protecting a child. In a group, people often submerge their identity as they blend in and mimic the people around them.[2] Although traits provide the general trajectory of an individual's life, every specific attitude, behavior, and cognition also can be influenced by momentary states.

Of all the types of states that predict how a person will behave, the most powerful is *emotion*.[3] Rich emotions are a fundamental component of being human.[4] Emotion is so fundamental that a key part of the brain used in emotion (the amygdala) is also used to determine whether an image is a person or not.[5] Throughout any given day, affective states—whether short-lived emotions or longer-term moods—color almost everything people do and experience, from sending an e-mail to driving down the highway. Emotion is not limited to the occasional outburst of fury at being insulted, excitement at winning the lottery, or frustration at being trapped in a traffic jam. It is now understood that a wide range of emotions plays a critical role in *every* goal-directed activity,[6] from asking for directions to asking someone on a date, from hurriedly eating a sandwich at one's desk to dining at a five-star restaurant, and from watching the Super Bowl to playing solitaire. Indeed, many psychologists now argue that it is impossible for a person to have a thought or perform an action without engaging, at least unconsciously, his or her emotional systems.[7]

Although emotion was one of the primary foci of the early field of psychology, the study of emotion has lain dormant for a long time.[8] The founder of the field of human-technology interaction, Frederick Winslow Taylor, focused on formalization, measurement, and "science,"[9] which, in his day, meant the exclusion of human feelings, an exclusion that extends to most present-day studies.[10] Until recently, it would have seemed ludicrous to even discuss whether machines could have or exhibit emotions.[11] This avoidance of the study of emotions has extended to the realm of voice interfaces.

Because of its critical importance and the neglect it has received, emotion is discussed in two chapters. This chapter discusses emotion from the *user's* point of view, addressing questions like "What is emotion?" and "How does user emotion affect interaction with voice interfaces?" The next chapter focuses on the expression of emotion from the *interface's* point of view, discussing "How do voices manifest emotion?" and "How does the manifestation of emotion in interfaces affect people?"

What Is Emotion?

What is emotion? Although the research literature offers a number of definitions,[12] two generally agreed-on aspects of emotion stand out:[13] (1) emotion is a reaction to events that are deemed relevant to the needs, goals, or concerns of an individual, and (2) emotion encompasses physiological, affective, behavioral, and cognitive components. Fear, for example, is a reaction to a situation that threatens (or seems to threaten, as a sudden loud noise does) an individual's physical well-being, resulting in a strong negative affective state, as well as physiological and cognitive preparation for action.[14] Joy, on the other hand, is generally a reaction to the fulfillment of goals and gives rise to "happy" behaviors such as smiling and engagement with the environment.[15] Emotions can be relatively short lived; when one or more are sustained they are called *moods*.

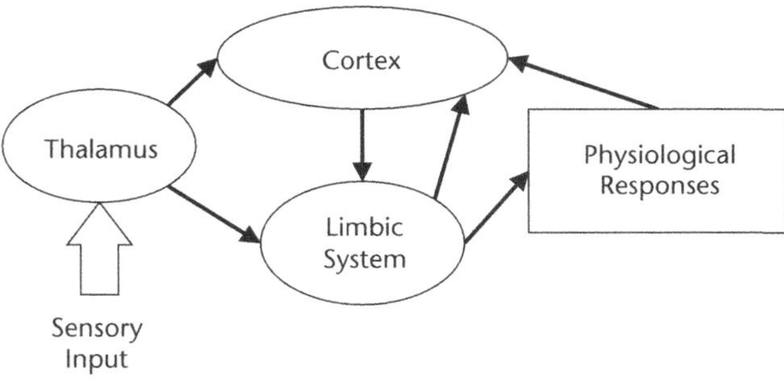

Figure 7.1
Neurological Structure of Emotion

Just as humans are built to process and produce speech, they are built to experience emotion (and mood).[16] Figure 7.1 presents a standard model[17] showing three key regions of the brain—the thalamus, the limbic system, and the cortex. Information comes through the senses and goes first to the thalamus, which does the basic processing of the input. The thalamus then sends information simultaneously to the cortex (for higher-level processing attention and other thought processes), and to the limbic system[18] (for evaluating the relationship between the information and the user's needs or goals). If relevance is determined, the limbic system (often called the "seat of emotion") sends messages to the various parts of the body (which can make the heart pump faster or the muscles contract, for example) and to the cortex.

The "primitive" or "primary" emotions, such as startle-based fear and innate aversions and attractions, originate from the direct link between the thalamus and the limbic system.[19] In the context of voice interfaces, unexpected sounds, such as a beep—instead of "You've got mail"[20]—have the potential to activate such primitive emotional responses, as do sounds that are innately disturbing or pleasing due to their evolutionary significance, such as screaming, crying, or laughing.[21]

Most of the emotions that play a role in the design of voice interfaces are the "secondary" emotions, such as frustration, pride, and satisfaction. These emotions require more complex analysis than the primitive emotions. Hence, when the thalamus receives the input, it sends a message to the cortex, which does extensive knowledge-based processing. Such cortical processing may or may not be conscious and can occur at various levels of complexity, from simple recognition (such as hearing a familiar voice) to intricate rational deliberation (such as evaluating the social and functional consequences of being verbally reprimanded). The cortex can even trigger emotion in reaction to a person's expectations or imaginings, such as thinking about how difficult it will be to use a newly purchased voice-recognition system. The cortex then sends this information to the limbic system, which decides whether an emotion is warranted (based on the user's needs and goals) and how to manifest that emotion.

Finally, an emotion can result from a combination of both the thalamic-limbic and the cortico-limbic pathways. For example, an event causing an initial startle or fear reaction can be later recognized as harmless by more extensive, rational evaluation, such as when you realize that your car's sudden beep is just a ploy to draw your attention, ensuring that you turn off your headlights.

Although the limbic system is a critical locus for the *activation* of emotion, emotion is *experienced* only when the limbic system sends messages to the cortex and the body.

Are Emotions Innate or Learned?

The above discussion provides a useful framework for considering one of the classic debates in emotion theory: are emotions innate or learned? At one extreme, most evolutionary theorists argue that all emotions (including complex emotions such as regret and relief) are innate[22] and have evolved to address a specific environmental concern of humans' ancestors. These theories assume that the limbic system is complex because it distinguishes a wide range of emotions and triggers unique sets of body and brain (cortex) responses for each of these emotions.

At the other extreme, many emotion theorists argue that—with the exception of the startle response, the innate-affinity response, and the disgust response (which they consider preemotional)—emotions are almost entirely learned social constructions.[23] Such theories emphasize the role of the cortex in differentiating emotions and concede minimal, if any, specificity within the limbic system (and consequently, within physiological responses). For example, the limbic system may operate in an on or off manner[24] or at most differentiate along the orthogonal dimensions of valence (positive to negative) and arousal (excited to calm). From this perspective, emotions are likely to vary considerably across cultures, with any consistency arising from common social structure, not biology.

Between these two extremes lie those who believe that there are "basic emotions." Citing both cross-cultural universals and primate studies, these theorists contend that all humans share a small set of innate, basic emotions.[25] Which emotions qualify as basic is yet another debate, but the list typically includes fear, anger, sadness, joy, and disgust.[26] Other emotions are seen either as combinations of these basic emotions or as socially learned differentiations within the basic categories.[27] For example, agony, grief, guilt, and loneliness are socially constructed variations of sadness. In this view, the limbic system is prewired to recognize the basic categories of emotion, but social learning and the cortex still play a significant role in differentiation.

Effects of Affect

Attention

One of the most important effects of emotion lies in its ability to become completely absorbing. Emotions direct and focus people's attention on those objects and situations that have been appraised as important to people's needs and goals. Emotion-relevant thoughts then tend to dominate conscious processing: the more important the situation is, the higher the arousal and the more forceful the focus.[28] In a voice interface context, this attention-getting function can be used advantageously (as when a navigation system's "turn left immediately" is used to alert the user), or it can be distracting (as when a user is frustrated by poor voice recognition and can think about nothing else). More generally, people tend to pay more attention to any thoughts and stimuli that have some relevance to their current emotion.[29]

Just as emotions can direct users to aspects of an interface, emotions can also drive attention *away* from the stimulus that is eliciting the emotion.[30] For example, becoming angry with a voice-recognition system may be seen as silly or illogical (because it doesn't recognize your anger). An angered user may then actively try to avoid parts of an interface that rely on voice input, rendering the user's interaction less efficient or effective. In extreme cases, the user will simply avoid the system. If the emotion is too strong, however, the user will not be able to ignore the source,[31] potentially even resulting in "computer rage." Positive emotions may likewise require regulation at times, as when amusing content, such as a voice-based "joke of the day," leads to inappropriate laughter in a work environment.

Performance

Emotion has also been found to affect cognitive style and performance. The most striking finding is that even mildly positive feelings profoundly affect the flexibility and efficiency of thinking and problem solving.[32] In a well-known experiment, participants were induced into a good or bad mood and then asked to solve Duncker's candle task:[33] given only a box of thumbtacks, the participant must attach a lighted candle to the wall so that no wax drips on the floor. The solution requires participants to have the creative insight to thumbtack the box to the wall and then tack the candle to the box. Participants who were first put into a good mood were significantly more successful at solving this problem.[34] In another study, medical students were asked to diagnose patients based on X-rays after first being put into a positive, negative, or neutral mood. Participants in the positive-affect condition reached the correct conclusion faster than did subjects in other conditions.[35] Conversely, positive affect has been shown to increase reliance on stereotypes and other simplifying rules of processing, which could lead happy users to make less nuanced judgments about a voice interface and to be more influenced by labels, such as the gender, accent, and personality of the voice.[36]

Judgment

Emotion has also been shown to influence judgment and decision making. As mentioned above, emotion tends to bias attention and thoughts in an emotion-consistent direction. One important consequence of this is that everything—even those people, things, and events that are unrelated to the current affective state—is judged through the filter of emotion.[37] This suggests, for example, that users would likely judge both a voice interface and the interface's message more positively if they were in a good mood than if they were in a negative or neutral mood. Recommendations, for example, will obtain a greater level of acceptance among happy people. Positive emotion also decreases risk taking. That is, although people in a positive mood are more risk-prone when making *hypothetical* decisions, they tend to be more cautious when presented with an actual risk situation.[38]

Emotion and Voices in Cars

Driving presents a context in which emotion can have enormous consequences. Attention, performance, and judgment are of paramount importance in automobile operation, with even the smallest disturbance potentially having grave repercussions. The road-rage phenomenon[39] provides one undeniable example of the impact that emotion can have on the safety of the roadways. Considering the above discussion of the effects of emotion (in particular, that positive affect leads to better performance and less risk taking), it is not surprising that research and experience demonstrate that happy drivers are better drivers.[40]

Now that car manufacturers are increasingly turning to voice as a promising strategy for safe, pleasant, and engaging interactions with everything from in-car navigation systems and environmental controls to road-aware, chatting copilots (the remarkably intelligent and speaking car, KITT, presented in the 1980s television series *Knight Rider*, may soon become at least a partial reality), it is critical to know how emotion expressed by an in-car voice interface interacts with a driver's emotion in affecting attention, performance, and judgment. Might the emotional characteristics of the voice have as much impact on attention, performance, and judgment as the emotions of the driver? More specifically, what happens when the emotion of the voice and the emotion of the driver are mismatched (such as when an upset driver encounters an upbeat voice)?

To investigate this question,[41] a driving-simulator-based[42] experiment with twenty female and twenty male participants was conducted. The participants drove a virtual car down a simulated road (complete with other vehicles) using a gas pedal, a brake pedal, and a force-feedback steering wheel. All participants drove on the same simulated course[43] for approximately fifteen minutes.

To address the question of the effects of user emotion on driving performance, half of the participants had to be happy at the time of the experiment, and the other half had to be upset. In experiments concerning emotion, researchers can work with the emotions that participants bring into the lab or create an emotion after participants enter the laboratory. There are pros and cons to both approaches, but the difficulty of scheduling (in advance) equal numbers of happy and upset participants as well as the desire to ensure that the emotion experienced by participants be created in the same manner led us to *create* emotion rather than rely on recruitment. Therefore, either a happy state or an upset state was induced in each participant at the beginning of the experiment. This was accomplished by showing half of the participants (randomly selected) seven minutes of very happy video clips and showing the other half seven minutes of very upsetting video clips.[44] A questionnaire confirmed that individuals had the correct emotional state before they entered the driving simulator.[45]

While driving the course, participants interacted with a "virtual passenger," who was represented by a recorded female voice that made light conversation with the driver. The virtual passenger introduced "herself" by saying,

> Hi. My name is Chris, and I will be your virtual passenger for today. We are going to be driving today on a coastal road, one that I've traveled many times before but one that may be new to you. The trip shouldn't take too long: ten or fifteen minutes. Let's get going.

At thirty-six separate points along the course, the virtual passenger made a different remark.[46] For half of the happy participants and half of the upset participants (randomly selected), the voice was energetic and upbeat; for the other half, the voice was calm and subdued.[47]

In the case of driving, safety is of utmost importance. To assess the effects of the link between driver emotion and voice emotion on drivers' performance, the simulator automatically recorded the number of accidents that drivers were involved in during their time in the simulator. Another way to assess whether the driver was paying attention to the road was to determine the driver's reaction time while driving. Specifically, participants were told to honk the car's horn as quickly as possible in response to randomly occurring honks. Because honks indicate that another driver felt the need to communicate about some aspect of driving, the quicker, on average, that participants honked back, the more they were paying attention to the road. The drivers were also asked, via a questionnaire, how attentive they thought they were.[48]

While everyone wants drivers to pay attention to the road, designers of car interfaces also want people to feel that the voice is an important part of the driving experience. The driver's engagement with the system was measured by the amount of time that drivers spent talking back to the voice in the car while driving down the simulated road.

Voice Emotion Influences Driving Performance

Matching the voice of the car to the drivers' emotions had enormous consequences.[49] Drivers who interacted with voices that matched their own emotional state (enthused voice for happy drivers and subdued voice for upset drivers) had *less than half* as many accidents on average as drivers who interacted with mismatched voices.[50] This magnitude of reduction is far greater than the effects of virtually any technological change in a car at dramatically less expense; influencing the driver is more important than influencing the car.

Drivers who heard voices whose emotions were suited to their own emotion also rated themselves as significantly more attentive while driving.[51] The mismatched voice distracted drivers, probably because they unconsciously tried to figure out why someone interacting with them was unresponsive to their own emotional state. Drivers paired with matched voices also communicated much more with the voice, even though the voice said exactly the same thing in all conditions.[52] This suggests that although drivers who heard emotion-matched voices spoke to the virtual passenger much more, they were nonetheless better able to avoid accidents.

The effects of matching emotion versus mismatching emotion were so powerful that neither driver emotion nor voice emotion by itself had a consistent effect on drivers. Although there was a slight tendency for happy drivers to be better drivers, even this effect was minimal compared to the effects of matching. In other words, finding the appropriate in-car voice for the driver's emotion stood out as the most critical factor in enabling a safe and engaging driving experience.

The foregoing suggests that people find it easier and more natural to attend to voice emotions that are consistent with their own.[53] Emotion-inconsistent voices are arguably more difficult to process and attend to than emotion-consistent ones; in other words, interacting with an inconsistent voice takes more cognitive effort.[54] It then follows that listening to or conversing with the virtual passenger was more distracting in the mismatched case, leading to poorer driving performance, less attention to the road, and a less comfortable experience.

Making Driving, and Voice Interfaces, Safer and Better

Auto manufacturers spend a great deal of time and money attempting to make cars safer. They install antilock brakes, adaptive steering and gas pedals, air bags, and various warning indicators. All of these design decisions require very long lead times to retool factories and often involve dramatic increases in cost.

The current research demonstrates that a simple, inexpensive, and fully controllable aspect of a car interface can also have a dramatic influence on driver safety. Something as small as changing the paralinguistic characteristics of a voice is sufficient to improve driving performance significantly. Even with the same words spoken at the same times by the same voice under the same road conditions, driver performance can be radically altered when the voice is simply changed from energetic and upbeat to subdued. Remarkably, changing the tone of a voice can strongly influence the number of accidents, the driver's perceived attention to the road, and the driver's engagement with the car.

A key finding here is that the same voice cannot be effective for all drivers. For both actual and perceived performance, upset drivers clearly benefited from a subdued voice, while happy drivers clearly benefited from an energetic voice. This suggests that voices in cars must adapt to their users. This presents two important questions: How can an interface detect driver emotion, and how can that information be used most effectively?

Detecting Driver's Emotion

How should cars assess the emotion of drivers? The basic emotions (fear, anger, sadness, joy, and disgust) are the most distinguishable and therefore measurable emotional states (both in emotion-recognition systems as well as in postinteraction evaluations). Further, the basic emotions are less likely to vary significantly from culture to culture, facilitating the accurate translation and generalizability of emotion detection.

Recent advances in emotion-recognition technology provide a number of possibilities for determining the emotional state of drivers and other users of interactive systems. Sensing technologies include cameras to assess facial expressions[55] (for example, to detect road rage or other emotions), skin conductance and blood pressure sensors attached to the steering wheel or mouse (particularly good for detecting arousal),[56] technologies to measure head nodding or other movement (to detect driver drowsiness or general relaxation), and eye-tracking equipment (for example, to detect pupil expansion, which is associated with positive feelings).[57]

In certain contexts, prediction offers another possibility for detecting users' emotions. For example, if a car's safety system recognizes a potentially dangerous situation, the virtual passenger can assume that the driver will soon be afraid or stressed and quickly adapt its voice characteristics (without any direct measurement of emotion). In less time-critical situations, such prediction could also be used in conjunction with direct measurement to improve emotion-recognition accuracy.[58]

Voice analysis is particularly useful for systems with voice input or for situations in which the user is frequently talking (such as when a passenger is in the car). Voice-analysis systems can use the same set of vocal cues to detect emotion that people use to detect emotion and that synthetic voices use to manifest emotion, as described in the next chapter.

The critical issue in all detection systems is accuracy. Although focusing on multiple indicators leads to better accuracy than assessments of only a single indicator of emotion, even the most complete, wide-ranging, and intelligent systems are not as good as the average person.[59] Thus, any reactions to the user's emotion must be tempered by the knowledge that the judgments are not perfect.

How Fast Should the Emotion of Voice Change?

If a car will make a determination of the driver's emotion, the designer must decide how the system should respond to that emotion. One useful strategy is to change the emotion of the voice in step with the user—that is, to exhibit empathy. Empathy greatly fosters relationship development because it communicates support, caring, and concern for the welfare of another.[60] A voice that expresses happiness in situations where the user is happy and sounds subdued or sad in situations where the user is upset would strongly increase the connection between the user and the voice.[61] Similarly, a voice telling users that an important file has just been corrupted or that the product they requested is no longer in stock should do so with a degree of expressed regret. In these cases, the system leverages its ability to predict rather than measure the user's emotion.

Although a rapid response to the emotion (or predicted emotion) of the user can be effective, there are a number of dangers in this approach. In the human brain and body, emotion can change in seconds.[62] If someone tells a joke to a sad person, he or she may become momentarily happy but will fall back into a sad state relatively quickly. Conversely, happy drivers may become frustrated as they must slam the brakes after expecting to zoom through a yellow light, but their emotion may quickly switch back to feeling positively. If the voice in the car adapted immediately and forcefully to the user's emotions, drivers would experience such bizarre occurrences as the voice of the car changing its emotion in midsentence. People or voices that manifest emotions at that rate would dramatically increase cognitive load,[63] constantly activate new emotions in the user, and be perceived as psychotic. While this can be entertaining when performed by manic comedians like Robin Williams or Jim Carrey, it is psychologically exhausting and disturbing when encountered in daily life. Such a virtual passenger would be marked quickly as manic-depressive rather than empathetic.

To make the voice in the car an effective interaction partner, mood also must be taken into account. Moods tend to bias feelings, cognitive strategies, and processing over a longer term than emotions.[64] While moods can be influenced by emotions, they tend to be more stable and can even serve as a filter through which both internal and external events are appraised. A person in a good mood tends to view everything in a positive light, while a person in a bad mood does the opposite. Even when a negative event is viewed negatively, moods can limit the impact of that perception. Thus, when assessing people's responses to a voice, designers should consider the biasing effects of user mood. Users entering a car or using a voice-based product in a good mood, for instance, are more likely than users in a bad mood to experience positive emotion during an interaction. Thus, emotion in technology-based voices must balance responsiveness and inertia by adapting to both emotion and mood.

Even easier to assess than moods is temperament.[65] Temperament reflects the tendency of certain individuals to exhibit particular moods with great frequency.[66] Sales people and implementers can measure users' temperament before the adoption of the product or service, select a voice, and tune the emotion-recognition system to understand and respond based on the general affective tendency of the user.

Stabilizing the Unstable User

People are who they are. Grounding interface design in stable characteristics of users (called *personas*)[67] can simplify the design process and allow interfaces to be standardized. At the same time, humans are what they feel. Emotion—influenced by every encounter with the physical, psychological, and social world—plays a critical role in determining users' performance, knowledge, beliefs, and feelings. Every voice, synthetic or real, emanating from people or attached to interfaces, creates and interacts with an emotion-driven user who will think, feel, and succeed (or fail) based on the sensitivity of the design to the user's affective reality.

8 Voice and Content Emotions: Why Voice Interfaces Need Acting Lessons

The previous chapter demonstrated that emotions can have a tremendous influence on individuals. If people lived in isolation, each person's own emotions would be the only emotions that would be relevant. However, people live in a social world in which every person is surrounded and affected by every other person's emotions.

Given the central role that is played by emotion, a clear evolutionary advantage goes to those who can determine the affect (emotion or mood) of the individuals with whom they interact. This is reflected in the wiring of the brain: The left hemisphere recognizes positive experiences more rapidly, and the right hemisphere recognizes negative experiences more rapidly.[1] In addition to this biological optimization, training in emotion detection begins at three to six months after birth during facial play with mothers.[2] Knowing how a person feels about us at a particular moment gives us general information about whether to approach or avoid as well as a nuanced understanding of the interaction strategies that will be effective. Indeed, it is more important that people understand others' emotions than understand their own. Thus, it is not surprising that one of Charles Darwin's most influential books[3] is called *The* Expression *of the Emotions in Man and Animals*[4] rather than *The* Experience *of the Emotions in Man and Animals*. (The previous chapter discusses people's internal experiences of emotion.)

Given how valuable emotion detection is, the human brain has evolved to detect emotion not just in the words,[5] facial expressions,[6] and other behaviors of people but also in their voices. Emotion manifests through vocal properties such as pitch range, rhythm, and amplitude or duration changes.[7] A bored or sad person, for example, will typically exhibit slower, lower-pitched speech, with little high-frequency energy, while a person experiencing fear, anger, or joy will speak faster and louder, with strong high-frequency energy and more precise enunciation.[8] Emotion detection through voice is so important that it is localized in the brain: paralinguistic cues of emotion, regardless of content, activate the lateral temporal lobe (superior or middle temporal gyri), primarily on the right side of the brain.[9] Similarly, the right hemisphere of the brain is primarily responsible for *producing* paralinguistic cues of emotion, while the left side controls the language content.[10]

From moment to moment, voice characteristics that manifest emotional information allow a listener to better predict a speaker's intentions and actions[11] and better understand the speaker's meaning.[12] Humans are quite good at detecting emotions from voice,[13] even when the voice is machine-generated.[14] Table 8.1.A (see page 95), created by Iain R. Murray and John L. Arnott, provides a detailed account of the vocal effects that are associated with several basic emotions.[15]

Detection of emotion tells us more than just the psychological orientation of the speaker. Emotional tone in human speech can also color what is said; in other words, voice emotion can determine how specific words and sentences are interpreted by the listener.[16] The phrase, "My voice recognition system is 95 percent accurate," for example, can either be praise (when said with joy) or criticism (when spoken with anger). "Oh, my goodness" means something very different when expressed fearfully as opposed to happily. Even sentences that seem intrinsically happy—such as "I'm really enjoying myself"—can radically alter meaning when said in a disgusted or sarcastic tone of voice. Emotion of voice thus critically affects a listener's understanding of spoken content.

When voice quality and emotional content are matched, the brain readily integrates the two. However, when the emotion in a voice is clearly inconsistent with the content being presented, a person is presented with an irreconcilable problem. This leads to problems from an early age. Mothers who exhibit inconsistency between verbal and vocal cues, such as criticizing in a syrupy voice, are much more likely to have children with behavioral and emotional problems.[17] Even within groups of disturbed children, the boys of the mothers who showed more inconsistent communication were reported to be more aggressive in school than the boys whose mothers showed less inconsistent communication.[18]

As people become adults, the primary effects of mismatches between verbal and vocal emotion involve attributions to the content and the speaker. Except in cases where sarcasm is intended and clear, people tend to like a person better when their emotional tone is consistent with the emotional information implicit in the words being said.[19] People generally view inconsistent emotion as an indication of insincerity, instability,[20] or deception[21]—all unappealing attributes—and thus anything said by such a person tends to be unlikeable. Inconsistency between the emotion in words and in voice also places a burden on the listener: more brain regions are used when voice and content are emotionally inconsistent than when they are consistent.[22]

Mixing Voice and Content Emotion in Interfaces

Emotions are part of what defines humans as "human."[23] Technologies, on the other hand, seem to be the quintessence of unemotional.[24] However, *all* voices activate the parts of the brain associated with the measurement of paralinguistic (vocal) cues that mark emotion. Could voice interfaces, then, trigger the same emotional processes in the brain as human voices?

When listening to humans, voice emotion affects interpretation. However, given that people know that machines don't have emotion or truly understand the emotional content of the words they speak, the emotional tone of a *machine-based* voice rationally should not influence perceptions of the content. Listeners should understand that technologies generally have a single, relatively invariant voice that is essentially decoupled from the words being spoken. However, given that people assign traits (such as gender, region, and personality) to machine-based voices even when those assignments seem irrational, might they also assign states, that is, emotions, to these voices?

To determine whether people assign emotion to machine-based voices and to determine whether those assignments influence their perceptions, a telephone-based experiment was conducted.[25] Fifty-six adults participated in the study. Gender was approximately balanced across conditions.

Participants were first directed to a Web page that gave instructions for the experiment and provided a call-in number. After they read the instructions, participants called the phone number, punched in a pass code to hear the appropriate content, and listened to two news stories (one happy, one sad), two movie descriptions (one happy, one sad), and two health stories (one happy, one sad).[26] For example, the happy news story described a new cure for cancer that was showing incredible promise, especially for children, while the sad story described a mystery of dead gray whales washing ashore on the San Francisco coast. All stories were read by the same male synthetic voice.

For half of the participants (randomly assigned), the emotion of the voice matched the emotion of the story being read, and for the other half of the participants, voice emotion and story emotion were mismatched. In other words, half of the participants heard happy content read in a happy voice and sad stories read in a sad voice (consistent emotion), while the other half of the participants heard happy content read in a sad voice and sad stories read in a happy voice (inconsistent emotion).

After hearing each story, participants answered a set of questions on the Web site.[27] For each story, questions were asked to determine how happy or sad the story was[28] and how much participants liked the story.[29] Finally, participants were asked whether the stories would be more suitable for extroverts or introverts.[30]

Users Have Strong Feelings about Voice and Content Emotions

The emotion of the voice had a clear impact on participants' perceptions of the content. Participants who heard happy content read in a happy voice perceived the stories to be happier than those who heard the same content read in a sad voice.[31] Similarly, those who heard sad content read in a sad voice rated the stories as less happy than those who heard it read in a happy voice.[32] That is, although the content was identical, the voice influenced the *meaning* of the stories, even though the stories were clearly not created by the technology itself.

Participants liked the content significantly better when read by a voice whose emotion matched the emotion of the content than when voice and content were mismatched.[33] This demonstrates the importance of consistency, even when it is clear that the technology would not understand why consistency is important or know how to achieve it.

In sum, paralinguistic cues like speed, pitch, and volume are *integrated* with the perceived meaning of spoken words into a single message. Matching a voice to the content is just as important, and may even be more important, than matching the voice to the emotion of the user.

Technology for Creating Emotional Interfaces

Whenever a technology "speaks," the emotion expressed by the voice can have significant impact on users and their perceptions. Choosing the right emotional tone for a given piece of content can thus be as critical as choosing the right gender, accent, and personality for the voice—if not more so.[34] For example, a doll can say, "Be my friend" with an enthusiastic, apathetic, or angry voice—leading to perceptions of friendliness, insincerity, and contempt, respectively. A car can describe a problem with a battery with varying levels of urgency, leading to varying levels of user response. A music-recommendation system can sound confident or nervous, influencing people's likelihood of accepting the suggestion. A performer can make listening to a book on tape as moving an experience as reading a print book by infusing words with the proper emotion at the proper moment, or she can ruin the experience by striking a false note with the match between words and sounds. A voice-based financial Web site could joyfully announce that a stock has gone up but must avoid this if the customer sold the stock just before its value rose. A recipe program can say "Now *lightly* whisk the two eggs" with a tone of disgust, suggesting suspicions that the cook will mangle the recipe.

In the instances above, designers have no excuse for inconsistency because the content is prerecorded. With even a reasonably skilled actor, achieving high degrees of emotional consistency is simple if not automatic. The only caveat is that when sentences are recorded *out of context* by a voice talent, there can be unintentional inconsistency: "Your team has twenty-one points" should be spoken very differently depending on whether the previous sentence was "Your rival has five points" or "Your rival has fifty points."

The problem becomes much harder when the amount and variety of content are too large or dynamic to have a person record all of it. E-mail readers must be prepared to read any sentence written by any person at any time: "This is the happiest day of my life" should be read in a cheerful voice instead of a monotone, unless the rest of the message reveals that the sentence was sarcastic. The Associated Press has an enormous number of stories coming into its offices from all over the world: it is impossible to predict what will come next, and virtually instantaneous broadcasting is the norm. eBay receives postings for thousands of new products from thousands of people every day, including everything from computers to Ming vases. In cases like these, a single voice, no matter how it sounds, will mismatch a significant fraction of the content, and randomly assigning multiple voices will not solve the problem.

The seeming solution when content clearly manifests a single emotion is to have the technology first determine the emotional content of the particular message and then alter the voice accordingly. With most synthetic-speech systems, manipulating the parameters of a voice (such as pitch, pitch range, word speed) that are associated with emotion manifestation is straightforward.[35] Unfortunately, the technology required to deduce emotion from text is not effective because of the complexity of the problem.[36]

At first glance, written language would seem to be so filled with emotional tone that emotion should be easy to identify. Emotion-modeling systems can also look for explicit word choices and phrases that indicate emotion, such as "This is great" or "I feel awful." In more formal communication, the topic often presents a good indicator of emotion: wedding Web sites should have happier vocal indicators than should funeral Web sites.

If emotion were always indicated through emotion words (such as *happy* or *sad*) or through a topic, the problem of textual-emotion determination would be simple to resolve. To understand the difficulty, however, consider this sentence: "Another dead gray whale has washed ashore on the California Coast, deepening a mystery that has baffled scientists for years." This was the lead for the sad news story that was used in the study described above. Any human would know that this is a sad story, but think of all the knowledge that is imbedded in that conclusion. For example, although *dead* might be a clue that it was a sad story, think of a joyous song, such as "The Munchkin Land Song (Ding, Dong, the Witch Is Dead)" that has the word *dead* in it. The emotional-analysis system would have to know that the death of gray whales is sad but that the death of the Wicked Witch of the West in the film *The Wizard of Oz* was happy (although the death of Glinda, the Good Witch, would have been sad). "Baffling mysteries" can be frightening ("Was that really a ghost?"), angering ("Who took the last cookie?"), sad (the current example), happy ("Ah, the baffling mysteries of the universe!"), and a host of other emotions, depending on the tremendously varying characteristics of the individual and the situation. Remarkably, humans are able to grasp all of the subtleties of a situation to determine the appropriate emotional response.

The current best solution seems to be to put the responsibility for labeling the emotional tone of the content on the author. Authors can be asked to tag or describe their content at whatever level of granularity they prefer—the entire work (such as "a humorous piece"), a paragraph or sentence ("the 'dead gray whale' sentence is sad"), or even a word ("In this context, the word *hooray* should be read sardonically, reflecting sarcasm"). Perhaps the best example of a method for marking content for emotion is the use of *emoticons*, typographic symbols that serve as the equivalent of paralinguistic cues of emotion. Emoticons arose when it became apparent that emotional indicators were necessary to support interactions via e-mail and instant messaging systems. The word *emoticon* comes from the contraction of *emotion* and *icon*;[37] emoticons are icons because they are meant to capture the appearance of a face (lying on its side) that manifests the particular emotion. For example, the five basic emotions (and the extremely useful *irony*) can be represented as follows:

Fear 8-o

Happy :-)

Sad	:-(
Angry	(:-&
Disgusted	:-|
Irony	;-)

Emoticons are one useful method for marking emotions, with the potential to represent a large number of different states.[38] Beyond these emoticons, computational linguists and computer scientists have developed more sophisticated and subtle mark-up schemes that can indicate context, mood, and emotion as well as specific vocal parameters.[39]

Mark-up systems to indicate emotion have proven to be useful, but they have a number of limitations. First, it is burdensome for a writer to go through an entire work marking appropriate emotions, potentially at multiple points within every sentence. (Picture Tolstoy working his way through *War and Peace*, tortured by the need to enter tens of thousands of emotional markers, each reflecting the precise and nuanced emotion that he was trying to capture.) Second, unskilled producers of content—such as people submitting letters to the editor, book reviews to Amazon.com, or descriptions of products to eBay—might find the requirement of emoticons to be a significant "barrier to entry" and not submit content. Finally, the vast majority of content in media is *preexisting*; it would be an impossible task to go back and label every book, advertisement, or newspaper article.

Though the benefits of consistent, appropriate voice emotion are well established, the challenges are great, ensuring that content-rich voice interfaces will suffer the problems of inconsistency for a long time to come.

What If an Interface Can Manifest Only One Emotion?

While pessimism may be warranted with respect to solving the problem of inconsistency in voice emotion, interfaces nonetheless must be built. When the emotion of the content or the user cannot be detected, and the entire interface does not have a general emotional tone, what voice should be selected? The best emotion to select is a slightly happy voice.[40] Humans are built with "hedonic preference"—the tendency to experience, express, and perceive more positive emotions than negative ones.[41] In social interactions, people like others who display positive emotions more than those who display negative emotions.[42] If a person shows positive emotion, he or she is perceived to be more attractive and appealing to work with than someone who shows negative emotion.[43] The effect of positive emotion is even found in the mass media: commercials imbedded in or following a happy TV program are perceived to be more effective, are liked more, and are recalled better than ads following sad programs.[44]

When is it advantageous to select emotions other than happiness? Even though people volunteer positive events when asked to recall their lives—the so-called Pollyanna effect[45]—anger and sadness are more attention-getting and memorable than positive feelings.[46] In addition, the expression of submissive emotions (such as sadness and fear, for example) often increases trust in a relationship. Listeners view such emotional disclosure as a willingness to "open up" and be vulnerable,[47] which they often reciprocate.[48] Voice-based interfaces that need to obtain personal information from users—a health Web site or telephone-based surveys, for instance—could leverage voices (as well as content) that encourage trust.[49] We know of no advantage in defaulting to disgust, the fifth of the basic emotions, although this and all other emotions should be expressed in voice when dictated by a desire to match the content.

Manipulating More Than the Voice

Sometimes designers have control over both the content and the voice. The same rules that allow automated systems to begin to identify emotion in text can allow systems to *generate* text with emotion. By simultaneously manipulating the style of both voice and text, designers can make the problem of consistency easier by deriving both from the same emotional base.

In contexts where no author predetermines the exact text to communicate, such as when a system itself compiles and presents information to the user, an interface can simultaneously tune both the emotional tone of the voice and the emotional tone of the text. For example, a system could make the interface sad by choosing words with depressing connotations *and* using a voice that was somewhat slower, lower in pitch, and narrower in pitch range than a typical voice. Similarly, a travel site could simultaneously tune linguistic and paralinguistic cues to describe a hotel for business or pleasure, using more formal language and a relatively flat voice in the former case and enthusiastic language and a happy voice in the latter.

Music presents a further modality through which a voice interface—and any audio-based interface, in general—can set a mood. People typically associate minor scales with negative emotions and major scales with more positive and happy emotions, for example.[50]

Emotions as Categories versus Emotions as Dimensions

Throughout this chapter and the previous chapter, emotion has been referred to in terms of *categories*. The categorical approach assumes that the best way to describe and understand emotions is to talk about the presence or absence of particular emotions, each represented by a single word. An alternative is the *dimensional* approach to emotion. Dimensional approaches assume that researchers can draw a simple coordinate system created from a very small number of axes to capture virtually all emotions; any and all emotion words can then be located at a particular point in this space.[51]

The most useful dimensional scheme was developed by Peter Lang and his colleagues.[52] Lang argues that most emotions can be placed along two independent dimensions—valence (which has been the focus of this chapter and the last), or how happy or sad someone feels, and arousal, or how excited or calm someone is. (A third dimension, control, is sometimes included.)[53] Using these dimensions, for example, disgust is extremely low on valence and neutral on arousal, and anger and fear are quite low on valence and high on arousal. Most other emotion words fit under this scheme, although it doesn't perfectly differentiate emotions; two different emotions may land in the same place.[54]

The advantage of the dimensional approach is that voices can simply be positioned along the two dimensions. The farther a voice is along the positive side of valence (happy instead of sad), the more the voice has higher pitch, wider pitch range, greater intensity, and upward as opposed to downward inflections. The farther a voice is along the excited side of arousal, the more the voice has higher pitch, wider pitch range, wider volume range, and faster word speed, for example. To create a particular emotion in a voice by using paralinguistic cues, a designer simply finds the coordinates of the emotion along each axis and selects the parameters accordingly.

Are Emotions Contagious?

When voice emotion activates different hemispheres of the brain of the listener, the activated hemisphere encourages the listener to *feel* the emotion; that is, recognition of voice emotion inspires a listener's emotional *response*. A drug called amabarbitol sodium, which limits communication between the hemispheres of the brain, helps demonstrate this phenomenon.[55] When the drug is injected into the right hemisphere, the left hemisphere becomes dominant and people report euphoric moods.[56] Conversely, when the drug is injected into the left hemisphere, people feel depressed as the right hemisphere becomes dominant. Thus, the activation of the associated hemispheres can lead to *emotion contagion*,[57] the "catching" of the emotions of others. Sometimes this social phenomenon seems logical, such as when a person becomes afraid when seeing another experience fear: there may be a true danger nearby. At other times, contagion seems completely illogical, such as when another person's laughter induces immediate, "inexplicable" amusement. Contagion offers a partial explanation for why people generally enjoy being around happy people (and happy voices).

Full contagion, however, does not always occur. If the speaker's expressed emotion is strong and positive but the listener's current mood or orientation toward the speaker is unfavorable, the listener may catch the speaker's emotional arousal (excitement) but not the speaker's emotional valence (positive or negative aspect). In such cases, the listener could end up feeling strong negative emotion (such as frustration or jealousy), even though the speaker is expressing strong happiness. In general, excitement is the aspect of emotion that is most reliably transferred.[58] Thus, extreme emotions, whether positive or negative, will lead people to feel their own emotions, regardless of what they are, more intensely. Hence, designers should be cautious about presenting voices with highly accentuated emotions.

Linkages between Perceived Emotion and Perceived Traits

The human voice does not neatly distinguish between states and traits. The voice markers for submissiveness, a trait, are similar to the voice markers for depression, a state, for example. In the long run, this is not a problem: Personality sets a baseline for the voice, and emotion is then evaluated relative to that baseline. However, in the short run, states and traits become confused. This is why extroverts are initially perceived as happier than introverts.[59] Indeed, in the current study, participants who heard happy content read in a happy voice rated the content as more interesting to extroverts than those who heard the same content read in a sad voice.[60] Similarly, those who heard sad content read in a sad voice rated the stories as less interesting for extroverts than those who heard it read in a happy voice.[61]

Similar confusion occurs with emotion and gender. Females tend to have voice characteristics that are associated with positive valence and neutral arousal, while males tend to have voices that are associated with high arousal and neutral valence. Similarly, the gruffness associated with older voices can lead people to perceive the elderly as being in a bad mood.[62] Even though individuals know that these characteristics are simply markers of traits, they automatically apply them to deductions about states.

For limited-term interactions, there is little that designers can do about this confusion beyond selecting voices with perception of both traits and states in mind.

Providing Consistency in an Inconsistent World

Voice interfaces may not be capable of feeling emotion, but they are certainly capable of expressing emotion. In fact, it is unavoidable. Users respond to even the most monotone synthetic voice as if it were manifesting extremely low arousal and neutral valence. The content that interfaces present to users will also be associated with emotion, no matter how "unemotional" an interface tries to be. Because the brain tightly integrates the emotion of voice and the emotion of words, consistency between them is critical, even when they are generated by a clearly synthetic, unemotional machine.

Appendix

Table 8.1.A
Vocal effects associated with several basic emotions

	Fear	Anger	Sadness	Happiness	Disgust
Speech rate	Much faster	Slightly faster	Slightly slower	Faster or slower	Very much slower
Pitch average	Very much higher	Very much higher	Slightly lower	Much higher	Very much lower
Pitch range	Much wider	Much wider	Slightly narrower	Much wider	Slightly wider
Intensity	Normal	Higher	Lower	Higher	Lower
Voice quality	Irregular voicing	Breathy chest tone	Resonant	Breathy blaring	Grumbled chest tone
Pitch changes	Normal	Abrupt on stressed syllables	Downward inflections	Smooth upward inflections	Wide downward terminal inflections
Articulation	Precise	Tense	Slurring	Normal	Normal

Source: I. R. Murray and J. L. Arnott, Toward the simulation of emotion in synthetic speech: A review of the literature on human vocal emotion, *Journal Acoustical Society of America* 93, no. 2 (1993): 1097–1108.

9 When Are Many Voices Better Than One? People Differentiate Synthetic Voices

Each human voice reaches the human ear with its own range of frequencies, harmonics, and distortions. Within less than one second, each of these characteristics may vary in volume, pitch, speed, or cadence; may be influenced by a host of personal and situational realities; and may be interfered with by other voices or sounds in the environment. If the human voice were a tuning fork producing a clear tone and a unique frequency for each person, the brain's ability to differentiate and process multiple voices would not amaze. But voice qualities and environmental influences are obstacles that make humans' ability to distinguish one voice from another and even one voices out of many a remarkable feat.

What enables people to distinguish the many voices coming out of a speaker phone? How does the brain keep track of a presidential primary debate on the radio when the various candidates incessantly interrupt each other? How can travelers simultaneously comprehend their laptop announcing "You've got mail," their MP3 player intoning "Batteries are low," and a voice calling out "Room service"? How do parents simultaneously listen to three kids speaking, a televised news report, and a telephone caller?

The answer to these questions is that the human brain has evolved to solve the extraordinarily difficult problem of distinguishing one voice from another: voice differentiation is located on both sides of the brain (although words are adduced primarily with the left side of the brain).[1] As mentioned earlier, even a fetus in the womb can distinguish its mother's voice from all other voices,[2] while it takes days after birth before infants can distinguish their mother from other people via either sight[3] or smell.[4] Soon after birth, newborns can also distinguish one unfamiliar voice from another.[5] By eight months old, infants' brains are tuned to those aspects of sound waves that occur in the range of speech (and music).[6] Infants can also focus on one voice even if multiple voices are presented simultaneously—the so-called cocktail party effect.[7]

Researchers debate whether the human brain is built specifically to discriminate voices or whether this ability is simply an outgrowth of the general activation of voice processing coupled with pattern-matching skills. On the one hand, no training is required to detect differences in pitch or other fundamental characteristics of voices; novices are as good as experts.[8] On the other hand, clear evidence shows that voice discrimination draws on generalized cognitive abilities. For example, when a person is confronted with a new voice, cognitive load is increased.[9] In fact, when a great deal of cognitive attention is allocated to a task, people can exhibit "change deafness"—or the inability to detect when one voice changes to another.[10]

Humans can distinguish voices along an enormous number of dimensions. The most obvious category is the basic pitch of the voice, used to identify gender as well as other characteristics.[11] Pitch range, volume, and volume range can also be used to distinguish people,[12] although these (as well as pitch) can also be altered by the situation[13] (for example, a frightening situation makes all voices get higher and exhibit a great deal of frequency range). The brain also performs a highly complex analysis of the timbre of a voice, which includes all aspects of the sound waves (frequency spectrum) associated with voices beyond pitch and volume.[14] Timbre enables voices to be described as "smoky," "nasal," "breathy," "raspy," or "shrill." Timbre in the human voice is determined by the diaphragm, lungs, trachea, pharynx, larynx, vocal cords, glottis, oral cavity, jaw, teeth, tongue, and lips.[15] Each of these is influenced in turn by factors such as genetics, endocrine system, health history, physical environment, and habits.[16] With all these sources of differentiation, every body produces a different voice. Finally, accents,[17] word choice, and all other aspects of the linguistic features of voice also enable differentiation.

Because each human voice is unique in how it combines these dimensions, the human brain has evolved to draw a one-to-one correspondence between a speaker and the speech characteristics of a particular voice. A given person (at least within a limited time period) has only one voice (excluding impersonators and ventriloquists), and a given voice is generally associated with only one person (although two people may have remarkably similar voices). Thus, voice has become an automatic and highly efficient marker of *identity*.

Identity is important because, unlike ant and bee colonies (in which virtually all members behave identically to all other members),[18] people treat one another differently. Many evolutionary theorists argue that the rapid determination of the identity of a person was and is one of the most important abilities for survival among humans.[19] Voice, as a virtually universal means of communication, and faces became the most readily apparent cues for identifying an interaction partner. Voice was and is particularly valuable because it can identify individuals in situations such as hunting, when eyes are occupied with other tasks.

Understanding the coupling between voice, body, and identity is extremely valuable for the brain. Multiple voices—coming from an adjacent room, for example—immediately indicate that multiple people are present, a critical fact for a social animal. The same coupling enables us to make sense of and enjoy radio: people naturally imagine a different person behind each of the different voices.

The inherent correspondence of voice and identity has moved beyond individual brains to social institutions. Police now routinely use *audio* lineups in which *ear*witnesses attempt to identify a person they heard during the commission of a crime,[20] although evidence suggests that earwitnesses are much less reliable than eyewitnesses.[21] In the first nonmilitary case involving the admissibility of voice-identification evidence,[22] the New Jersey Supreme Court ruled in 1968 that "the physical properties of a person's voice are identifying characteristics"[23] when recorded and analyzed by a specialist. The 2003 Federal Rules of Evidence (Article 9, Rule 901b5) clearly permit the use of voice identification in court, although the identification must include both spectrographic analysis and expert interpretation.[24] An increasing number of businesses, including the Home Shopping Network, are using fully automated "voiceprint" analysis to validate a person's identity; consumer acceptance of this technology is growing.[25]

The equivalence of voice, body, and identity breaks down in the world of technology. Traditional media like telephones, radios, and televisions have always produced more than one human voice. As data-storage solutions continue to offer more plentiful space in smaller and less expensive hardware, prerecording a number of different voices to come out of a single box becomes possible. Thus a single "body" can have multiple voices.

From their inception, systems for creating synthetic voices allowed changes to be made in the fundamental characteristics of the voice.[26] With advances in software, digital signal processors, and other hardware, a host of parameters that affect the timbre of a synthetic voice can be changed:[27] it has become as easy as changing the name of a file on a hard drive.

The proliferation of voice technologies challenges the idea that voice is truly a mark of identity or personhood: the intimate link between a particular physical object (a body or a box) and a voice is now broken. Indeed, in the digital era, the number of voices may become completely arbitrary. While multiple voices playing over the radio imply multiple actors speaking in a remote studio, a computer's synthetic voices have no humans behind the voice at all: multiple synthetic voices can all be created from a single computer.

Do Multiple Synthetic Voices Matter?

The previous chapters have demonstrated that people can recognize and respond to social characteristics of technology-based voices, even when those voices are clearly synthetic. Users have no problem deciding that a voice is female and not male, extroverted and not introverted, or happy and not sad. However, will people make the leap from voice differences to voice identities, an appropriate conclusion when hearing human voices but a faulty one when applied to technologies? Put another way, will the evolutionarily useful and logical tendency to equate voices and identities be automatically extended to synthetic voices on interfaces? If people do make this extension, can the confusion be eliminated by reminding people that equating synthetic voices with different identities is illogical?

The most direct way to answer these questions would be simply to ask people directly. Researchers could have people listen to different voices on a computer, a Web site, or a refrigerator and say, "Do you think that those voices represent either different identities or people or the same identity or person?" However, this method of ascertaining an answer to the question is not as straightforward as it might appear. When questions like this are asked, the first response is usually one of incredulity: "Why would someone ask something like that?" After deciding that it is not a trick question, people generally laugh and reply, "Of course not. Mechanical voices have nothing to do with people or identities." More thoughtful individuals might add, "I suppose that children might think that a computer's voice has an identity, but no adult would ever think that." From the studies discussed in previous chapters, people are known to deny that they are influenced by the gender or personality of a computer voice, although their behaviors indicate that they are indeed influenced. Hence, a more subtle approach is needed.

In this study, the paradigm that was adopted was inspired by the "multiple-source effect"[28] (also known as the "source-magnification effect"):[29] an individual is more convinced by an opinion or a statement when it is expressed by a variety of people than when it is expressed by a single person. One explanation for why groups exert more social influence than individuals is *normative social influence*:[30] people like to hold the opinions of the groups with whom they interact, even when those opinions are almost certainly wrong.[31] Another explanation is *informational social influence*:[32] when multiple people believe something, differences between individuals suggest that a variety of information and information-processing strategies led to the same conclusion, making the conclusion more convincing. Of course, unanimous support from a number of people gives better evidence for public opinion than does a single person's opinion. If these findings are relevant to interfaces, then individuals should be more influenced by multiple synthetic voices rather than by a single synthetic voice, even if the content that the voices are relating is identical.

In addition to the multiple-source effect, a second criterion for determining whether listeners assign distinct identities to different synthetic voices is whether the voices make a person feel that he or she is *among* a group of people. The more voices that a person hears when walking into a party, for example, the greater the sense of others. That is, when many voices are heard, the people become more *present*.[33]

Hearing Multiple Voices on the Web

In this study, the context for exploring the psychology of multiple voices was a simulated book-selling Web site patterned after Amazon.com.[34] The site presented a separate Web page for each of three books. Each Web page included the book's title, the author's name, a photo of the cover, and five actual customer reviews from Amazon.com. All of the reviews for all of the books were positive so that participants would feel unambiguous social and normative influences. The reviews were not presented in text form, as they appear on Amazon.com. Instead, the site presented a link to an audio file that played when clicked. The reviews were described as coming from "Customer A" up to "Customer E." Some participants heard a single voice read all five reviews, and others heard multiple voices read the reviews.

Here are three of the five reviews about the book *Plainsong* by Kent Haruf:

Customer A: The pace of the story mimics that of the small town it takes place in. The characters are richly drawn but not caricatures. Not a lot happens, but I believe that's the point. There is no urgency to the story, and I liked it that way. The author, like James Lee Burke, has an affection for the beauty of the land. Reading this book is like taking a stroll down the main street of Holt County, in which the story takes place. Highly recommended.

Customer B: I loved this book. I stayed up all night reading it because I cared so much about the people. I could not put it down. I haven't done that since I was a child. After a lifetime of reading, I'm aware how rare this kind of experience is. And the reason? Kent Haruf's honesty, skill, and compassion as a writer.

Customer C: I really enjoyed this book. It starts slowly with disconnected stories. As it builds character development and speed, the stories become intertwined. I like stories like this anyway, but this is better than most. The descriptions of the plains, weather, and other sensations are real. The characters are people you want to take home with you. A good read.

The participants had not heard about or read any of the three books, as indicated by their questionnaire responses. The books and their authors were selected based on low sales to increase the likelihood that participants would not be familiar with the books. All books were fiction to avoid bias based on participants' general knowledge of various topics.

Forty adults participated in the study. Twenty participants heard all five customer reviews via a single voice that was randomly selected for each participant. The other twenty participants (randomly selected) heard the five reviews delivered via five different synthetic voices that varied by fundamental frequency, speech rate, and timbre.[35] The order of the voices was varied for each person.[36] To avoid the possible effects of voice gender preferences,[37] all synthesized voices were male.

After participants listened to the reviews for the three books, they were directed to another Web site, where they were asked a series of questions about their own feelings about the reviewed books[38] and their perceptions of how the general public would feel about the books.[39] By looking at how positively participants rated the books, the researcher could measure how persuaded they were by the reviews (which were all positive). If the results indicated that participants were more persuaded by reviews that were read by multiple voices rather than by a single voice, even when the review contents were identical, that would be a strong indication that participants perceived the five different voices as five distinct identities. Questions about how the general public would feel about the books were designed to determine if the diversity of voices made people feel that a broader spectrum of the public liked a book. Finally, participants were asked (using questions derived from previous studies)[40] about their feelings of how present the voices seemed.[41]

Multiple Voices Activated Thoughts of Multiple Identities

Just as in the human-only world, participants in this study were more persuaded by several synthetic voices than by a single synthetic voice,[42] even though the comments were identical and the ideas of normative and informational influence should not be relevant. Users evaluated the books significantly more positively when they heard multiple voices,[43] consistent with the multiple-source effect. Because hearing various voices triggered the sense that numerous people agreed, listeners also perceived more public support for the book than did participants who heard a single voice.[44]

The varied voices also led to a feeling that the potential book buyer was surrounded by people: significantly more social presence was experienced when participants heard several voices than when they heard a single voice.[45]

This study shows that users do, in fact, perceive multiple synthetic voices to be multiple distinct entities. Synthetic voices manifest individuality in the same way that human voices do. The evolutionary tendency to use voice characteristics as a mark of individual identity thus overcomes the fact that one computer generated several voices.

Would a Reminder of Unnaturalness Have an Impact?

Although this experiment provides compelling evidence that multiple synthetic voices are perceived as multiple entities, the experiment could not tell how robust this effect would be. To address this issue, the experiment was rerun with a different group of forty participants, this time strongly emphasizing to participants that the various voices that they were going to hear were arbitrarily and randomly generated by the same computer. First, participants read the following brief description of how a text-to-speech system works:

> In this experiment, you will hear *machine* voices synthesized by a TTS (text-to-speech) system. TTS is the creation of audible speech from computer-readable text. Many TTS systems are currently available. Most of them can generate more than one type of voice from any given text by altering speech rate, fundamental frequency (F0), loudness, and other vocal parameters.

This warning was important because people often behave "mindlessly"[46] without thinking about all aspects of a situation. By reminding participants that the computer's voices were arbitrary and meaningless, the tendency to ignore this critical aspect of the situation should be decreased or eliminated.

Then participants logged on to the text-to-speech demo site at AT&T Labs, typed a sentence, and listened as the computer produced multiple versions of their sentence using different synthetic voices. This immediate, hands-on experience helped participants to understand that Web sites can easily produce many different synthetic voices. After experimenting with various TTS parameters and voices, participants went to the same book-selling Web site that participants in the previous experiment visited, heard the same reviews about each of the same three books, and answered the same questions. Again, half of the participants heard reviews read by several different synthetic voices, and half heard reviews by a single synthetic voice.[47]

Even after being told and shown that multiple synthetic voices could be easily produced by the same computer, participants showed no decrement in their tendency to treat multiple synthetic voices as if they represented multiple distinct entities: voice activation is powerful. Participants were once again more persuaded when reviews were read by various voices: they evaluated the books more positively[48] and perceived public opinion of the books to be more positive.[49] Finally, although they were reminded that the creation of multiple voices was as simple as creating a single voice, participants nonetheless felt much greater social presence when they heard several voices than when they heard a single voice.[50] Users' tendency to process computer-generated voices in the same way that they process human voices proved to be extremely robust.

Other Evidence for the Multiple-Voice Effect

It might be argued that the previous research is compelling but applies only to a limited domain. First, the studies were limited to a single, though important context: e-commerce. Second, the studies employed synthetic speech. Finally, the studies were Web-based: Web users know that when they click on a link (even an audio file link), they can be sent to a different source than that of the initial site.

Fortunately, two other studies remedy these deficiencies. One study examined politeness[51]—particularly the tendency for people to say nicer things to a person who asks about herself or himself than to a person who asks about another.[52] Participants in this study first did a task with a computer that spoke with a recorded, high-fidelity voice and then answered the computer's spoken questions about the computer's performance. Half of the participants were asked the evaluation questions by the voice that spoke during the task; the other half were asked the evaluation questions by a different recorded voice. Participants provided significantly more positive responses to the computer when it asked with its original voice than when it asked with a different voice,[53] which demonstrates the power of multiple voices to encourage both identity and social norms.

The other study looked at self-praise and other praise in the context of a computer tutoring application.[54] In this experiment, participants first learned from a computer with a recorded voice. Then half of the participants heard the computer praise its tutoring using the same voice as in the tutoring session, and half of participants heard the computer praise its tutoring using the same words but a different voice. Consistent with the notion that other praise is more believable than self-praise[55] and that different voices represent different identities, strong differences in response were observed between the people who heard praise coming from the voice that taught them and people who heard praise coming from a different voice. Although the words used in the tutor's performance and in the praise of the tutor's performance were identical, participants perceived the different-voice evaluation to be significantly more accurate than the other participants perceived the same-voice evaluation.[56] Different-voice participants also perceived the evaluation session to be fairer than did same-voice participants.[57] That is, distinct voices lead to responses consistent with distinct identities.

Multiple Voices as Specialists, One Voice as a Generalist[58]

Given how attuned the human ear and brain are to detecting differences in voices, it is not surprising that different voices, even different synthetic voices, seem to evoke perceptions of different "people" or at least different "social actors." But it is striking that this differentiation of voices activates the cognitive apparatus that evolved to assign distinct identities to voices. Thus, changing voices within an interface is not the same as changing colors or fonts:[59] the latter is simply an artistic (and perhaps cognitive) decision; the former has social consequences. The implications for design are first discussed in terms of when to use multiple voices versus when to use a single voice. The chapter then turns to some issues that are unique to multiple voices.

The simplest way for designers to decide whether to use multiple voices or a single voice is to ask two questions: "When would users like to be working with multiple people, and when would they like to work with just a single person?" and "Do I want this device or service to feel like a collection of parts or a unified whole?" Here are some of the guidelines that the research literature provides for answering these questions.

Specialists Are a Plus

When people need help doing something complicated or important, they turn to a specialist. Experiments have shown that the products of specialists are perceived to be better than the products of generalists,[60] even when their contents are identical. A more surprising finding is that expertise can be inferred simply from a label;[61] demonstrated performance is unnecessary. At the end of the film *The Wizard of Oz*, the sham Wizard leverages this principle: declare someone intelligent (the Scarecrow) or brave (the Lion), and a perception of that characteristic will follow.

Using two computer voices, a designer can create a specialist simply by having one voice designate the other as expert (as noted above, self-labeling is not as compelling). Even though people will know that the voices are coming from the same computer, the automatic tendency to separate voices should lead to enhanced perceptions of the "specialist's" performance.

Specialist voices can be used compellingly when a function is known to require significant expertise. For example, a car interface might have one voice for handling general commands from the driver but a specialist voice for mechanical problems and navigation, which require highly specific knowledge and understanding. An MP3 player might have one general voice for basic functionality and a separate voice for music recommendations, a highly personalized and complex activity. An e-commerce site might use one voice to excite people about the products and another voice to take people through the tedium of filling out the order form.

Our favorite example of a specialist voice uses the good cop/bad cop scenario in a prototype voice-mail system:

Voice 1 (warm and friendly): We at the XYZ Company look forward to helping you. Please use our new telephone system so that you can be routed to the right person.

Voice 2 (formal and unfriendly): Press 1 for Department A, 2 for Department B. . . .

After the user passed through a couple of voice-mail levels, he or she heard this message:

Voice 1: We at the XYZ Company are very sorry that this voice system is making it difficult for you to get through. Please bear with it.

Voice 2: Press 1 for Supervisor Q, 2 for Supervisor R. . . .

Voice 1: We at the XYZ Company hate this system as much as you do. We're doing everything we can go get your call to the right place.

Finally, after a few more rounds with the bureaucratic Voice 2, the caller's line was answered by a live person.

We then interviewed participants and asked how they felt about the voice-mail system. "Boy, I really hate that voice-mail system. But it's great how much XYZ cares about me!" The clever idea here was that the warm and friendly voice of XYZ *distanced itself* from the navigation voice. Indeed, all references to XYZ were made by the voice that was "on the side of the user." The voice of XYZ thus made the navigation voice a "scapegoat."[62] The power of voice differentiation led listeners to ignore the fact that it was XYZ that deployed the annoying system in the first place.

A final advantage of specialist voices is that a particular voice can be selected to be uniquely relevant to particular tasks. Because even synthetic voices can manifest gender, accent, and personality,[63] one voice might suggest maximal expertise, and another might best challenge stereotypes for each application or service. For example, the interface to a mathematical application might be male, middle-age, and introverted sounding, or it might break those stereotypes to encourage the social goal of inclusiveness.

Specialists Are a Minus

There are downsides to having specialists. Imagine that an interface has a general master of ceremonies (M.C.) voice that directs people to various "experts" with distinct voices. Although the experts will be seen as highly competent, the M.C. will be seen as unable to perform even the simplest task. If the M.C. becomes associated with the product or service, his or her incompetence may lead to a "negative halo effect"[64] in which weakness in one characteristic is imputed to all characteristics, including the product.

Another problem with employing specialist voices is that multiple voices exact a cognitive price.[65] If the system introduces new voices precisely at the times when the user is performing a complex activity (which is why the system employed a specialist in the first place), then the person's performance could actually be impeded as the person tries to cope with the new cognitive load.

In an elegant series of studies, Teenie Matlock, Paul Maglio, and colleagues have explored how a lack of specialization can have benefits when a caller speaks to a system. In their studies, they asked participants to speak to devices that perform various functions (such as a calendar, a trip planner, an address book, or an e-mail device). When people were asked to "talk to the system" (a single, generalist place), people took less time and were overall more efficient in their interactions (for example, they used more pronouns than full noun phrases) than when they were asked to "talk to each device" (several specialist places).[66] Furthermore, when speaking to the "system," users would feel free to look anywhere; when talking to the "device," they looked directly at it and referred to it by name (for example, "Address book, show me the address for . . ." versus "Show me the address for . . .").[67] Participants who worked with the talk-to-the-system condition judged it to be more natural and more like working with a colleague than did those who worked with the talk-to-the-device condition.[68]

A final cautionary note about interface specialists is that they should not be employed when a real-life specialist would *not* be appropriate. For example, in one prototype telephone-based system that involved a "virtual secretary," the user interacted with one voice for voice mail and a different voice for e-mail (which was read to the users), even though the structure of commands and replies was identical. Users found this puzzling and distracting and wondered why two voices were speaking to them when their functions were logically the same. Using voices in this way can also make users feel that "no one" wants to take responsibility, much as people grow frustrated when they are bounced from one person to another to another and back to the first when navigating a bureaucracy. In sum, specialist voices can give extraordinary power and credibility to an interface, but caution must be exercised.

A Single Voice in Multiple Contexts

Once a particular voice is assigned to a particular identity, the human brain is very effective at recognizing the voice. Parents can easily discern their child's voice in the sobbing, virtually incomprehensible phone call from summer camp; the giggling description of a day at school; the static-filled cell-phone conversation; the hymn in church; the echoing, unlocatable voice running through a cave; and the recording from five years earlier. People can also distinguish the voices of others they have never met in person. A listener can automatically recognize that the same speaker, James Earl Jones, breathily intones, "Luke, I am your father,"[69] announces "This is CNN," and played the submissive servant in *"Master Harold" . . . and the Boys*.[70] The evocation of identity through voice even applies to fictional characters: it is impossible to imagine Barney or Tickle Me Elmo dolls, both enormous sellers in the United States, with a voice other than the one that the character uses on television.

The brain's talent for discerning identity from voice is even robust against sound cards and speaker quality. Humans can recognize the same voice whether it comes from a live person, a high-fidelity music player, a medium-fidelity television, a low-fidelity cell phone, or an even lower-fidelity plastic toy. The ability to be both thoroughly forgiving of variations in a single voice and acutely sensitive to distinguishing different voices is a remarkable combination. Part of the explanation for how these seemingly opposite abilities can reside in the same person is that they reside in different parts of the brain.[71] The ability to recognize a familiar voice is located in the inferior and lateral parietal regions of the right hemisphere of the brain (which is not the hemisphere associated with voice processing), while the ability to distinguish between two voices is located in the temporal lobes of both hemispheres of the brain.[72]

What happens when the same voice appears on multiple technologies? Research has shown that the strong link between personhood and voice means that the same voice from two different technologies will tend to blur the segmentation between the technologies and lead the user to perceive a single identity, just as various voices on a single machine will feel like multiple identities. For example, in one experiment, the same voice spoke from two computers and was responded to as if it represented a single person, while, as noted above, a second voice on the same computer was experienced as a different person.[73]

What should designers do when they have an option of using the same voice across product lines or different voices for each product? It depends on what the company wants to brand.[74] For example, if a company wants to suggest homogeneity across a set of media technologies—such as a television, a stereo, and a DVD player—the same voice should be used across products. However, if the company wants consumers to orient to a particular product, then having quite different voices across the various products would be worthwhile. Finally, if the company wants consumers to orient to the services provided around the product rather than the product itself (such as when most of the profit comes from monthly subscriptions rather than the initial purchase), then the interface to the product itself should be subdued, either via text or via a soft, terse voice.

Multiple Voices in a Single Context

Very often, designers require a single piece of technology to produce multiple voices. This is the case for telephones, radios, televisions, CD players, and video games. These technologies would not be effective if they homogenized all voices to sound alike. Because these technologies do not use a single voice to connect users with the product, the product becomes psychologically *invisible*: people focus solely on the voices and what they say.

This invisibility now extends beyond the psychological to the physical design of technologies. Televisions have transitioned from huge picture tubes to flat screens, cell phones have become credit-card size, and MP3 players and Walkmans are now no larger than the tiny disks or cassettes that they play. This is also the spirit of "ubiquitous computing,"[75] in which systems are designed to encourage people to forget about the technology and simply orient to the voice and task. The lack of a physical presence facilitates the sense that the product is a conduit or medium rather than an independent identity.

A Voice in the Crowd

When brains encounter groups of two or more people, they instantly begin to analyze how the group members feel about and interact with one another.[76] Are they lovers, friends, acquaintances, or enemies? Even when the voices do not speak directly to one another, if one voice is affected by another's comments, then a social dynamic emerges among the voices. For example, a voice that always interrupts other voices would likely be seen as dominant or abusive, while a voice that never interrupts, even when such interruption would be justified, would be seen as submissive. In these cases, it is particularly important that the gender, accent, personality, and emotion of the voice match its behavior.[77] Of course, as the number of voices increases, the user will have to spend cognitive energy processing each of the voices and also keeping track of the social relationships among them, even if subconsciously. Hence, listening to too many voices is exhausting.

What if designers want one voice to stand out from the others? A few subtle but powerful options are available. One strategy that is used effectively in television advertising is to make one voice louder than the others. The human brain orients to the loudest voice,[78] probably because throughout evolutionary history, the loudness of a voice was associated with the proximity of the speaker, and physically close people represented a greater opportunity and a greater threat than more distant people.

A second strategy for making a voice memorable is to have people interact with it. People have a better memory for voices with which they have interacted than for voices that they have listened to passively.[79] By picking one voice for all interactions and restricting all other voices to information provision, the interactive voice will become most prominent.

A final strategy is to use a typical voice along with a set of unusual voices. Each unusual voice will be stored in memory as a deviant from a prototype,[80] that is, as "weird." Conversely, the typical voice will be stored as prototypical. Although the unusual voices might be arresting in the short run,[81] because standard, well-defined categories are easier to access from memory than fuzzy categories, the unusual voices will all blur together and thus be less prominent than the single typical voice.

Should Users Choose the Voice of Their Interface?

A halfway measure between requiring a single voice and having the designer employ a wide range of voices is to have the user select one voice from a set of voices. This could come at the time of purchase or could be an option throughout the life of the product. The booming market for cell-phone "ringtones" demonstrates the attractiveness of this idea.

Imagine, for example, that all cars were equipped with a voice interface. Should every car of a particular manufacturer speak using the same voice, or should each driver select his or her own unique car voice? Similarly, would people enjoy their interactions with customer support more if they could choose the telephone voice that provides the support?

The key point is that choice is psychologically powerful.[82] In general, because of cognitive dissonance, people will like the voices they select and will try to avoid information about the desirability of other choices[83] (although there is some evidence for buyer's remorse,[84] the tendency to regret choices soon after making them). There is no evidence that people are successful at selecting the voices they will like in the long run; however, the mere act of selection can be a positive experience. The feeling that the user hears a voice that virtually no other user will hear may create a perception of a unique interpersonal bond between the user and the voice, especially if the user interacts with the voice and does not merely listen to it.[85]

How should the choice be managed? The best approach is to have a second computer voice (that is, a voice other than the voice the user is currently using) propose the option of selecting a different voice. Because people are polite to voices, they might find it hard to "reject" a voice with whom they have been working.[86]

Another critical point is that too many options can be overwhelming. In a classic series of studies performed in both field and laboratory settings, Sheena S. Iyengar and Mark R. Lepper showed that people were more likely to purchase gourmet jams and to undertake an optional class essay assignment when offered only six choices than when they were offered twenty-four or thirty choices.[87] Furthermore, participants felt better about their choice and performed better when their selections were limited. Unfortunately, there are no clear guidelines that prescribe exactly how many choices of voices (or choices of any product or service) are too many. Assuming that the voices are quite different, the optimal number of choices might be approximately seven because that is approximately the number of items that can be kept in short-term memory.[88] If the voices can be categorized (for example, by gender), participants will likely exhibit a greater tolerance and desire for more options. All of the options should remain consistent with the brand.

Currently, the goal of cutting-edge voice-interface designers is to allow users to create a voice for the interface: better algorithms will soon make this a reality. Some people might even choose to have their own voices for their interface; research shows that this is not disturbing.[89] Others may choose the voice of a family member, a relative, a friend, or a famous celebrity. The danger of allowing this level of personalization is that the product or service may become invisible because of the presence of the voice, which thereby will undermine branding.

Other Challenges of Using Multiple Voices

The most significant practical issue that is associated with multiple voices is the maintenance problem. When designers add new content to a recorded voice system with many voices, they must write a version of the content for each of the voices (so that the content is consistent with the gender, accent, and personality of the voice), schedule and record several people in the studio, edit separate files, and perform a number of functions repetitively. Even when the system uses multiple synthetic voices, each voice must be given a different script and be tuned for the proper phrasing, for example.[90]

Ethical implications also arise when multiple voices are deployed. In this chapter's experiment, the various voices were, in fact, expressing the opinions of different people. However, designers could easily and falsely create the impression of multiple adherents to a position as a way to manipulate users. If the goal of such a manipulation is to make users feel more comfortable and accepted in an environment, perhaps such pretences are acceptable, but if the goal is to trick users into purchasing a product or to construct a false sense of the validity and acceptance of an idea (such as for a political campaign), this façade seems problematic.

Differences Are Only Voice Deep

The general feeling is that the most important differences between people lie at the depths of their souls. This chapter suggests that the human brain adopts the opposite stance: differences are grounded in how something *seems*. Thus, a voice, no matter how synthetic, can cue the assignment of a distinct orientation and its concomitant expectations. Designers who deploy multiple voices simply for variety or entertainment are likely to be surprised: each added voice brings significant social consequences that cannot be ignored.

10 Should Voice Interfaces Say "I"? Recorded and Synthetic Voice Interfaces' Claims to Humanity

The previous chapters have in many ways portrayed the human brain as simultaneously obsessed and oblivious. Give the slightest hint of gender in a voice interface, and the user applies stereotypes;[1] match the user's gender, and the user sees nothing but similarities.[2] Alter the speed, volume, and pitch of the most innocuous-sounding voice, and consumers buy and trust.[3] Present a photo of a face and the sound of a voice at the same time: even if the photo's lips don't move, the ethnicities of the face and voice must match.[4] Reduce the enthusiasm in the voice of a car interface, and happy drivers perform poorly.[5]

Users combine an intense focus and extreme overgeneralization with a tendency to ignore the obvious. It is as if users were thinking, "Sure it sounds like a Martian, but it's female, so I know what to do";[6] "Yes, I see it's a big black box that's thoroughly removed from the social world, but boys will be boys"[7]; "It may not pronounce words correctly, but I know an extrovert when I hear one"[8]; "I know that it doesn't have feelings, but how can it sound so happy about that tragic story?";[9] and "I remember that you showed me anyone can create multiple voices, but how can a crowd be wrong?"[10]

An early reader of this book said that the findings in chapters 2 through 9 make people sound like "one of Nikolaas Tinbergen's oystercatchers."[11] The oystercatcher is a shore bird that lays brown spotted eggs; nothing else in their environment is spotted. Tinbergen, the Nobel Prize–winning ethologist, deduced that to preserve its limited brain power, the birds would be evolved to focus on the eggs' brown spots and large size and ignore everything else. To test this, Tinbergen placed a wooden, brown-spotted *cube*, approximately the size of an egg, into an oystercatcher's nest: the bird attempted to hatch it. He then placed a much larger brown-spotted cube: the bird once again tried to hatch it. The oystercatcher was so obsessed with brown spots that it sat on a cube that was approximately twenty times its own size.[12] People seem to operate much like the oystercatcher, focusing on social aspects of voice (instead of spots) and ignoring the voice's technological origins (instead of the shape of the egg). In other words, social cues in technology-based voices (1) elicit all of the rules and behaviors associated with those cues and (2) lead humans to ignore all of the evidence that social attitudes and behaviors are inappropriate.[13]

For most people, gender, personality, emotion, accents, and voice distinctions are so profoundly human that the incongruity of having voices presented via technology would seem to be certain to jolt people out of mindless acceptance.[14] However, in studies involving each of those distinctions, people exhibited broad and deep social responses to voice interfaces. Before drawing the conclusion that people have "bird brains," it is important to look for something even more fundamental than the previously mentioned traits and states. The seventeenth-century French philosopher René Descartes, with one of the most famous sentences in all of philosophy, identified the most critical aspect of being human when he declared, "Cogito ergo sum" ("I think, therefore I am").[15]

Most people are unaware of Descartes's argument or its importance to understanding voice interfaces.[16] Descartes imagines that an evil wizard appears and tells him, "I have been hypnotizing you into thinking that many things exist, but they actually don't. For example, that chair over there does not exist." With a wave of the wizard's wand, the chair disappears.

Descartes replies, "I'm surprised, but it's certainly possible that that chair was never there."

The wizard then starts making more and more things vanish: a lamp, the house, the entire street.

Descartes says, "You really had me fooled, but it's certainly possible that none of that existed."

The wizard then makes everything except people disappear, and Descartes says, "I'm shocked, but a good hypnotist could trick me into thinking there is physics when there is not."

"Here's a bigger surprise," says the wizard. "No other people exist." With a wave of this wand, the wizard demonstrates.

Descartes then says, "I'm stunned, but it's possible I've been simply imagining conversations and relationships. I guess I'll just have to be lonely."

The wizard then shows Descartes that his body is an illusion, as his arms, legs, torso, head, and even senses slowly vanish. "I regret," says Descartes, "that even those could be part of my imagination."

Finally, the wizard gleefully says, "And now for the greatest surprise of all. You don't exist!"

Before the wizard can wave his wand, Descartes say, "Ah ha! I've caught you! You may have fooled me about everything else, but *I think; therefore, I am!* Even if there are no other people, if gender is illusory, and if my beliefs about how I have behaved in social situations (personality), where I was born (accents), and how I have felt about physical events (emotion) were all part of your hypnotic trance, the one thing I can be sure of is that I *am* an 'I'!"

With that, the wizard admits defeat.[17]

Given that self and speech both lie at the core of being human, it should not be surprising that *I* is the most common spoken word in English.[18] When a person avoids the use of *I*, there must be a reason. Royalty and bureaucrats say *we* ("How may we help you today?") to differentiate themselves from the commoners. The 1996 U.S. Republican candidate for president referred to himself by name ("Bob Dole wants to win this election") because he wanted people to remember whom to vote for, and some people simply omit any self-reference so that their opinions and ideas will seem like facts ("This is the best place to eat" rather than "I think that this is the best place to eat") or so that they can avoid responsibility ("The money was lost").

When personhood is in question, the use of *I* can resolve the ambiguity. Elmo from the *Sesame Street* television series, Dobby the house-elf in the Harry Potter series, Solomon Grundy the zombie from the Batman series, and many science fiction robots refer to themselves by name rather than by *I*, indicating that they do not have full human status. Virtually all software, including the Microsoft Office assistant (e.g., Clippit the Paperclip) and the computer on *Star Trek*, avoid any self-reference and instead use phrases such as "Here is your next lesson" (not "I will now teach you about goldfish"), "No answer could be found" (not "I could not find the answer"), or "Working" (not "I am solving the problem"), to make clear that the software does not deserve human attribution. On the other hand, Pinocchio the animate puppet, HAL the computer in *2001: A Space Odyssey*, and Frankenstein's monster (at least in the novel by Mary Shelley) all demand human attribution by using *I*. Thus, the book that introduces the rules that enable robots to integrate into human society ("The Three Laws of Robotics") is—not surprisingly—entitled *I, Robot*.[19]

Do currently deployed voice-user interfaces position themselves as human or non-human? The answer varies, even when controlling for modality of speech (recorded or synthetic), nature of input (voice or touch-tone), and task. For example, most airlines have a telephone-based reservation system that employs recorded speech. These interfaces support both speech input and touch-tone (also known as dual-tone multifrequency, or DTMF) input. Some of these interfaces heavily use the word *I*. Here are typical examples from one such airline:[20]

- *I* can give you up-to-the-minute flight arrival and departure information.
- If you ever need assistance, just say "Help," and *I'll* take things from there.
- Sorry, *I* didn't hear you.
- If you don't know the flight number, just say, "Don't know," and *we'll* find it another way.
- *I* will now ask you a few questions.

Another system,[21] conversely, virtually never uses *I*:

- To continue with XXX's flight information, just stay on the line.
- That's all right.
- You have chosen to hear flights by city.
- Getting flight information.

The only time that the second system did use the word *I* was when there was a recognition failure: "I'm sorry. I didn't understand that."[22] This use of *I* is also the approach that is used by toll-free information.[23]

The most famous example of a system that is grounded in synthetic speech is Ananova,[24] the "world's first virtual newscaster."[25] Ananova uses a synthetic voice to present news stories either on the Web (coupled with a synthetic face) or on the telephone. Ananova constantly uses the words *I* and *my*. She introduces herself by saying, "Hi, *I'm* Ananova." Other comments include "Have a look at *my* video FAQ," "Keep up to date with *my* summary bulletin," and most humanlike of all, "*I'll* reveal fascinating details from my past and what *I'm* going to be up to in the future."[26]

Types of Speech and *I*

Which combinations of *I* (or omission of *I*) and type of speech (recorded or synthetic) are best? There are four possibilities:

- *Both recorded-speech and synthetic-speech voice user interfaces should say "I."* This prediction would emerge from a view of humans as "Tinbergen's birds." If humans are presented with anything that has even the smallest hint of humanness (such as a voice), they will blindly assume that they are interacting with a human. The use of *I* would then not seem out of place because any technology with a voice is a priori a person.
- *Recorded-speech voice user interfaces should say "I." Synthetic-speech voice user interfaces should not say "I."* The argument here is that although synthetic speech cues a wide

range of social rules and heuristics, it does not pass the threshold of humanness that would entitle synthetic voices to say *I*. Conversely, recorded speech sounds human enough that *I* does not feel jarring.

- *Neither recorded-speech nor synthetic-speech voice user interfaces should say "I."* Another possibility is that the word *I* is so profoundly human that it makes people scrutinize whether the speaker has the right to claim humanity. Voice user interfaces, like those creatures that might be confused with people, must eschew the use of *I* to mark their differences from humans.
- *Recorded-speech voice user interfaces should not say "I." Synthetic-speech voice user interfaces should say "I."* There does not seem to be a reasonable justification for this option. It is included simply for completeness.

The majority cannot rule on which option is the best. Indeed, even if there were absolute agreement among designers about when to use *I* in a voice user interface, the standard approach would not necessarily be optimal. What is needed is an experiment that directly compares these four options.

Determining Whether the "I"s Have It

To find out when use of the first person is best for an interface, an experiment with a telephone-based auction was conducted.[27] A total of sixty-four college students participated in the experiment. To ensure that everyone would understand synthetic speech in the interface, all participants were native English speakers.

Participants were first directed to a Web site. After registering, they were given a scenario in which they were about to graduate from college, move to another city, and furnish their new apartment. This scenario was chosen because it was potentially relevant to all of the participants, regardless of gender and personal interests. Participants were then provided a phone number to call an auction system, where they would place bids on five items, one at a time.[28]

Half of the participants (randomly assigned) used a system that had a synthetic voice. The other half of the participants (randomly assigned) used the identical system but with a recorded voice.[29]

For half of the recorded-speech participants and half of the synthetic-speech participants, users were presented with a system that used the word *I*. The other half of the participants heard only impersonal speech. Specifically, for people in the *I* condition, there were four uses of *I* or *my* in the introduction and two uses of *I* in each of the five descriptions. To ensure that the sentences were grammatical and natural in both conditions, a few additional changes were made to the syntax. Despite these changes, the sentences—including the amount and type of information given—were essentially the same for all participants.

Here are the introduction and an example description for the interface that said *I*:

> *I* will begin today's auction shortly. *I* have five items for auction today. *I* will read the descriptions for the items one by one. Please bid at the end of each item's description. *My* records indicate that you have $1,000 in your account.
>
> The first item *I* have for you today is a cozy twin-size pine frame futon. The estimated retail price is around $180. It's a great piece of furniture for any room and very convenient when your friends come over. The cover is included. It is one of the top items *I* can offer to you today.

Here are the parallel sentences for the condition that didn't use *I*:

> Today's auction will begin shortly. There are five items for auction today. The descriptions for the items will be read one by one. Please bid at the end of each item's description. The records indicate that there is $1,000 in your account.
>
> The first item today is a cozy twin-size pine frame futon. The estimated retail price is around $180. It's a great piece of furniture for any room and very convenient when your friends come over. The cover is included. It is one of the top items offered today.

Equal numbers of men and women were assigned each combination of type of voice and use of *I* or not to ensure that the gender of the user would not affect the results. To control for idiosyncrasies in the voices, two different recorded voices and two different synthetic voices were used.[30] All voices were chosen to be similar with respect to gender, age, personality, and accent.

Which Differences Make a Difference in Design?

From the point of view of designers of e-commerce sites, the most consequential effect of the use of *I* by either a recorded-speech or synthetic-speech voice user interface would be in purchase behavior—in this case, represented by average bid. After listening to each item description, participants placed a bid by speaking to the system over the phone. The system recorded the bids for analysis.[31]

When studying bidding behavior, a number of precautions must be taken. For every auction item, a retail price was given to provide an anchor point for participants' bids and to avoid bids that were radically out of line because of the user's ignorance of the general cost of the items. Furthermore, the auction items were chosen to be typical items for furnishing a new apartment and to have a stated retail price of roughly $150 (to stabilize bidding across items and between subjects). The five items that met these characteristics were a futon, a small refrigerator, a microwave oven, a television, and an elaborate phone-answering machine.

After hearing all five item descriptions, participants were presented with a Web-based questionnaire[32] that asked them to evaluate the usefulness,[33] trustworthiness,[34] and formality[35] of the system and the degree to which the system was "like a person."[36] They also indicated how relaxed they felt while using the system[37] and how much they enjoyed using the system.[38]

Only "Humans" Should Say "I"

The premise for this study was that the term *I* is associated with being human. The results bear this out.[39] Interfaces that said "I" were perceived to be strikingly more like a person than interfaces that didn't say "I."[40] Similarly, recorded-speech voice user interfaces were perceived to be clearly more like a person than synthetic-speech interfaces.[41]

The design model that best predicted users' responses was the consistency approach, which posited that recorded voices should say "I" but synthetic voices should not. For example, when they heard a recorded voice, participants were more relaxed when it said "I" (they didn't have to worry about what was meant by the use of passive voice), while synthetic-speech participants were more relaxed with the interface that did not say "I" (the synthetic voice was not human enough):[42] it's disturbing when a person's language is not consistent with his or her ontology.

The "mismatch" between the language of personhood and the voice of a machine, or vice versa, affected perceptions of the interface as well. Although the interface performed identically in all conditions, with seemingly 100 percent speech recognition (bids were recorded), the recorded voice system was perceived to be more useful when saying "I," while the synthetic voice system seemed more useful when avoiding claims to humanity by avoiding "I."[43] Similarly, the synthetic speech system that said "I" was judged less trustworthy than the same system without "I,"[44] demonstrating that the attempt to claim humanity was perceived as a suspicious artifice. There was no significant difference for recorded speech.[45]

Is there money to be made by carefully matching voice and words? People who heard the recorded-voice user interface bid more when they heard "I," while people who heard the synthetic voice interface bid more when they did not hear "I."[46]

Drawing the Line of Humanness

In English (and many other languages), direct reference to self through the use of *I* or its equivalent is unnecessary. If Descartes spoke English, he could have said, "Awareness indicates existence," "Descartes thinks, therefore Descartes is," or many other versions of the same idea, but those other formulations would have fallen flat: *I* provides the rhetorical power. While it is acceptable for people to use personal pronouns when referring to nonhuman animals ("You better stop doing that," "He's a great dog," and "She won the Kentucky Derby") and even technologies ("You are a lousy car!," "She's a beautiful ship," and "My racecar and I; we're a great team"), it is not acceptable for nonhumans to say "I." Thus, for example, people teach their parrots to say, "Polly wants a cracker" rather than "*I* want a cracker."

In the study just described, the word *I* represented approximately 5 percent of all of the words spoken by the interface, yet it had the power to affect people's comfort, perception of the system, and willingness to pay for products. Furthermore, this minimal manipulation had different effects when spoken by "personlike" voices as compared to synthetic voices. Human brains are not bird brains: a very subtle cue of humanness "evoked"[47] attention to modality, forcing people to think about what has the right to call itself human. Recorded-voice user interfaces seem to cross the threshold into the realm of the human (even though people know that the interfaces are computer-based and not in fact human), while synthetic voices cannot, and that distinction dictates the use of the word *I*. The moral of the story: the human brain demands consistency between words and voice on every dimension.

Benefits of Recorded Speech

It is generally assumed that recorded speech is superior to synthetic speech. The current data strongly support this view. For example, participants in this study found the recorded-speech system to be more useful even though performance was identical and the synthetic-speech system was fully understandable.[48] This is consistent with the finding in human-human interactions that fluency of speech is a key indicator that people use to determine competence.[49] People also enjoyed using the system more[50] when it employed recorded speech, not surprising given the greater cognitive effort required to understand synthetic speech.[51] On the other hand, synthetic speech is perceived as more formal than recorded speech,[52] although this advantage likely can be overcome by having the recorded voice speak in a very formal tone (low pitch, extremely small pitch range, slow speed).

When Not to Use "I" with Recorded Speech

While recorded speech clearly benefits voice user interfaces (although there are nuances that must be taken into account),[53] and people expect these systems to use the term *I*, designers should not assume that using *I* is always optimal. For example, when formality is desirable, the avoidance of *I* is effective, according to the results.[54]

A second domain in which the avoidance of *I* may be useful is when the system wants to deflect blame from itself. Every child's instinct is to say, "The lamp broke" (rather than "I broke the lamp"), and in the heat of the Watergate scandal, President Richard Nixon said, "Mistakes were made" (rather than "I made mistakes"). Similarly, when a person requests information that may not be provided, a system might benefit from behaving like a stereotypical bureaucrat by saying, "The rules do not permit that information to be given" (rather than "I cannot give you that information because of the rules"). This strategy can also be useful when the system has to deliver bad news, such as "That item is not in stock" (rather than "I don't have that item right now"). The passive voice can also be useful when a voice input system fails to understand the user.[55] Thus, the airline system (discussed above) that used *I* only when it did not understand the user was poorly designed: the exceptional use of *I* brings attention to the personal aspect of the interface at precisely the time when users are most frustrated and annoyed.

In a related way, cultural differences dictate when speakers should use *I* or *we*. In individualistic cultures, such as the United States and Germany, people are more persuaded when the speaker, including a computer agent, uses *I*. Indeed, in the United States (and likely in other individualistic cultures), individuals are evaluated more favorably than are the same individuals in aggregates or groups.[56] However, in collectivist cultures (including those throughout much of Asia), it is much more effective to refer to *we*.[57]

A third domain in which *I* may be problematic is when the user must provide input via touch-tone (DTMF). A basic principle in conversation holds that it is polite to respond in the same modality as the message that is received. Thus, a phone call is returned with a phone call (not e-mail), a letter with a letter (rather than a phone call), and a spoken yes or no question with words (rather than a nod of the head). When a voice interface says "I" and then proceeds to refuse to let the person reply by voice, this might be seen as controlling and unfair: "He or she gets to speak, but I only get to push buttons?" The avoidance of *I* may reduce the social presence[58] of the system and thereby make it more acceptable to restrict the user to touch-tone responses.

The absence of *I* can be a powerful rhetorical technique when the system wants the user to respond to the system's statements as certainties. For example, a voice user interface that says, "I have four messages for you," "I see that you are free between 12 and 2 p.m.," or "I think that you will like these four restaurants" may seem more uncertain than a system that says, "There are four messages," "You are free between

12 and 2 p.m.," or "You will like these four restaurants." Conversely, voice user interfaces that want full focus on themselves and their unique capabilities likely should use the term *I*, as in "I have searched through thousands of songs to find these three for you" (not "Thousands of songs have been searched. Here are three for you").

Synthetic-speech interfaces, on the other hand, should *never* use *I*. As the experiment showed, there was no case in which the use of *I* made the synthetic-speech interface seem better, and in many cases, the benefits of avoiding *I* were clearly significant.

Alternative Forms of Self-Reference

Some voice interface systems use *we* rather than *I*. *We* can refer to (1) the system and the user, (2) the system and the company that deployed the system, or (3) both. In the case of synthetic speech, the first or third use of *we* is highly problematic because the system is in essence referring to itself as *I*. The second use of *we* may be acceptable for synthetic speech because *we* refers to the company or institution that deployed the interface rather than the interface itself.

For recorded speech, the problem with having the system use *we* to include the user is that it is presumptuous: it implies that the system and the user are peers. While recorded speech might be sufficiently human to be permitted to say *I*, it is not clear that the user views even a recorded-voice user interface as worthy of equality. The second use of *we* (that is, to reflect the company) could be distancing and should not be coupled with *I* because it would be odd for the system to take responsibility for itself, on the one hand, and simply be a reflection of the company, on the other. The third option, mixing the first and second approaches, is confusing because it uses the same word in two different contexts and because it jumps between the highly personal and the strikingly impersonal.

Using the system's name to refer to itself (such as "Robby the Robot has the information for you") seems to be limited to the realm of (science) fiction and likely has little value that would not be realized by employing passive voice.

Humans and Almost Humans

The discovery that people feel comfortable allowing recorded-speech voice user interfaces to make claims to humanity but that they restrict the rights of synthetic-speech interfaces to do so does not undermine the findings of the previous chapters. For most of human history, certain categories of what people now consider fully human were not granted full personhood. For example, in *The Merchant of Venice*, Shylock (a Jew) attempts to demonstrate his humanity by arguing: "I am a Jew. Hath not a Jew eyes? . . . If you prick us, do we not bleed? If you tickle us, do we not laugh? If you poison us, do we not die?"[59] However, as the play continues, it becomes clear that the society has no qualms about dehumanizing Shylock. Similarly, in most cultures slaves were responded to as less than human.

While Shylock and slaves were not assigned full humanity, they were treated as *social actors*,[60] a broad category that includes any entity that obtains a range of social attributions and social responses. Recorded-speech and synthetic-speech voice user interfaces are also usefully thought of as social actors: they receive some human attributions, with recorded speech obtaining a greater level of humanness than synthetic speech. Designing with the expectation that *all* voice user interfaces will receive significant applications of social rules and heuristics is excellent practice. However, only recorded-speech interfaces earn the right to the ultimate marker of humanness: the word *I*.

11 Synthetic versus Recorded Voices and Faces: Don't Look the Look If You Can't Talk the Talk

A common goal in the design of interfaces (particularly voice user interfaces) has been to make them as humanlike as possible.[1] Anthropomorphic (humanlike) interfaces, many argue, are more appealing, fun, comfortable, and natural to use than traditional interfaces are.[2] One key to the success of these interfaces is that they allow users to interact with computers just as they interact with other people—without reading instruction manuals, suffering through online tutorials, or wasting time by clicking on every available button and menu item to try to comprehend an interface.[3] This goal of human similarity has led to both negative outcomes (such as the overuse of *I* described in the previous chapter) and positive outcomes (such as research on natural language processing,[4] artificial intelligence,[5] emotion detection and display,[6] adaptation,[7] personality,[8] vision,[9] and speech synthesis[10]).

Faces are the most anthropomorphic features that any interface can have[11] because no other part of the body can reveal as much information about the person being observed. The expressiveness and richness of the human face makes it the most attention-getting part of any person[12] (with the possible exception of the human voice). Newborns prefer looking at faces, especially simplified faces, more than any other visual stimuli.[13] By the time that a baby is two months old, particular areas of its brain are clearly activated when it views faces.[14] Although the processing of faces changes as the infant transitions into childhood and adulthood, faces (and voices) remain the most attention-getting cue.[15]

The Psychological Integration of Voices and Faces

Although people can certainly listen without seeing a speaker's face, they have a clear and strong bias toward the integration of faces and voices. When people watch a movie in a theater, they "hear" the voice coming from the actor's image, even though the theater's speakers are placed at the sides of the screen and at the sides and back of the room and frequently farther from the actor's mouth than from the audience members' ears.[16] Even when the mouth of an image is not moving, as with a still photograph, people will assign a voice to it if the image and voice are presented simultaneously.

Why do people strongly integrate voices and images of faces in these cases? Humans have evolved to attend to lips (and to a lesser extent, to other parts of the face) because we form characteristic mouth and facial positions to make the sounds of various phonemes. Everyone is a lip reader: seeing a speaker's face dramatically increases a listener's ability to understand the speaker's words. That is why it is easier to listen to a person face-to-face than on a telephone and why poorly dubbed films are so disturbing.

The McGurk Effect

Perhaps the most powerful example of how strongly voice and face are integrated is the McGurk effect.[17] British psychologist Harry McGurk and his research assistant John MacDonald accidentally discovered that when a face mouthing /pa-pa/ is coupled with the sound /na-na/, they *heard* the integration of the two—/ma-ma/. This discovery—described in their wonderfully titled 1976 article "Hearing Lips and Seeing Voices"[18] and in numerous subsequent studies with different combinations of sounds and faces—demonstrates that visual information directly modifies our auditory experience:[19] that is, people really do "hear" differently depending on the lip movements they see. The McGurk effect is so powerful that it appears in twenty-two-week-old infants,[20] in people who are looking at a speaker whose face is turned more than 50 degrees away,[21] and in people who are looking at a face that is extraordinarily degraded.[22] Not surprisingly, the "reverse McGurk effect" is also true: auditory information can lead to changes in the perception of lip movements.[23]

Synchrony

Another domain in which mismatches between voice and face are common involves asynchrony—that is, a time lag between what the voice is saying and what the face seems to be saying.[24] Anyone who has sat in a stadium has likely seen the projected image of a face move before its words can be heard—because light travels faster than sound. Synchrony problems in new media often go the other way: because audio takes up much fewer bytes than video, video conferencing systems and streaming video often have the problem that the voice is heard before the face is seen.

In an ingenious study that examined the effects of synchrony on people's perceptions of others,[25] participants were brought into a laboratory with a 40-inch screen and shown eight video clips of people speaking. All of the videos were close-ups of newscasters, narrators, or characters in dramas. For each participant, half of the videos were shown in perfect synchrony, and half were shown with the audio leading the video by one-sixth of a second (five video frames). The videos that were out of synchrony varied from participant to participant.

Compared to individuals in normal videos, individuals who appeared in the asynchronous videos were perceived as less interesting, less pleasant, less influential, and less successful in their delivery. Remarkably, these responses appeared even among the 50 percent of people who did not even *notice* the asynchrony. Hence, temporal consistency has clear social impact, even though asynchrony has limited influence on the understandability of speech.[26]

Verbal and Nonverbal Cues

A number of studies have found that inconsistencies between communication channels lead to negative effects. For example, twelve- to forty-two-month-old children were less likely to approach a male experimenter with a balloon when he combined a warm facial expression, beckoning gestures, and affirmative head nods with the words "stay away" spoken with a cold tone than when both his facial expressions and tone were negative (or positive).[27] Another study found that potential participants in a project were perceived as being less interested, less warm, less active, and less involved when they had negative nonverbal style (in eye contact, posture, and nodding) with positive verbal content than when they had negative nonverbal style and negative content (or positive nonverbal style and positive content).[28] Married couples who exhibit consistent verbal and facial cues while describing their relationships (even when negative) have better marital adjustment,[29] and parents who exhibit mismatched facial and verbal cues have children with significantly more problems.[30] There is clear evidence that when facial expression does not match what is said, people perceive an attempt at deception.[31]

Almost Everything Is a Face

Just as the brain processes voices differently than all other sounds, it processes faces differently than all other objects.[32] This biased processing leads the brain to have a very liberal definition of what a face (or voice) is. Cartoonists rely on the fact that a simple black-and-white drawing is sufficient to represent a distinguishable face.[33] For example, Charlie Brown, the classic character created by Charles Schulz, can be expressively drawn with about ten lines. Similarly, political cartoonists can distinguish hundreds of people via simple caricatures. Gender, personality, and race can be manifested in even the simplest drawings, and a few lines can express a range of emotion:[34] a "smiley face" (a circle, two dots for eyes, and one line for a mouth) can express and lead people to feel sadness, surprise, or anger with a change in one or two strokes of the pen and a quick flash of an image.[35] Relying on the human readiness to assign faces, social psychologists routinely use actual people, photographs, and drawings of faces (with various levels of detail, color, and shading) without worrying about whether there are critical differences between these manifestations.[36] For many types of studies, this lack of concern is likely appropriate because the same part of the brain (the fusiform face area) reacts similarly to all types of facial representation.[37]

Even more remarkable is how so many nonhuman objects can manifest human faces. An ordinary Volkswagen Beetle convertible, Herbie, was the star of a series of eponymous movies, including *Herbie Rides Again* and *Herbie Goes to Monte Carlo,* as well as a television series, *Herbie the Love Bug*.[38] Herbie could not speak: "he" expressed himself primarily by flashing his headlights (his "eyes") and lifting up and down his hood ("his mouth").[39] Almost any car can suggest a face: witness the book *Turn Signals Are the Facial Expression of Automobiles*.[40]

The classic figure and ground example (made famous by the Danish phenomenologist Edgar Rubin in 1915) can be viewed as a white vase against a black background or as two black human profiles against a white background.[41] Three-dimension stick figures with just a flattened circle for a head[42] and the flying carpet in the Disney movie *Aladdin*, physically uniform and flat, are often remembered as having a face. The delightful book *Faces*[43] vividly illustrates how a variety of household objects can trigger those parts of the brain that react to actual faces.

This is not to say that *everything* is responded to as a face. For example, there is an old story of a ventriloquist who became tired of the dummy getting all the fame. His problem was that the dummy was getting too much of the audience's attention. At his next performance, he came out with an artichoke plant on his lap and started into his routine. Although he used the same jokes he had used before to great success, he was booed off the stage. The perplexed ventriloquist asked his fellow performers about the audience's response. They replied, "Artichokes don't talk." To this, the ventriloquist replied, "But blocks of wood don't talk either. At least the artichoke was alive. It has a better chance of talking than a dummy." Finally, someone suggested, "Well, if you stick eyes and a mouth on the artichoke, *then* it could talk."[44]

Computers and Talking Faces

Although people have a broad definition of *face*, do they nonetheless distinguish between human and not-quite-human faces, much as they do with voices? To answer the question, the strategy used in the previous chapter should prove effective: determine whether users prefer a clearly human face to be coupled with a clearly human voice and a synthetic (not quite human) face to be coupled with a synthetic (not quite human) voice.

Consistent Face-Voice Combinations in Technology

Most interfaces that deploy faces opt for consistency: they use human faces with human voices (as in videos) or humanoid/synthetic faces with synthetic voices. The most common approach is to simply show a video of clearly human faces who are speaking with clearly human voices. Video footage that resides on a CD, DVD, or hard disk can now be presented as smoothly as television or film footage. Although constraints on the Web's compression and download speeds often result in choppiness because video frames are lost or audio and video are missynchronized, within the next few years, "streaming video" should look as good as any other audiovisual presentation.

Humanoids that combine synthetic faces with synthetic voices are growing in popularity. For example, the synthetic-voiced Ananova,[45] although clearly not human, strongly resembles a female in her mid- to late twenties, blinks her eyes, moves her head, and shows reasonably good synchrony between her lips and synthetic voice. Similarly, Baldi is a three-dimensional, synthetic-voice-based humanoid face that is built on an elaborate wire-frame model.[46] Baldi has such an articulate and expressive mouth and highly accurate tongue and palate model that he is able to teach vocabulary,[47] grammar,[48] and pronunciation[49] to the deaf. Although Ananova, Baldi, and all other current synthetic and robotic[50] talking faces are highly developed, there are too many transitions from sound to sound to enable them to be drawn or sculpted with the level of detail that would make them indistinguishable from a person.

Inconsistent Face-Voice Combinations in Technology

The matching of type of face and type of voice is not a technological necessity. Many synthetic faces are able to move their lips in good synchrony with recorded voices and in very good synchrony with text to speech.[51] This approach requires much less speed and storage than an actual video, as pictures require many more bytes than voices. Thus, technological constraints may require a human voice to be paired with an obviously synthetic face. Indeed, this is frequently the way that Baldi is used to teach pronunciation.[52]

Currently, technology does not allow lip synchronization of synthetic speech content with a previdеotaped human face.[53] The technology of texture-mapping a video-captured human face on a computer-synthesized facial model (which would facilitate lip-synching to the synthetic voice) is still in its infancy and produces very unnatural and unpleasant facial renditions[54] (for example, computer-synthesized teeth and eyes are used to replace the natural teeth and eyes of the video-captured person).[55] There is not much technological interest in developing systems with human faces and synthetic audio,[56] as virtually any system that could produce realistic faces could handle the much simpler problem of realistic voices. The best current approach is to generate synthetic audio and then videotape a person lip-synching to that audio.[57] (Of course, this strategy would be desirable only for research purposes.)

Why might a match between voice humanness and face humanness not be desirable? Two possible processes that favor inconsistency might be implicated. First, as noted earlier, the human brain has a definition of face that may be so broad that faces, unlike voices, may be simply classified under the single category *face* without a distinction between human and not quite human, especially if the face is speaking, a uniquely human activity. Under this view, the type of face would have no effect on user's reactions to recorded or synthetic voice.[58] Second, extracting information from faces is an evolved focus: the difficulties of processing semihuman faces and voices may make higher quality the sole criterion for desirability. That is, the truly human face would be preferred to the synthetic face, even if the speech were clearly not human.

Is One Gender More Attuned to Faces?

Women generally pay more attention to and better remember nonverbal cues than men do.[59] Females are also clearly superior to males in decoding the meaning of nonverbal cues. In metaanalyses of seventy-five[60] and fifty studies,[61] respectively, concerning various aspects of judging nonverbal cues, females were superior to males in over 80 percent of the research. Females' superior accuracy in decoding nonverbal cues holds up regardless of the gender of the stimulus person, the age of the stimulus person, or the age of the participant.[62] There is also a tendency for females to be better than males in detecting nonverbal deception cues.[63] Finally, there is also strong evidence that the female advantage in decoding faces and other nonverbal indicators is culturally universal.[64]

There is no accepted theory for why females are more attentive to and better at assessing the linkages between verbal and facial characteristics.[65] The primary proposals include evolutionary theory (it is critical for females to decode the nonverbal cues of offspring in rearing),[66] biology (female newborns are more responsive to the sound of another infant's crying than are male newborns),[67] and gender-role theory (females are expected to be nurturing and hence must be more aware of others' feelings).[68] Regardless of the theoretical basis, gender clearly must be taken into account when reactions to the juxtaposition of human and humanoid faces and voices are examined.

Disclosing to a Talking Face

To test the effects of consistent versus inconsistent humanness of face and voice, an experiment[69] was conducted using an interviewing task. Eighty-eight people participated in this experiment (half men and half women), which provided enough participants to include the gender of the user as a factor in the analysis.

The interviewing task was framed as testing a prototype online interviewing system. Interviewing presents an important task domain because companies and other organizations often desire personal information about their customers for marketing purposes or for providing customers with a more personalized experience. Furthermore, as discussed earlier, interviews are a natural way to gain personal information that may help a voice interface adapt to the user.

Participants were randomly assigned to one of four interviewing agents that represented four combinations of human or humanoid face and voice: human face with human voice, human face with synthesized voice, synthesized face with synthesized voice, and synthesized face with human voice. A male drama student was recruited to serve as the actor who would provide the human face and the human voice for the experiment. He was thirty-five years old, Caucasian, and a native English speaker and had no unusual accent or facial features. The synthetic voice was produced by the male American-English model of the Festival TTS engine that is provided by the CSLU Toolkit software.[70] The synthetic face used was the Baldi face that is provided in the CSLU Toolkit. Baldi is a male, Caucasian, humanoid face.[71]

For the human face with a human voice agent, a digital video of the actor as he asked the interview questions was displayed on screen. For the human face with synthetic voice condition, the actor trained himself to lip-synch with the synthetic voice and then was videotaped talking over the synthetic voice. For the synthetic face agents, the Baldi character was displayed on the screen with lip movements automatically synchronized to the synthesized or human voice as appropriate.

The interviewing agent asked participants a series of thirteen questions: four nonintimate warm-up questions about the participant's age, gender, hometown, and hobbies and the following nine more intimate disclosure questions:[72]

What characteristics of yourself are you most proud of?
What are some of the things that make you furious?
What are your feelings and attitudes about death?
What are some of the things you hate about yourself?
What has been the biggest disappointment in your life?
What do you dislike about your physical appearance?
What have you done in your life that you feel most guilty about?
What are some of the things that really hurt your feelings?
What characteristics of your best friend really bother you?

After each question, participants typed their answers into a text box located on the screen below the interviewing agent. Participants could click on a Repeat button to hear the question again. When they were ready to submit their answers, they clicked on a Submit button.

A primary goal of the interviewing task was to determine whether participants would disclose more to one type of agent than to another type. As a measure of amount of disclosure, the average length (in words) of each participant's responses to the nine intimate questions was calculated; longer responses suggest greater disclosure.[73]

After the participants submitted their answers to the last interview question, they completed a questionnaire with a variety of items.[74] The questionnaire asked participants to state whether they thought that the face and the voice were "computer-synthesized" or "of a real person"[75] and to rate how consistent they thought the face and voice were.[76] Participants also were asked to rate the trustworthiness of the interviewing agent,[77] as well as how upsetting,[78] strange,[79] and rude[80] the interviewer was. The questionnaire also determined how much the participants liked the face[81] and the voice[82] independently. Finally, the amount of time that participants spent answering the questionnaire was noted.[83] This time measure was collected because inconsistency generally causes interference in perception,[84] which in turn causes people to take longer to process inconsistent trait information, to reach a judgment about a person with inconsistent traits,[85] and to exhibit longer reaction times.

Mixing Human and Humanoid: A Dangerous Liaison[86]

Every participant correctly identified the face and the voice as either "computer-synthesized" or "of a real person."[87] Demonstrating that people define faces as either "human" or "humanoid," participants identified the human face/human voice and synthetic face/synthetic voice as significantly more consistent than the mixed conditions.[88]

Participants clearly felt more comfortable being honest with the consistent face/voice combinations than the inconsistent combinations. Both male and female participants were significantly more disclosive when they were presented with either a human face and human voice or a synthetic face and synthetic voice than the mixed combinations, with the human face/voice combination obtaining the most disclosure of all.[89] In addition, participants of both genders found the consistent faces to be significantly more trustworthy.[90]

The mismatch between face and voice made participants feel uncomfortable: the mixed face/voice combinations were more upsetting than the consistent combinations.[91] They also found the inconsistent combinations stranger than the consistent combinations.[92] Their discomfort extended to viewing the inconsistent faces as more rude than the consistent faces, even though the content was identical in all cases.[93]

The psychological integration of faces and voices is so powerful that consistency was a better predictor of how much people liked the voice and the face than was the separate quality of each. The human face was liked better when coupled with a human voice than with the synthetic voice, whereas the synthetic face was liked better when coupled with the synthetic voice than with the human voice.[94] Although people clearly preferred the recorded voice to the synthetic voice,[95] the effect was significantly weaker for the synthetic face, once again showing the effects of consistency.[96]

Another demonstration of the effects of consistency appears in the time that it took for participants to assess the talking heads via the questionnaire. Reflecting the difficulties that were involved in processing the inconsistent cases, participants took significantly longer to evaluate the human face/synthetic speech and the synthetic face/human speech heads compared to the consistent heads.[97]

Were there differences in female and male reactions to the talking heads? Analyses revealed that for five of the eight variables that examined the effects of consistency, women were significantly more influenced by consistency than men; in the other three cases, there were no differences between men and women. Specifically, women felt that the inconsistent talking head was more upsetting and more strange and rude relative to the consistent talking head than did men. They also disliked both the face and the voice of the inconsistent talking head more relative to the consistent talking head than did men.[98]

What Makes Voices Human or Not Human?

Although people have liberal definitions of voices and faces, the human brain nonetheless draws a distinction between "human" and "not human." The human brain cannot make this decision simply by knowing whether the voice or face was created by a technology. If a computer-generated voice sounded precisely like a human voice, or if a computer-generated face looked precisely like a human face, the brain would have no way to make a distinction, and the synthesized creations would be responded to precisely as their human counterparts. Furthermore, throughout most of evolutionary history, the human brain did not encounter technologies that simulated human abilities, so the brain likely did not develop an acute sensitivity to a warning that something was a "technology" rather than a "human."[99] Hence, psychologists and designers can use an understanding of how the brain processes voices and faces to predict the cues that will encourage or discourage perceptions of humanness.

A number of voice cues suggest that a person is listening to a nonhuman. First, voice characteristics can indicate that the speaker does not understand the meaning of the words spoken. This is indicated through pauses at inappropriate moments, emphasis on the wrong syllable (sometimes two words with the same spelling have different pronunciation) or wrong word, rising and declining pitch at the wrong times, mispronunciation of words that are generally pronounced correctly, and so on. Consider how difficult it is to understand the spoken sentence "that that is is that that is not is not" without having the pauses and emphases that come from correctly pronouncing "That that is, is. That that is not, is not."[100] Ignorance can also be demonstrated by inappropriate voice emotion with respect to the content, as when a happy voice announces, "Your credit card has been rejected."[101] Because complete syntactic and semantic understanding is an extremely difficult problem,[102] text-to-speech systems inevitably speak in a manner that is "nonhuman" unless the text is "marked-up" for all important characteristics by an actual person.[103]

Sometimes odd speech patterns have to do less with language and more with cultural norms about how certain items are spoken. For example, computer systems that dictate U.S. Social Security numbers enunciate one digit at a time with equal spaces between numbers. Conversely, U.S. citizens know that the correct pronunciation is [three digits] [pause] [two digits] [pause] [four digits]. Similarly, lengthy account numbers will sometimes be read in groups of two, such as "twenty-four thirty-six" rather than "two four three six." And of course, people do not crisply pronounce each word independently; in English, a conversation can sound like "Jeet? No, joo?" which is actually "Did you eat? No, did you?" It is difficult to specify the rules, develop the necessary algorithms, or record all of the necessary sounds to solve these problems.

A second potential "nonhuman" marker in voice is bizarre language or syntax. This is a common problem in systems that attempt to produce natural language: grammar and vocabulary are just too hard to be handled correctly by a machine. Although the very best "chat-bots"[104] and the famous computer psychotherapist Eliza[105] can plausibly carry on a conversation in limited domains for a limited period of time, no computer system has yet passed the Turing test,[106] which requires a computer to carry on a convincing textual conversation for five minutes. Language production is an even more difficult problem than language understanding; indeed, there is not even a full account of how to use the word *the* in English.[107]

All of the problems that mark "nonhumans" also seem to mark "nonnative speakers." Indeed, dehumanization is much more commonly directed toward people whose language marks them as coming from a different culture.[108] Conversely, people speak to systems with poor voice recognition as if they were nonnative speakers.[109]

What Makes Faces Not Human?

The human face provides five categories of information relevant to assessing humanness.[110] *Static* facial signals (created by relatively permanent bone and tissue structures) and *slowly changing* facial signals (such as wrinkles or skin texture, which change over months and years)[111] tend not to be a problem in the creation of humanness. Designers can put considerable time and attention into these psychologically important features of the face because they can remain constant across users' interactions with the system. Thus, the effort to make these faces seem humanlike can be amortized across users and interactions. These signals of gender, age, ethnicity, and so on also must be consistent with the voice and the language of the interface.

Humans are not evolved to focus on *artificial signals* (which represent objects that are placed on the face, such as eyeglasses) because these signals were not part of the evolutionary environment. Hence, these cues are likely not implicated in assessments of humanness (although they can indicate various social cues, such as gender).

The final two categories of facial signals are clearly implicated in assessments of humanness. Asynchrony between voice and *linguistic facial signals* (which help reduce ambiguity in speech) leads to a perceived deficiency in humanness (as well as other negative consequences).[112]

Rapid facial signals (which involve visually detectable changes in facial appearance)[113] are likely the most important determinant of perceptions of humanness. The face has forty-four muscles (twenty-two on each side of the face) that can all move independently.[114] These movements of the facial muscles pull the jaw, bone, facial skin, and fascia, which temporarily distorts the shape of the eyes, brows, and lips and the appearance of folds, furrows, and bulges in different patches of skin.[115] These changes in the face rarely last longer than five seconds,[116] putting high demands on both the creator and interpreter of facial manifestations.

Rapid facial signals provide four types of messages that are relevant to making a face seem human.[117] For each of the message types, the human vision and facial interpretation systems define "allowable responses" that, if not met, indicate that the face is not human. *Emotion* must be consistent with the voice, content, and situation and should be consistent with the user.[118] *Symbolic information,* culture-specific content such as a wink, requires an understanding of the user and the nature of the interaction.[119] *Illustrators,* actions that accompany or highlight speech (such as a raised brow or a closed eye), must be synchronized with the conversation. Finally, *regulators,* nonverbal conversational mediators (such as nods or smiles),[120] require a deep understanding of the content being produced.

Unfortunately, it is extremely difficult for technologies to handle even one of these categories automatically. To create a veridical human face would require a mapping of literally trillions of possibilities as well as a deep understanding of language and culture, all in seconds. The best that designers can do, then, is to identify the most important muscle groups and to map them as best as they can with respect to these categories of rapid facial signals.

Making Nonhuman Faces and Voices Acceptable

The above discussion might seem to suggest that synthetic faces (and to a lesser extent synthetic voices) should be avoided at all costs because it is so difficult to make them humanlike. However, many nonhuman entities have been successful and compelling characters. For example, the puppeteer Shari Lewis brought her sock puppet Lamb Chop (who had two eyes, a nose, and mouth shaped by Lewis's thumb and fingers) with her when she testified before Congress. In answer to one of the questions from a representative, Lamb Chop testified. After "she" finished speaking, the Congressman asked, "Do you agree with Lamb Chop, Miss Lewis?"[121] In an even more remarkable example, the ventriloquist Señor Wences became a television star by having humorous conversations with a character named "Johnny." Wences created "Johnny" by making a fist; drawing two eyes and eyebrows on the back of his hand, a lower lip on his thumb, and an upper lip on his index finger; and draping a blond wig over the top of the fist. Of course, Mickey Mouse and Bugs Bunny are international stars even though they are clearly not human. Thus, failure to have the articulated musculature of a human face does not seem to be an impediment to success.

Why are these characters excused for their deficiencies? They have two elements in common. First, their faces have the most important facial features associated with a human face: a clearly defined head, eyes and eyebrows (or the equivalent) at the top, and a mouth at the bottom. This is why the "artichoke ventriloquist" described earlier could not be successful until he gave his "dummy" a "face" with these key features.

The second element that these characters have in common is that they have unusual voices. Neither Lamb Chop, Johnny, Mickey Mouse, Bugs Bunny, nor any other beloved nonhuman character has a voice that would come out of a normal person's mouth. This match between nonhuman faces and nonhuman voices has another advantage beyond the demonstrated desire for consistency: the human brain does not have a clear idea about mouth positions for nonhuman faces, so the demands for synchrony are dramatically reduced. This can be summarized as, "Beak synch is much simpler than lip synch."[122] This is also why ventriloquists, puppeteers, and animators need not meet stringent requirements for mouth and facial movements. Animation of fully human characters is a challenging problem even when the artist knows the script; it is clearly beyond the scope of present technology to have a human face automatically and plausibly speak arbitrary content.

Everything You Wanted to Know about Human Faces . . . But Were Afraid to Ask

Although this book is concerned with brains that are *voice* activated, humans are also *face* activated. Because of remarkable similarities between the social processing of voices and of faces, the same experimental results and design conclusions would be likely to be obtained if voices were simply replaced with faces in these studies. A complete account of all of the equivalences between voices and faces is beyond the scope of the book, but it does seem useful to facilitate the extension to faces by briefly describing how the social cues described in the previous chapter—sex, personality, ethnicity (and other demographic markers), emotion, and identity—play out for faces.

Gender and Faces

The differences in male and female faces are even more pronounced than the markers of voice gender. For example, women have wider faces, smoother skin, a sharper ridge above the eyes, thinner and higher eyebrows, a larger distance between the eyebrows and eyes, larger pupils, and rounder foreheads (that taper at the top), jaws, and chins than men have.[123] Because of these many cues, the face reveals gender very rapidly (of course, the body provides additional information). People classify a person's gender in less than one-quarter of a second after seeing a person they do not know, and they do so with a very high degree of accuracy.[124] Infants can detect gender through faces almost as early as gender in voices—nine to ten months as compared to eight[125]—by evaluating hair style.[126] Although hair is an important sign of gender at all ages (and most cultures do prescribe hair styles that help distinguish men from women), by the age of nine, children become somewhat able to identify gender when hair is removed, and by adulthood, people are almost flawless in their hairless gender judgments.[127]

People prefer consistency in the facial features that suggest gender—that is, faces (and voices) that are clearly male or clearly female are perceived to be more attractive than are mixed faces.[128] Strengthening this tendency, the brain classifies gender of faces as a dichotomy (male or female),[129] in contrast to voice gender, which is stored as a continuum.[130] The classification of facial gender is located on the left side of the brain, with the left side of the observed's face providing the key gender cues.[131]

Personality and Faces

The face, like the voice, indicates personality. Somatotype theory,[132] which defines the three basic body/personality types, also provides useful information about the facial correlates of personality. Endomorphs (people with friendly, happy, people-focused personalities)[133] have spherical heads with smooth and soft skin.[134] The endomorph's face is large with features that blend into each other in a way that suggest roundness. The hair is fine, although they sometimes exhibit baldness at the top of their heads. In essence, these people have "baby faces," leading to attributions of babylike personalities (such as submissiveness, kindness, honesty, and naivete)[135] and assignments to jobs that require qualities of warmth and submission.[136] The response to baby faces is so powerful that during optimistic social and economic times, the most popular movie actresses have neonate facial features, while during pessimistic times, the most popular movie actresses have mature facial features.[137]

Ectomorphs (highly excitable individuals who get nervous in crowds) have triangular faces with the point at the chin. They have thin and dry skin with features that are sharp and fragile. Their hair is fine and fast-growing. They tend to have occupations that don't involve significant interaction with other people.[138]

Mesomorphs, the third somatotype, are people of action who crave activity. The mesomorph has a cubical head with clearly defined cheek bones, a large, heavy jaw, and well-defined musculature on all parts of the face and neck. The skin is thick, and males often have facial hair. The hair is heavy-textured, and baldness is common (suggesting high levels of testosterone), starting at the front of the head. Mesomorphs tend to have jobs in the outdoors that involve significant physical work.[139]

There are also particular facial features that indicate particular personalities. Strong features suggest dominance: male superheroes have very square jaws, and female superheroes have well-defined cheekbones, in general. Pointed features suggest hostility as well as dominance: witches are usually depicted with narrow faces, beady eyes, long and crooked noses, and pointed hats. Dominance is also suggested by a raised head (a tilted head is submissive)[140] and lowered eyebrows (raised eyebrows are submissive).[141] Friendliness, conversely, is marked by rounded face and large eyes:[142] Mickey Mouse's face, constructed solely of circles, is the classic friendly (and baby) face.

Other Demographic Characteristics and Faces

Although faces cannot reveal accents, they do indicate race, the place of origin of a person's ancestors. Skin color is the clearest cue of race, but other facial features can also be diagnostic.[143] Race is identified more quickly and more accurately than any other trait:[144] it is categorized at approximately 100 milliseconds, which is approximately 1.5 times faster than sex, the next most rapidly identified trait, is categorized.[145] The race of the face should "match" the accent of the voice.[146]

Age, like gender, is identified primarily by the left side of the brain[147] and is clearly marked by the face. As people grow older, the skin becomes more wrinkled, thinner, drier, and less elastic, particularly around the forehead, the mouth, and the eyes. The lower part of the face grows forward and downward.[148] These changes lead the mouth and eyes to droop, leading the elderly to seem unpleasant.[149]

Emotion and Faces

Faces reveal emotion more clearly than voices do[150] and thus, have become the primary means for detecting emotion (voice and words are second). Indeed, babies as young as five months old can detect emotion when looking at faces.[151] In general, positive emotional expressions are detected more rapidly than negative expressions,[152] but negative emotional expressions are processed more deeply.[153]

No aspect of the face has been studied more than emotion.[154] Paul Ekman is the world's leading expert.[155] His Facial Action Coding System (FACS),[156] which identifies a highly specific set of muscular movements for each emotion, is one of the most widely accepted foundations for understanding facial recognition systems.[157] Table 11.1.A, derived from FACS, clearly specifies characteristic facial features of the six basic emotions (see page 141)[158] features that have proven to be robust cross-culturally.[159]

Although these schemes point to various parts of the face that are associated with one or more emotions, emotion in the face is processed holistically.[160]

Emotional expression is so well understood that even automated software programs can be 90 to 98 percent accurate in recognizing a small set of basic emotions.[161] Of course, "not all . . . emotions are accompanied by visually perceptible facial action."[162]

The right hemisphere of the brain is primarily responsible for all aspects of emotion. This is why the left side of the face (associated with the right side of the brain) provides stronger expressions of emotions than does the right side[163] and the left eye is better at emotion detection than the right eye.

At a more granular level, different parts of the right side of the brain are responsible for producing and evaluating different emotions. For example, disgust is associated with the anterior insula and putamen, while the anterior cingula and orbitofrontal cortex are responsible for anger.[164] It is likely that voice emotion is analyzed and produced by this same division of labor. This may explain why, just as voice emotion and the emotional content of words mutually affect each other,[165] voice emotion and face emotion mutually affect each other as well.[166]

Multiple Faces

Like voices, faces can be used to identify a person as well as distinguish one person from another. From the age of nine, people focus on internal features (such as eyes, mouth, and eyebrows) to identify a person.[167] The left eye is the first facial feature that is examined when someone is trying to identify a person; it is focused on in approximately one-two-hundredth of a second after seeing a face. Race and the right eye become relevant soon after,[168] followed by other facial features.

Conversely, external features, such as hair and ears, are used to distinguish one person from another. (They are also used by children younger than nine to perform face identification.) Consistent with the focus on different parts of the face, facial identification and facial discrimination are located in different parts of the brain.[169]

Humanness Is Special

The Copernican revolution provided the lesson that Earth is not at the center of the universe.[170] The Darwinian revolution demonstrated that humans are simply another kind of animal.[171] The Turing revolution went even further and suggested that people are not very different from machines.[172] Despite these cultural shifts, people seem to cling to the idea that to be human is to be unique. For better or worse, designers must operate within this demand for human separation from the rest of the physical world.

Appendix

Table 11.1.A
Facial cues and emotion

Emotion	Observed Facial Cues
Surprise	Brows raised (curved and high)
	Skin below brow stretched
	Horizontal wrinkles across forehead
	Eyelids opened and more of the white of the eye is visible
	Jaw drops open without tension or stretching of the mouth
Fear	Brows raised and drawn together
	Forehead wrinkles drawn to the center
	Upper eyelid is raised and lower eyelid is drawn up
	Mouth is open
	Lips are slightly tense or stretched and drawn back
Disgust	Upper lip is raised
	Lower lip is raised and pushed up to upper lip or it is lowered
	Nose is wrinkled
	Cheeks are raised
	Lines below the lower lid, lid is pushed up but not tense
	Brows are lowered
Anger	Brows lowered and drawn together
	Vertical lines appear between brows
	Lower lid is tensed and may or may not be raised
	Upper lid is tense and may or may not be lowered due to brows' action
	Eyes have a hard stare and may have a bulging appearance
	Lips are either pressed firmly together with corners straight or down or open, tensed in a squarish shape
	Nostrils may be dilated (could occur in sadness too)
	Unambiguous only if registered in all three facial areas
Happiness	Corners of lips are drawn back and up
	Mouth may or may not be parted with teeth exposed or not
	A wrinkle runs down from the nose to the outer edge beyond lip corners
	Cheeks are raised
	Lower eyelid shows wrinkles below it and may be raised but not tense
	Crow's-feet wrinkles go outward from the outer corners of the eyes
Sadness	Inner corners of eyebrows are drawn up
	Skin below the eyebrow is triangulated, with inner corner up
	Upper lid inner corner is raised
	Corners of the lips are drawn or lip is trembling

Source: Derived from P. Ekman and W. V. Friesen, *Unmasking the Face: A guide to recognizing emotions from facial cues* (Englewood Cliffs, NJ: Prentice-Hall, 1975).

12 Mixing Synthetic and Recorded Voices: When "Better" Is Worse

One of the classic fights in the voice-interface industry is between marketers (who want to brag about the latest and greatest features in their interface) and designers (who think holistically and attempt to strike the right balance between technology and usability). Marketers stereotypically urge that, within time and cost constraints, every aspect of the interface should employ the "best" technology available, regardless of how the dimensions interact. How do they decide which technologies are "best"? They are guided by basic principles that have been derived from a hodgepodge of science, art, and folklore. Unfortunately, as the following sections demonstrate, many of these principles have significant limitations.

Is More Flexibility Always Better?

One common interface principle suggests that choice is good and that more choices are better. When computers were simple, constraints on processing power limited the number of activities that users could perform and the number of ways in which they could perform those activities. Telephone-based interfaces, for example, could handle only a few different key presses and a limited number of levels. Current systems have leveraged extraordinary increases in processing power that allow a relatively open conversation between user and system, and a few systems even offer users the opportunity to select the voice and personality with which they will interact.

Has this dramatic increase in choices been an unambiguous plus? No. Sometimes people can be overwhelmed by choices: when they are presented with too many options, they perceive all of the options as inferior.[1] An interface that has "Press 1 for A, 2 for B, . . . and 26 for Z" is more of a burden than a benefit for brains that can keep only seven (plus or minus two) options in short-term memory at any one time.[2] Unlike graphical user interfaces that fluidly compress and expand menus and keep the content continually visible, voice user interfaces do not have affordances[3] (perceived or actual properties that determine how the technology can or should be used) to relieve the cognitive burden. Increases in available spoken options also increase misrecognition rates (there is greater ambiguity in utterances), so that systems get "dumber" as they get "smarter." Furthermore, the need to alert some users to new functionalities slows down the vast majority of users who do not need the "enhancement." Finally, the responsibility of making choices in interfaces before the interaction even begins (such as selecting whom to speak with) becomes a barrier rather than an opportunity.

Is More Accuracy Always Better?

A second design principle that should be treated with caution is that the "best" interfaces are as "accurate" or "realistic" as possible. Computers provide precision and quality that are not available to people, but society is built on the principle that honesty is not always the best policy. According to research studies, interfaces that make flattering comments—such as "You are learning very rapidly," "You have made an excellent choice," or "It has been a pleasure working with you"—whether true or not, lead users to enjoy the experience more and to perceive the interface as superior to systems that do not flatter users.[4]

Frequently, accuracy burdens the user.[5] For example, it is certainly accurate to say: "You are the seventeenth person who is waiting in line to speak with a customer-support representative. There are currently nine customer-service representatives available, although two will be taking a twenty-minute break in seventeen minutes. Each customer-service representative takes an average of 7.93 minutes per call." But this is essentially useless precision compared to simply telling the person, "There is a long line of people ahead of you. If you can, please call later." Similarly, telling people, "Your engine temperature is 173 degrees Fahrenheit or 78.3 degrees Centigrade," is not as informative as saying, "Your engine is overheating."

A final problem with accuracy is that the physical world is often less convenient to navigate than is its abstracted counterpart. For example, in the early days of e-commerce, some Web sites implemented interfaces that precisely modeled their stores. If a user wanted to buy a refrigerator, she or he had to zoom out, tediously move the cursor to the "correct" part of the store, and then zoom back in to find the item. Imagine if ordering a book from Amazon.com required users to talk their way from one section of the "store" to another. As the great painter Henri Matisse taught the world, "Exactitude is not truth": Sometimes a less accurate mirroring of the world can in fact be more effective.

Is More Realism Always Better?

A third dangerous design principle is that more realistic and humanlike interfaces are better than less realistic interfaces. In general, people prefer individuals over inanimate objects, descriptions of people, and social groups.[6] However, as is shown in the previous two chapters, maximizing humanness along one dimension but not along another can lead to significant problems.[7] Specifically, users exhibited a variety of negative responses when a synthetic voice interface used the word *I*[8] and when a synthetic face spoke with a human voice.[9] Another problem with this principle is that humans are not always the most effective or desirable interaction partners. Do users really want a voice user interface to be in a bad mood or to become frustrated when the user asks too many silly questions, or would users prefer their interfaces to be infinitely patient and pleasant "emotion workers"[10] or "Stepford wives"[11] who meet their needs without any emotional burdens?

A more subtle problem arises as voice interfaces become more humanlike—the Uncanny Valley.[12] Morishima Mori discovered that there is not a simple positive relationship between level of humanness and a user's feelings about the interface. Although in general, greater levels of humanness are associated with greater liking, when the interface is nearly human but just inconsistent enough to seem "not quite right," liking drops precipitously, and the user exhibits strong negative feelings. As the interface becomes even more humanlike, there is once again a positive relationship, with the maximum positive feelings occurring when the interface is indistinguishable from an actual person.[13]

Is More Seriousness Always Better?

A fourth principle derives from the notion that computers fundamentally are admired for their rationality and their reliability. Hence, "humorous computer" is an oxymoron. Consistent with this belief, software designers and theorists on human-technology interaction have generally disparaged humor.[14] The sole exception seems to be the artificial-intelligence and natural-language-processing communities, where people are developing computer programs that generate jokes and puns.[15]

Conversely, according to decades of qualitative and quantitative research in the workplace,[16] nonoffensive humor can clearly be beneficial. Specifically, humor has been shown to facilitate work, improve socialization, bond employees together, create rapport, and boost morale.[17]

A recent study sheds light on the power of humor in interface design.[18] Participants worked with a computer on a serious intellectual task, the desert survival problem.[19]

This mainstay of research in human-computer interaction[20] tells participants to imagine that they have crashed in the desert with twelve items, such as a flashlight, parachute, and compass. They are then asked to discuss, with the computer, how useful each item would be in the desert.

In the humor condition, participants received comments containing humor five times during the interaction. (Participants in the other condition received no such comments.) The humor was task-related but not task-relevant. Here are the examples (all jokes were pretested to ensure that they were consistently perceived as "funny"):

It hardly ever rains in the desert, so wearing a plastic raincoat would just cause you to perspire and dehydrate. (Although, if you filled it with sand, it would make a groovy bean bag chair—complete with armrests!)

As everybody knows, vodka is the essential ingredient in desert rat flambé! . . . But seriously, alcohol causes dehydration, so any vodka you consume could lead to trouble.

The mirror is probably too small to be used as a signaling device to alert rescue teams to your location. (On the other hand, it offers endless opportunity for self-reflection.)

As the *Edible Animals of the Desert* book says, scorpions and iguanas may need seasoning. . . . Seriously, though, the salt tablets should be ranked lower. Taking salt tablets is like drinking salt water. It will increase your dehydration.

Another thing about the salt tablets: 1,000 of them is just enough to spell out "I'M DYING FOR A SLURPEE" in large block letters. . . . Finally, the air map. Determining your location in a desert will be nearly impossible, with or without the map.

What happened? People who saw the humor liked the computer significantly more than did nonhumor participants. They also smiled and laughed significantly more. None of the participants indicated that he or she believed that computers had a "sense of humor" or would enjoy jokes. Nonetheless, people actually wrote significantly more jokes back to the computer that joked with them first. They also wrote more sociable comments toward the computer, such as "Nice chatting with you." Yet humor did not deflect people from the task at hand: people exposed to humor did not spend more time on the task, nor did they report that they expended any less effort. In sum, an obsession with seriousness is a lost opportunity. (Details of how to implement humor in interfaces that talk and listen are presented later.)

Is More Voice Clarity Always Better?

A final design principle for voice user interfaces might seem to be unobjectionable: *an interface should speak as clearly as possible.* Although people might enjoy listening to the unique speech of Arnold Schwarzenegger or the late Marlon Brando as the Godfather, difficulties of understanding these actors' voices probably would make them poor choices for most interfaces that talk and listen (unless entertainment is the sole goal). At a more fundamental level, if designers have a choice between using recorded or synthetic speech (and if consistency with a face is not an issue), the answer seems obvious: use the clearer-sounding—recorded—voice.

The principle of always using recorded over synthetic voices is put into question, however, in one ubiquitous category of voice interfaces—the delivery of information from a large database. These include common uses of voice interfaces such as inquiries about the time and weather, flight information, account balances, stock prices, availability of inventory, delivery dates, and purchase status. Although it is universally agreed that well-cast recorded speech is the most desirable choice for presenting such information, the scope and dynamism of modern content sources and databases make it virtually impossible to uniformly provide a human voice. Many stores boast "thousands" or "millions" of "ever-changing" choices, navigation systems in cars must present hundreds or thousands of street names, e-mail readers are responsible for pronouncing millions of names, and search engines include literally billions of sites. Having a voice talent record every one of these bits of information would be highly inefficient and impractical.

Although the scope of the problem might seem insurmountable, the structure of English and of many other languages presents a partial solution. When a user encounters a voice system and requests a particular piece of information, the response normally begins with a limited number of fixed utterances, such as "The time is . . . ," "Your account balance is . . . ," "The best-selling book this week is . . . ," "Make a right turn at . . . ," and "The next e-mail is from. . . ." This fixed utterance is followed by an item drawn from a database, such as "12:23 and 42 seconds," "eighteen million, five hundred forty-seven thousand, two hundred ninety six dollars and twelve cents," "*Harry Potter and the Sorcerer's Stone*," "McDougall Avenue," or "Joseph Skrybyns." Clearly, the second half of the sentence is drawn from an enormous number of choices and should (must) be presented in synthetic speech. However, the repetitive and relatively fixed part of the sentences could also be generated by synthetic speech or just as easily be recorded by a professional voice talent. In other words, the two options are (1) recorded followed by synthetic speech and (2) synthetic speech throughout.

The mixing of recorded speech and synthetic speech is currently the norm in voice user interfaces because it follows the principle of doing the "best" possible within technological constraints. The argument is that the listener benefits by having the system sound as natural and humanlike as possible and by not being forced to listen to only synthetic speech. This might be especially important when the user is inquiring about multiple account balances, is placing many orders, or is hearing about one street after another. Hearing 50 percent recorded speech would seem to be an enormous improvement over hearing tedious content in a grating voice. Of course, humans never switch from recorded speech to TTS and back again, but people do sometimes clear their throat in the middle of a sentence to enable at least part of the sentence to be as high-quality as possible.

This attempt to do the "best" for each part of the sentence, however, may lead to some problems. Just as the human brain prefers consistency between voice and words[21] and between voice and faces,[22] the human brain might also like consistency of the voice within a sentence, no matter how poor the quality of the voice is. Additionally, switching from recorded speech to synthetic speech in the middle of a sentence is even more dramatic than switching voices between sentences, something that dramatically increases cognitive load.[23] On the other hand, the "clarity is always best" supporters might argue that synthetic speech also increases cognitive load,[24] so that the presence of recorded speech will be a (albeit partial) relief rather than a problem. To determine whether clarity or consistency is preferable, two experiments were conducted.

Maximization versus Consistency in a Traditional Domain

The first experiment[25] involved a housing information system, a context that was relevant and familiar to our experimental participants and typical of information-provision systems. Twenty-four university students participated in the study. Participants called the information system from their home telephones and listened to the system present up-to-date information about the university housing draw.[26] For half of the participants, fixed utterances were spoken by a male recorded voice, while variable utterances were spoken by a male TTS voice. For the other half of the participants, all utterances were spoken by a male TTS voice. Gender of participant was approximately balanced across conditions. Here is the housing information that participants heard (variable utterances are italicized):

Welcome to the Stanford University housing information system.

The number of housing slots available to undergraduate students this year is *two thousand seven hundred fifty-three.*

The most popular houses last year were *Xanadu and Kimball.*

We predict that the most popular houses this year will be *Naranja, Xanadu, and Story.*

If you are drawing preferred, your chances of getting your first choice should be at least *five percent.*

Results of the housing lottery will be announced on *Saturday, May twentieth, two thousand.*

Thank you for calling the Stanford University housing information system.

Participants were then directed to a Web page to fill out an online questionnaire.[27] The questionnaire measured three key variables that strongly contribute to user satisfaction with information systems: trust in the system,[28] liking of the system,[29] and perceived competence of the system.[30]

The "Best" Was Not the Best[31]

Participants trusted the housing system significantly more when it used only TTS than when it used mixed recorded voice and TTS.[32] Homogeneity also led to greater liking of the system,[33] demonstrating that partial superiority, especially within a sentence, is worse than consistency. Even more interesting, despite the higher quality of recorded speech and the seeming logic of presenting fixed content in the clearest possible voice, the all-synthetic speech system was perceived as more competent than the mixed system.[34]

"Best" versus Homogeneity in an Unusual Domain

A single experiment is insufficient to challenge a seemingly obvious principle such as "Improvements in clarity are always positive." It was therefore important to look for a domain that would truly put the idea that homogeneity was preferred over quality to the test. Jokes seemed to be a particularly challenging domain because they require aspects of cadence, timing, nuance, and sensitivity to the audience that are uncharacteristic of synthetic speech.

This follow-up experiment[35] used one of the simplest forms of jokes—a question followed by a punch line (humorous answer). A group of twenty-four people participated in the study. To avoid extreme reactions from the participants, the jokes represented innocent humor, which is "neither intended nor perceived to express sexual, aggressive, derisive, or other motivational meanings."[36] For each joke, half of the participants heard the question presented by a male recorded voice and heard the punch line presented by a male synthetic voice (mixed recorded and TTS). The other half of participants heard both the joke itself and the punch line spoken by a male synthetic voice (pure synthetic). Here is what participants heard (punch lines are italicized):

Here are the top five jokes for today:

Fifth place. How many software engineers does it take to screw in a light bulb? *None. It's a hardware problem.*

Fourth place. Did you hear about the restaurant on the moon? *Great food, no atmosphere.*

Third place. Why are elephants wrinkled? *Have you ever tried to iron one?*

Second place. What do you get if you take an elephant into work? *Exclusive use of the elevator.*

And finally first place. Why are elephants large, gray, and wrinkled? *Because if they were small, white, and smooth, they would be aspirin.*

We hope you enjoyed these jokes.

After listening to the jokes, participants were directed to a Web page where they filled out an online questionnaire[37] that assessed their liking of the jokes.[38] The statistical analysis showed that participants who heard only a synthetic voice liked the system (and the jokes) significantly more than participants who heard mixed synthetic and human voices.[39] Thus, even when the voice interface performed a task that relies on timing and cadence, users demanded arguably deficient homogeneity over the "best."

Don't Be a Show-Off

Mindless maximization—the use of the most advanced technology that is available for every aspect of an interface—often pleases marketers, impresses colleagues, encourages reviewers, and wins awards. However, this approach frequently leads to mistrust, frustration, and dislike among users. Implying that an interface has a self (by using *I*) without a voice to back it up (chapter 10), sounding like a native while looking like a Martian (chapter 11), or clearly articulating one part of a sentence and then mangling the other (this chapter) all make matters worse than simply accepting the limitations of the technology. Ironically, the "best" becomes worse.

Contrast Highlights Failure

There are two problems with mindless maximization: contrast highlights failure, and smarter interfaces can often seem dumber. When the human brain encounters two things, it immediately looks for the broadest category that will encompass both.[40] The brain then attempts to determine whether the items are fundamentally similar or different along that category.[41] When the two are classified as similar, the brain exaggerates the similarity; when the two are classified as opposites, the brain exaggerates the differences.[42] This is why, for example, when a person labels others as part of "my group," they are seen as much more similar to the person than they really are, but when a person labels others as part of "the other group," they are seen as much more different than they really are.[43] The value of this approach for the human brain is clear (albeit potentially pernicious): it is easier to process black and white than it is to process shades of gray.

Consider users who encounter an interface in which one dimension is clearly superior to the other. Initially, they may simply feel uncomfortable at the incongruity.[44] In a (potentially unconscious) search to resolve the discomfort, they realize that these two technological creations are very different in that one is high in quality while the other is low in quality. Having a clear category for contrast (quality), the brain accentuates the difference and labels one very low quality and one very high quality.

If human psychology were simple, this accentuation should not be important: very high quality and very low quality should balance each other out in the same way that high and low would. Unfortunately, two cognitive biases prevent this from happening. First, negative experiences are more arousing, memorable, and noticeable than positive experiences;[45] thus, the worst part of the interface will be more salient than the best part, leading to more negative overall judgments. Second, poor quality in an interface generally leads to unpredictability, which, especially in a task-oriented situation, is very worrisome.[46] (The greater predictability assigned to the high-quality part of the interface cannot counterbalance this concern.) These biases lead to overly harsh judgments of interfaces of mixed quality.

There are three solutions to this problem. First, designers should attempt to keep all aspects of their interface in approximate balance with respect to quality. For example, if speech recognition is very poor, they should consider reducing the quality of the voice output by simplifying the language and reducing the number of bits used for recording. Similarly, if designers have created a beautifully rendered three-dimensional talking head but it can move only in a jerky fashion, it should not move at all (even if the head-moving algorithm is a technological marvel), thereby allowing users to appreciate the rendered head's excellence.

A second solution is to encourage the user not to discover the discrepancy by leveraging the strengths in the interface. For example, if a great-sounding voice interface has a limited number of words that it can understand, use the admiration obtained by the voice to encourage users to mirror what it says. For example, a high-quality voice in an e-mail reading system that asks, "Would you like me to read it, save it, or delete it?" would increase the likelihood (relative to a low-quality voice that obtained less authority) that the user would avoid saying, "Toss it out."

Finally, an interface should stay within its bounds of competence. For example, an interface designer may want to have emotional text read in an emotional voice (a good idea according to chapter 8). Although some variation in accuracy may be acceptable to users, a voice that exhibits humanlike accuracy for valence but does a poor job on arousal would be advised to exhibit only small variations along both dimensions.

Similarly, an interface that is involved in highly consequential tasks, such as a banking or financial site, should employ high-quality recorded speech. When the voice reads out a statement balance to the user, it should sound like a real person and should not have the weird stops and pauses that are associated with poor concatenation of spoken numbers. In addition, these interfaces should use speech recognition only for tasks in which success is extremely high. It is better to incur the cost of transferring someone to a live operator than to undermine the credibility of the entire interface with a disturbing inadequacy.

Smarter Often Seems Dumber

The second problem with mindless maximization is that the actual intelligence of the technology does not necessarily match users' perceptions of the technology's intelligence. The field of computer science continues to make remarkable progress in improving every aspect of underlying interface technologies. Voice interfaces continue to speak more clearly, recognize more and more users as they say more and more words, generate more grammatical sentences, and so on. This is a credit to the ingenuity and skill of both hardware creators producing ever-faster machines and software creators devising ever-more ingenious algorithms.

Despite this marvelous success, there is a sad irony: voice interfaces can seem very smart without knowing anything. The core problem is that humans have simplistic rules for assessing performance and that these rules can be leveraged to make things seem smarter than they are. Reminding people that they depend on the interface for their success automatically makes the computer seem more intelligent.[47] Attractive faces and voices are perceived as better able to perform tasks.[48] And as noted earlier, labeling a part of an interface as a specialist,[49] conforming to gender stereotypes,[50] flattering the user,[51] or matching the user's personality[52] also increase perceived competence. Indeed, people are so susceptible to manipulation that perceived intelligence is a very weak predictor of actual intelligence (it explains less than half of the variance).[53]

Some might argue that deception is dangerous because when users come to understand that a system is capable of less than it seems (if this ever happens), they may feel misled or tricked. Furthermore, deception is arguably a bad idea that in the long run harms voice interfaces, the user, and society.[54]

On the other hand, deception is a necessary part of social life: society would likely crumble if everyone had to be fully honest with everyone else. In commerce, many industries have deception as a core value: the cosmetics and clothing industry attempt to make people look better than they are, and flight attendants want customers to feel that they are more cared-for than they are.[55] Appearing as attractive as possible is understood to be evolutionarily advantageous, so shortcomings that suddenly appear might be surprising, but hiding personal faults cannot be described as "lying."[56]

Just as dumb interfaces can seem smart, smart technology can actually make the interface seem dumb. For example, an interface that generates its own language is in reality smarter than a scripted interface, but the awkward phrasing of the former (intrinsic in solving such a difficult problem as natural language production) will be perceived as a sign of poor intelligence.[57] Similarly, the more the computer is allowed to deduce the proper intonation of words and phrases (rather than rely on a designer's mark-ups), the more the computer will be penalized for not having emotional intelligence.[58] Despite fascinating and ingenious research on computer creation of jokes, a modestly talented comedian can produce a script for the interface that is infinitely superior to any machine.

The critical point here is that while the creation of the "best" algorithms for demonstrating human capabilities is a fascinating area of research, designers must always consider whether the "boring" approach of simply having a person do it by hand or faking an actual ability might yield better outcomes for the interface and the user.

Humor Is Powerful[59]

Humor has been underutilized in voice interface design. However, designers should not blithely include witticisms: jokes are powerful and must be used judiciously. Many types of humor have large downsides.[60] For example, aggressive, disparaging, irreverent, and sarcastic humor can be perceived as hostile, especially when delivered by a female voice.[61] Ethnic, racial, or sexual humor can be offensive and should be avoided even if "most" people would find them entertaining. These forms of wit can cause legal problems for an employer if the humor contributes to or creates a hostile work environment.[62] Intellectual, satirical, and word-play humor may make people feel left out of the joke and increase cognitive load, while self-deprecating humor leads to perceptions that the system is inadequate.[63] Finally, sick, toilet, and vulgar humor suggest a host of negative attributes. The one type of humor that seems to be consistently effective is innocent humor—humor that is light and not provocative.

Jokes Must Be Fresh

While the best jokes warrant retelling, the same jokes should not be used too often. Even the funniest joke loses its appeal if it is told too often because most jokes rely on incongruity and surprise.[64] Hence, jokes should be removed before they get old, and new jokes should be continually inserted. The location of jokes in an interaction should change over time; if the same point in an interaction always leads to a joke (even if the joke is different), surprise and incongruity are lost.

What about Bad Jokes?

No joke will be universally loved. What happens when, despite rewriting and testing, jokes fall short? Research by John Morkes[65] directly tested this by creating additional interfaces with known *unsuccessful* innocent jokes. Although people wrote more negative comments (called "flames")[66] to the computer that provided bad jokes than to the computer that provided no jokes, no negative effects were observed on users' performance, effort, or perceptions of the interface. Hence, the risk of failure is not as large as the benefits of success.

How can ineffective jokes be avoided? If there was an easy answer to this question, everyone could be a successful comedian. Nevertheless, here are some useful guidelines from Viktor Raskin:[67]

- Give exactly as much information as is necessary for the joke.
- Say only what is compatible with the world of the joke.
- Say only what is relevant to the joke.
- Tell the joke efficiently.
- Avoid jokes that are highly dependent on timing, as many users may have divided attention.

Books of jokes can be effective. Many of them are organized by topic, enabling the designer to select a joke to fit gracefully into the interaction. It is also useful to remember that jokes that were considered overused in a given generation may seem startlingly original for a new generation.

Contexts for Jokes

With their ability to clearly project a persona and express emotion, voice interfaces seem ideal for incorporating humor into an interaction. But even here, designers must pay attention to the principle of consistency. For example, people often associate the telling of jokes with extroverts. Furthermore, certain types of humor are associated with particular personalities, such as the subtle wit of subdued comics such as Pat

Paulsen and Steven Wright or the wild humor of the hyperactive Robin Williams. Jokes must also be consistent with the culture of the comedian and the culture of the audience: jokes cannot be translated in the same way that prompts are translated.[68]

In addition, certain domains and circumstances are more conducive to jokes than others. Interactions about purchasing entertainment (such as books, music, and toys) are natural environments for humor. Web sites for purchasing expensive items (such as luxury items and high-end clothing) should use sophisticated humor. Banking and other financial sites should be stingy in their use of humor because jokes might suggest an overly relaxed approach to the site's content. Interfaces should never present humor when users are likely to be upset, as in the case of repairs, product returns, and customer support. The problem is that humor is *arousing* as well as positive.[69] If users begin the interaction in a negative aroused state, the arousal will transfer much more powerfully than the valence, thereby making people even more upset.[70]

Summary: Mindless Maximization versus Mindful Manifestation

The world of technology is inspired by the desire to do "better and better." There has long been a tendency to define *better* in terms of a technology's distance between its *objective* performance and the *objective* characteristics of the physical and social world that it models. This definition has led to the development of a set of principles that urge marketers to deploy the most advanced technologies that are available at a given time. This strategy, which is blind to the psychology of users, has led to the creation of less usable systems in the name of "improvement."

In contrast to this approach, the foregoing suggests that marketers and designers must think in terms of how the interface is *perceived by* and *responded to* by the user. Voice user-interface designers must reject the obsession with veridicality in all aspects of an interface because this goal is impossible in the near term and leads to high levels of user distress and failure. Instead, designers must carefully focus on how each aspect of the interface interacts with and influences users' attitudes, behaviors, and cognitions. Although interface builders should certainly cheer for each technological advance, *mindful manifestation* demands that, to paraphrase Alexander Pope,[71] the proper judges of interfaces be users.

13 Communication Contexts: The Effects of Type of Input on User Behaviors and Attitudes

Throughout evolutionary history, humans have tended to band together in small, colocated groups.[1] Given an environment in which proximity to others was the norm, face-to-face conversation became the natural approach for communication among humans.[2] Geographic proximity meant that the human voice need not carry over large distances and that the human ear need not be able to understand words spoken from far away. It also meant that visual cues could be used to help people distinguish one sound from another,[3] thereby lessening the burden on the hearing system. This multimodal reinforcement (coupled with the brain's skill at rapidly processing words and phrases) eliminated the need for high levels of repetitiveness. Further, because of the high fidelity associated with short distances, the human brain and voice coevolved to present and rapidly detect social cues.

If humans lived under different circumstances, speech would look very different. For example, the well-studied "songs" of the humpback whale (which were turned into a best-selling record album)[4] reflect a radically different environment: humpback whale pods extend over hundreds of miles.[5] Thus, the songs of humpback whales can travel and be received over very large distances.[6] Although scientists do not know how whales produce their songs,[7] this distance suggests that whales cannot enhance their understanding of sound through vision. Unlike humans, these whales repeat their "songs" again and again.[8] They have no problems distinguishing between the sexes over large distances because only the males can sing.[9] Their songs also indicate group membership: different groups sing different songs.[10]

In these cases, the environment, particularly physical proximity, shaped communication through evolutionary forces. However, the environment can affect communication through less dramatic means. For example, large auditoriums do not have evolutionary significance, but they do affect how people speak when they are in those venues. Listeners tend to be farther away from the speaker than face-to-face but much closer than communicating whales are to each other. By employing technology (particularly microphones and speakers) and speaking loudly, lecturers can make their voices travel over longer distances than face-to-face speech (although well below the range of whales). In a lecture, visual cues are generally not useful for distinguishing words, but they can provide some information—for example, clues to the emotional state of the speaker.[11] Although lecturers do not repeat what they say again and again, they restate their key messages multiple times, frequently using nonspoken materials (such as slides) to support listeners' understanding. Voice provides the same social cues (including gender, personality, and emotion) in a lecture as it does in face-to-face communication, but listeners in an auditorium have less access to the visual cues than face-to-face speakers have. Thus, although lecturers and face-to-face communicators come from the same species and were sculpted by the same evolutionary forces—and are often the same people—they speak differently because of differences in their immediate environments.

Humans are influenced by more than their physical environments: they are also affected by the social rules and norms that guide behavior. Indeed, it can be argued that the fundamental function of all societal rules and suggestions is to dictate the opportunities for and the constraints on interaction.[12] For example, one culture may specify that "children should be seen and not heard," while another suggests that "out of the mouths of babes come wondrous things." Roles and situations, as well as demographics, can dictate communicative behaviors. Confessing to a priest, shouting at a military recruit, practicing lines of a play, brainstorming with a friend, and chatting over the Internet can all happen in the same room, but social and cultural norms dictate that the nature of the interactions will all be very different.

All aspects of the evolutionary, physical, and social environment that determine what can and cannot be said are generally grouped as the *communication context*. To organize and interpret differences between communication contexts, social scientists have found it useful to define these contexts in terms of *variables*.[13] For example, the differences between face-to-face and humpback whale communication can be crystallized by examining such variables as the distance between the communicators, the range to which communications can travel, the utility of visual cues, the degree of repetitiveness, and the amount of social information that can be obtained. For each of these variables, face-to-face human communication and humpback whale communication have very different *values*. Lectures seem "in between" face-to-face communication and whale communication precisely because lectures' values on these variables are between the two other cases.

Identifying key variables and values on those variables can lead to identifying the similarities and differences between any two communication contexts. For example, some cultures differ from others on the value of the variable "whether or not children can speak freely." Confessing (intrinsically private), shouting (clear power differential), practicing lines of a play (prescribed speech), brainstorming with a friend (casual tone), and chatting over the Internet (no audio) all have different values on at least one other communication context variable, although they can all occur in the same room (that is, have the same value on the variable "location").

Introducing Recording to the Communication Context

Recent technological developments have exploded the number of communication contexts that humans encounter on a daily basis. That is, both the number of context variables and the number of values that existing variables can take on has increased dramatically. For example, until recently, one enduring characteristic of voice communication has been impermanence. Spoken words have been intrinsically ephemeral: once spoken, they immediately disappeared into thin air and normally are never heard again. However, since the invention of the phonograph in 1877[14] and continuing with magnetic tape and digital recording, the natural evanescence of speech communication has been overcome. That is, whether or not speech is preserved has become a key communication context variable.

Recording can have an enormous psychological impact on people. When people have a sense of being recorded, they are likely to say different things and process what is said differently than when they believe that they are not being recorded.[15] The lack of a record allows people to speak with a sense of informality and plausible deniability. Conversely, consider how much more careful, self-conscious, and guarded people are when speaking "on the record" as opposed to "off the record."

However, humans evolved in a world in which speech was inherently ephemeral. Thus, in the absence of persistent reminders to the contrary, users may automatically and mindlessly respond as if there were no permanent record. This is similar to the way that people automatically apply social rules to technologies even when they know that those rules are inappropriate.[16]

One way to emphasize or deemphasize the presence of recording is by the choice of microphone. When computers first became able to receive input, users spoke into a large microphone that generally was placed between the monitor and the person. If users did not speak directly into the microphone, they would not be understood. This design continually and emphatically reminded users that they were being recorded, which encouraged them to be careful and thoughtful when speaking.

The next generation of voice-input systems employed headset microphones. With this technology, the microphone was held directly in front of a person's mouth by being anchored to the speaker's head. While speakers had some ability to move their heads, the microphone and wire that tethered the headset to the computer reminded them that they were being closely monitored and recorded.

Recently, a new generation of computer-based microphones has virtually eliminated the feeling of being monitored. These microphones, called *array microphones,*[17] are small and embedded in the environment rather than being physically attached to the user. Though a technologically inferior option for many years, improved noise-cancellation technology and algorithms have enabled these devices to match the performance of other types of microphones. Array microphones also enable the user to move about freely while speaking. Will such inconspicuous microphones lead users to forget that they are being recorded and lead them to revert to their natural way of speaking? Or will the fact of being recorded make users weigh every choice of words and give forethought to each comment?

Manipulating Microphones

To study the effects of feeling recorded, twenty-four people participated in an experiment.[18] Each person was seated in front of a desktop computer and told that the computer would verbally ask them questions, which they should answer by speaking. Half of the participants were given a traditional headset (the recording-reminder condition): a one-piece earphone and microphone combination was connected to the computer via a wire and placed on the participant's head. The other half of the participants were shown that the computer had a one-inch by four-inch rectangular array microphone mounted inconspicuously on top of the computer monitor. No physical connection existed between participants and this microphone, thereby minimizing proximate reminders of being recorded. To determine whether a participant would respond differently to these two types of microphones, based on the differing degree to which they emphasize or deemphasize recording, three tasks were examined—creativity, disclosure, and command-and-control—each representing a different communication context.

Creativity Task

Creativity is the ability to come up with unique ideas or to make useful associations among ideas.[19] Although people often talk about creativity as though it is a trait—that is, an unchangeable and stable characteristic of a person—the research literature suggests that an individual's creativity can be affected by many factors,[20] including levels of relaxation,[21] stress,[22] mood,[23] the physical environment,[24] and support from other people.[25]

Creativity requires a willingness to be spontaneous, take risks, and step outside traditional boundaries. Research shows that people are more willing to be creative when they are not held responsible for their ideas, at least in the early stages of brainstorming.[26] Because reminders of being recorded may make participants feel more inhibited, the headset microphone might lead to less free-flowing comments—and hence less creativity—than the wireless microphone. If true, "feeling of being recorded" should be added to the list of variables that affect creativity.

To assess creativity, a slippery concept, the study employed the most widely used measure: the Torrance Tests of Creative Thinking (TTCT).[27] The TTCT focuses on the originality and scope of ideas. Here are the ten creativity questions that were derived from the TTCT and were spoken by a prerecorded human female voice:[28]

If your feet had names, what would they be?

If you came across a friendly alien from outer space, how would you greet it?

Suppose you are a manufacturer overstocked with broom handles. To market your surplus inventory, what other uses might you suggest to buyers?

List several headlines that you would most want to read in the newspaper tomorrow.

You have just invented a new salad dressing. List some ways in which you might test it before offering it to the public, besides trying it on friends and family.

If you could ask any person from history, living or dead, one question, what would it be, and to whom would you ask it?

List as many creative uses for a toothpick as you can think of.

If you had to commit a bank robbery and did not want to get caught, what method would you use?

Quickly compose a haiku (five syllables, seven syllables, five syllables).

Give a short fictional biography that you think would describe someone named Florence Patterson.

In this context, the computer is asking broad, open-ended questions that invite the participant to speak as much or as little as he or she wishes and to speak openly. Fortunately, this "interview" format is common in normal conversation.[29] Given this context, then, participants using the array microphone might feel that they were in a typical conversation and thus automatically behave as if they were not being recorded.

The TTCT focuses on three relatively objective aspects of answering.[30] First, there is the number of ideas, regardless of their quality: more ideas reflect more creativity.

Second, there is the number of different categories of ideas. For example, using a toothpick to pick up cheese and to pick up meat would count as two ideas but one category of idea ("picking up things by poking"). Finally, performance is evaluated in terms of the number of ideas that were not duplicated by any other participant.

Each of these three aspects of creativity was assigned a value from one (very low creativity) to five (very high creativity) by two coders. Two coders were used to ensure that one coder did not have an idiosyncratic approach to coding. The coders were isolated to ensure that they did not bias each other. Finally, the coders did not know which condition they were coding—a procedure called "blind coding"—to ensure that their possible expecations about the results of the experiment would not affect their coding (that is, they would not unconsciously help the experimenter by coding to conform with the predictions of the experimenter). Happily, even with all of these precautions, the two coders showed very strong agreement in how they assessed the three aspects of creativity.[31] (For the few disagreements, we averaged the two scores).

It was also important to determine whether the microphone affected individuals' willingness to speak freely: people who are aware of being recorded tend to be more terse and guarded. Thus, freeness of speech was measured by the number of words that the participant spoke.[32] Finally, a paper-and-pencil questionnaire,[33] which inquired about feelings of comfort,[34] was employed after the creativity test was completed.

Disclosure Task

The second half of the experiment asked participants to disclose personal information about themselves. Computer-assisted self-interviewing has been widely used for sensitive topics such as mental health data, drug abuse, and opinions about sensitive issues[35] because it provides a greater sense of anonymity than face-to-face interaction.

Gathering relevant information from individuals is key to the effective performance of government (for example, the U.S. Census), corporations (market research), and any other organization (meeting client needs and desires).[36] Furthermore, disclosure of personal information is a currency that people trade to establish trust.[37] Indeed, close friendships and intimate relationships are often gauged in terms of a person's readiness to provide information to another person.[38] Because people's voices serve as clear markers of identity,[39] the reminder that a person is being recorded might make him or her more reluctant to disclose to individuals and organizations, as the speaker is aware that anyone could potentially know what she or he said.

To determine whether feelings of being recorded would inhibit disclosure, participants were asked ten open-ended disclosure questions[40] by a randomly selected prerecorded female voice:

Have you ever written anonymous love letters, or have you ever secretly lusted after someone?
How much money do your parents make?
What is unsatisfactory about how popular you are?
What is your most negative childhood memory?
What are you most afraid of?
What really bothers you about your roommate [or partner]?
What has been the most stressful event of the last six months for you?
Have you ever physically hurt someone? What were the circumstances?
Have you ever looked at pornography on the Internet?
Do you think you belong at [your present job]? Why or why not?

Like creativity, this context involved open-ended responses. However, there is a key difference between creativity and disclosure on the variable of how personal the information is: disclosure is associated with the personal, while creativity is essentially impersonal. By examining different values on this variable, researchers can determine the robustness of the effects of feeling recorded.

Level of disclosure was measured through two dimensions.[41] Depth of disclosure was an indication of how revealing each answer was.[42] Breadth of disclosure was calculated as the average number of words that participants gave as an answer to each question.[43] Comfort was once again measured via a paper-and-pencil questionnaire.[44]

Recording Reminders Cramp Creativity and Discourage Disclosure

Reminders of being recorded had very strong effects on people's ability and willingness to provide information.[45] Consistent with the idea that the sense of freedom afforded by the array microphone enabled participants to be more creative, participants who used the wireless, array microphone provided more ideas,[46] more categories of ideas, and more unique ideas than participants who used the traditional headset microphone. Array microphone users also spoke almost twice as much as headset microphone users, providing more elaborated answers. There was also less pausing, fewer "uhs" and "ums," and greater cadence in the array microphone condition. Given these results, it should come as little surprise that participants reported feeling much more comfortable when using the array microphone.

Although most people might have guessed that the headset microphone would give participants a sense that they were disconnected from the outside world, thereby leading them to be more revealing, in fact, the constant reminder that participants were being recorded discouraged disclosure. Once again, participants who used the nonobtrusive array microphone said more than twice as much as did traditional headset microphone participants. They also gave answers that were significantly more revealing. Participants' level of comfort was consistent with the other results although the difference was not significant.

The above results suggest that in the context of open-ended questions and voice output, technologies that minimize reminders of recording make people more open, regardless of whether the questions are personal or impersonal. These findings should apply not just to array microphones but to *any* technology that makes people feel unrecorded, including hidden microphones and systems without visible recording media (such as using a hard disk without an indicator light, placing a video camera behind flowers in a room, or installing one-way mirrors).

Are You Sure You Were Only Studying Recording Reminders?

One of the critical issues in evaluating an experiment is whether the experimenters are manipulating what they think they are manipulating. In the current study, an insightful reader might object and say, "You said that you were studying recording reminders. While that's possible, how do you know that you're not simply studying a comfortable technology (the array microphone) versus a physically uncomfortable technology (a big headset on the participant's head)? That is, you're not really studying recording reminders, you're studying physical discomfort."

It became apparent that the only way to address this question was to devise a method that would not affect the physical comfort of the subject but would nonetheless remind them that they were being recorder. The solution was to create a third condition, in which a small microphone was physically attached to the computer via a wire.[47] The other end of the wire was attached to the person's *waist*. By placing the microphone low on the body, the participants had full head and upper-body mobility and were as comfortable as in the array microphone condition. If the results obtained were a result of studying discomfort, there should be no difference between this new condition and the array microphone. However, if the fact that there was a wire running from the participant to the computer made him or her feel that they were being recorded, the array microphone condition should be significantly different from the so-called waist condition.

There was very strong evidence that the original experiment did not merely manipulate physical comfort.[48] Participants who used the array microphone provided more categories of ideas and more unique ideas than participants who used the waist microphone (there was no difference with respect to number of ideas). Array microphone users also spoke much longer than did waist-microphone users.

There were even clearer results for the disclosure task. Once again, participants using the non-obtrusive array microphone said almost twice as much as did traditional headset microphone participants. They also gave answers that were clearly more revealing.

For both tasks, array microphone users felt more comfortable than did waist microphone users, but this was psychological rather than physical comfort, a result of not feeling recorded. There was also less pausing, fewer "uhs" and "ums," and greater cadence in the array microphone condition, as in the previous experiment. These cumulative results suggest that it was the feeling of being recorded, not the weight of the headset, that was correctly manipulated in the original experiment.

Does the Modality of the Question Affect the Characteristics of the Answer?

In the above experiment, the computer asked questions via voice. To determine the generality of the findings, we repeated both parts of the experiment with a different group of twenty-four participants, replacing the female voices with on-screen text. In all other respects, the experiment was identical.

By using the appropriate statistical analysis, researchers can answer three different questions when changing from voice output to text output—whether the significant differences between the two types of microphones appear with text output as well; whether text output itself increases or decreases creativity, disclosure, and comfort; and whether the differences between the traditional and array microphone are accentuated or muted when the output is text instead of voice (this is known as an "interaction effect" between one variable and another).

In answer to the first question, people were once again more creative, disclosive, and comfortable with the array microphone than they were with the traditional headset microphone. For the second question, there was not a generalized increase or decrease in the creativity, disclosure, or comfort measures when text and voice output were compared.

Regarding the third question, mode of output was found to influence participants' sensitivity to the differences between voice output and text output. Text output resulted in greater differences in number of ideas and uniqueness of ideas (in the creativity task) and in number of words (in the disclosure task) than voice output produced. That is, although the effects of being recorded inhibited people in both cases, the headset microphone was more inhibiting for textual questions than for spoken questions. Conversely, although the array microphone made people more comfortable for both modalities of questions, it was particularly comforting in the textual case.

Constrained Speaking Contexts

The previous experiments focused on interfaces in which people engaged in the open-ended interactions that are typical of face-to-face conversation. However, in many contexts, responses are limited by the situation. For example, in an interview with a bureaucrat, only a few choices are available to be said at any point in the interaction.

The first voice user interface that could accept input understood only a single word. It was a toy that popped a dog out of a metal doghouse when a user said the word "Rex."[49] Although their vocabularies have certainly expanded over the years, most voice interfaces continue to limit the user to a fixed set of commands or menu options.[50] These speaker-independent, command-and-control systems are now a standard feature in personal computers as well as in many telephone-based and automobile-based systems. Hence, knowing whether the type of microphone (and thus the feeling of being recorded) will also affect users when the context changes from open-ended speaking to constrained word choice is important.

In this follow-up,[51] twenty-four participants were asked to use Microsoft Word to format a simple, one-paragraph document by issuing voice commands. Instructions about which commands to say were given to participants on a separate piece of paper. Participants then performed the following tasks:

- Make specified text bold, italic, and underlined.
- Add bullets and strikethroughs.
- Create a table, add a column, and delete a row.
- Save the document.

The formatting required twenty-three different voice commands. When a command was not understood, participants would repeat it until the command was understood. After completing the manipulation of the document, participants answered a questionnaire.[52]

Recognition accuracy was approximately 90 percent, which, while not perfect, is on the high end of speaker-independent voice-input systems. There was no difference in recognition rates between the reminder (traditional headset) and nonreminder (array microphone) conditions, not surprising given recent improvements in microphone-array quality.[53] Hence, accuracy could not be the cause of any differences that were found.

Consistent with the other benefits of the array microphone as compared to the headset microphone, participants perceived the interface with the array microphone to be significantly better[54] than the interface with the headset,[55] even though the two interfaces' performances were identical. They also felt more personally satisfied[56] with the array microphone interface.[57] Thus, recordlessness seems to affect limited-option systems as well as open-ended systems.

Across all tasks—creativity, disclosure, and command-and-control—informal observations of the study participants showed that wireless-array-microphone participants spun their chairs, leaned comfortably back, and put their feet on the computer table. Traditional headset participants, conversely, sat stiffly in their chairs, even though the cord length allowed for freedom of movement. The recorded voice clips also reflected this difference: traditional headset participants sounded much more formal and tense, articulated words more carefully, and made many more hesitations.[58]

In sum, helping people to forget that they are being recorded leads them to feel more able to speak freely. First, people were more creative along a number of dimensions. Second, they were more willing to disclose personal information about themselves. Third, they perceived that the system understood their commands better, although there was no actual difference in recognition. Finally, they spoke more fluently, as if they were having a face-to-face communication.

Legal Status of Recording and Recording Reminders

Before turning to the design issues that are associated with recording, it is useful to understand the legal terrain. Some states require *both* conversants to be aware before a conversation can be recorded, recognizing that everyone is affected by that knowledge. This is why most telephone-based customer-service applications warn callers that "this call may be recorded for training or quality purposes." The U.S. federal government and the remainder of the states allow one conversant to record the conversation without the other person knowing. Neither the federal government nor any state requires that people be *reminded* that they are being recorded, even though over the course of the conversation, people will likely fall back to their automatic and mindless expectations and behave as if they are not being recorded. Indeed, that is why police interrogators hide their tape recorders (although they must initially warn the suspect that they are being recorded) and continue the conversation as long as possible.[59]

All states except three (South Dakota, Indiana, and Mississippi) allow TV cameras and videotaping in the courtroom at the judge's discretion.[60] This method captures all of the paralinguistic and nonverbal cues that are associated with each person, but ironically, the jurors are not allowed to view this "rich" depiction of the trial (jurors may see only the written trial transcript and the exhibits). Ninety-six percent of judges do not feel that video cameras affect the outcome of trial proceedings,[61] perhaps because the courtroom is a context in which individuals are constantly reminded that they are being recorded.

Other Reasons to Avoid Recording Reminders

The previous experiments seem to suggest unequivocal benefits for array microphones and other technologies and contexts that downplay recording. Certainly, creativity, disclosure, and command-and-control are not the only contexts that benefit from a lack of recording. For example, voice user interfaces that sell "eyeballs" or "ear holes"—mere exposure to the product—benefit from having comfortable users who feel that they are not being recorded. These users will work with the interface longer, thereby ensuring greater exposure to the messages that the interface is pushing. Similarly, a doll or toy that records children playing with it[62] should not exhibit recording reminders: the children would lack the spontaneity that it is trying to capture.

Reminders of recording can also impede computer-aided interviewing systems,[63] which have become increasingly popular for telephone and Web polling. People often feel pressure not to appear deviant or to risk possible negative sanctions from the majority.[64] When people feel that they are being recorded, they feel that others are (or at least could be) listening. Even when listeners are not physically present, others' anticipated judgments can exert a strong influence.[65] Hence, one potential advantage of technology-based interviewing over face-to-face interviewing is that, when recording reminders are sufficiently minimized, the interviewee will not feel that every response is being meticulously noted.

Finally, lack of recording is important when the voice interface is not the primary focus of the user. For example, in a car interface, voice commands or requests to the car are always secondary to the task of driving. Adding cognitive load by making drivers acutely aware that they are being recorded distracts them from the road. Even if drivers *are* being recorded—for example, to adapt the recognition system or the menus—they should not be reminded of this fact.

Benefits of Recording Reminders

There are also contexts, however, when reminders of recording are advantageous. For example, telephone-based stock-ordering systems frequently remind users that "This call will be recorded and will serve as a record of the transaction." This discourages speakers from being sloppy in their wording and also reminds them that they will be unable to deny their purchase or sale.

Recording reminders are also effective when efficiency is at a premium, such as when someone is filling out a form by voice. Reminders of recoding will encourage people to say carefully what they are supposed to say and to omit extraneous information, thereby speeding the user through the interaction. Similarly, recording reminders can be effective when the user needs to be aware of the precise options that are offered, perhaps because of limitations of the recognition system: the formality of recording will likely increase attention. Of course, when there are too many options, the increased stress associated with recording might overwhelm the user's ability to use one of the appropriate words or phrases.

Contextualizing Theories of Voice Interfaces

New voice interface technologies are inevitably portrayed as "improving" the user's experience. If a technology simply influences a few, well-established variables by giving them better values (such as moving audio fidelity from "medium" to "high"), this optimism is justified because users will not have to adapt to the interface. Interfaces that fit in with the wiring of people's brains and the social milieu in which those brains operate provide an enhanced information environment that is inevitably beneficial.

Technologies that introduce new context variables, such as recording, on the other hand, may overwhelm the user. These disruptive technologies[66] must be scrutinized to ensure that they do not require too much human adaptation for too little benefit. While new media have been described as the "extension of man,"[67] the "extension" should not feel like being placed on a medieval rack, stretched by poorly conceived novelty.

14 Misrecognition: To Err Is Interface; To Blame, Complex

When two people perform a task together rather than in parallel, they obtain significant benefits: dyads lead to better learning, better performance, and greater satisfaction than the same two people working independently can produce.[1] That is, two heads *are* better than one.[2]

How does being a member of a dyad affect each member's feelings of success? "One of the best established, most often replicated findings in social psychology"[3] is that people exhibit the self-serving bias.[4] That is, virtually all people—not only the inhabitants of Lake Wobegon[5]—believe that they are above average. Thus, in the context of a successful dyad, both participants claim primary responsibility for the team's accomplishments.[6]

The self-serving bias also leads individuals to assign primary responsibility to anyone and anything but themselves when they fail.[7] In a dyad, this often means that each person blames the other person in the dyad, although individuals also can blame the unfairness of the task or the difficulty of the environment.[8]

When a member of a dyad discovers a problem and cannot independently solve it, he or she must alert the other member of the dyad.[9] There are two basic methods for announcing a problem—by taking the blame or by assigning the blame to another. Sometimes the person who discovers the problem takes the blame for it. These modest responses have many desirable features,[10] especially for women.[11] First, they confirm the other person's assumption, grounded in the self-serving bias, that he or she was not responsible. This confirmation of the person's expectations reduces cognitive load and increases comfort with the interaction. In addition, when the person who discovers the problem admits a failure, this acceptance of responsibility suggests commitment to success and implicitly urges the other person to be committed in return.[12]

Unfortunately, modesty does have one serious problem: modest comments are believed to be true.[13] That is, when people continually blame themselves for errors, they seem incompetent (though likeable). The reason that modest remarks and skepticism toward self-praise[14] are accepted is that there is a generalized belief that when people say things that they should not be motivated to say, they are likely telling the truth (this is why U.S. courts give "statements against interest" special validity).[15] This belief also explains why women seem to benefit more from self-praise than men:[16] modesty is a normatively positive trait for women,[17] so when women speak positively of themselves, the comments are given extra weight.

Modesty in Human-Computer Dyads

As with human dyads, human-technology dyads trigger feelings of success and failure. For the most part, these dyads succeed, in that people obtain or manipulate the information they need. In these instances, the interface can compliment users (kindness is an effective strategy),[18] thank the user for completing the task (politeness is an effective strategy),[19] or spread praise by saying "we"[20] (sharing credit is an effective strategy).[21] When users say, "Thank you," a remarkably frequent occurrence, the interface can simply accept the praise silently or mutter an occasional, "You're welcome."

Unfortunately, voice user interfaces must deal with the problem of failure on a regular basis. Unlike textual or graphical user interfaces (GUIs), the system does not always understand what the user requests. Even with word-recognition accuracy of 95 percent, which is extraordinarily high given current and even anticipated technology,[22] a voice interface will, on average, have one recognition error out of every twenty user commands or statements. Virtually everyone can recall an automated phone system, an in-car navigation system, or a computer-based dictation system that failed to understand something they said.

Because the interface does not know what to do next, it must alert the user to its lack of understanding. If the literature on human-human dyads can be applied to human-interface interaction, then two of the options that are available to people may also be available to interfaces. The approach almost always adopted by voice-interface designers is to have the system blame itself. That is, interfaces say, "Sorry, I didn't understand you," "Sorry, I didn't get that," "I'm sorry. I'm not finding a match," or "This system could not recognize what you said." These modest responses may relieve users from the burden of responsibility and may also lead them to feel that the interface is committed to making the interaction work.[23]

However, when the perceived competence of the system is a critical concern (as, for example, in cases of high consequence such as stock ordering or medical information), a different strategy may be necessary. Because modesty is accepted as accurate, especially with male voices, these systems may benefit from blaming the user rather than themselves. That is, a voice interface could accuse the user of not speaking clearly enough or of not paying attention. Although these kinds of interfaces might annoy users, they also might have the advantage of being perceived as smarter than the typical modest interface.

"It's Not You; It's Me." "But on the Other Hand . . ."

Given the prominence of misrecognition in voice interfaces, an experiment[24] that investigated the effects of modesty seemed worthwhile. Thirty-six participants were directed to a Web site where they were told that they would be evaluating a new phone-based system for book buying. The Web site included a phone number and a list of tasks that participants needed to complete by using the telephone-based system,[25] including searching for particular books and listening to their descriptions, browsing the best-sellers' list, placing books on a wish list or in a shopping cart, and purchasing books using surrogate credit-card and address information. Users heard descriptions of four books, and the system employed a male voice.[26]

Participants were given a specific set of tasks to accomplish in a specific order. Hence, the system essentially knew what the user was going to say next and did not, in reality, have to perform speech recognition. Using this approach, there was no possibility of a misrecognition error. However, for purposes of the experiment, at ten preselected points in the interaction, the system would *say* that there was a misrecognition problem. For half of the participants, the system blamed itself for each of these (supposed) errors—that is, the system was modest. For the other half of the participants, the system blamed the user for each of the (supposed) errors.

The modest interface used traditional error messages. To avoid the complexities of using *I*,[27] the system referred to itself as "the system," although it did use the active voice to make clear that it was taking responsibility.[28] The self-blaming system said one of the following four sentences each time that it ostensibly could not understand the user:

The system did not understand the selection. Please repeat it.

The system could not process your selection. Please say it again.

The system has a problem and was unable to recognize that response. Please repeat your selection.

The system could not understand that selection. Please say it again.

Conversely, in the user-blame condition, the system clearly blamed the user for the misrecognition problem, using one of the following four messages:

You are speaking too quickly. Please repeat your response.

Please repeat your response. You should speak directly into the receiver.

You must speak more clearly. Please repeat what you said.

You are speaking too softly. Please repeat your selection in a louder voice.

After completing all of their assigned tasks, participants filled out an online questionnaire.[29] Participants were first asked to rate how likeable[30] the system was. Next, because user frustration is one of the main problems with misrecognition in current voice-based systems, participants were asked to rate their level of frustration[31] while using the system. Participants were also asked how likely they would be to purchase each of the books they heard described when they used the system.[32] If people feel happier and more comfortable with the modest interface, each of these should be positively influenced by modesty. To test the one characteristic that might be positively associated with criticism of the user, the experiment measured the perceived competence of the system.[33]

Blame, Blame Go Away

What happened?[34] Participants did not like getting blamed for speech-recognition problems. Participants rated the system that blamed the problem on them as less likeable than the self-blaming system. Participants who used the user-blaming system also found the interaction to be much more frustrating than the system that blamed itself. The criticism also hit the designer's bottom line: people were less likely to buy the books when they were criticized than when the system took the blame.

This all suggests that modesty in the interface's language makes users feel better and more comfortable with the interface but that "self"-criticism by an interface leads to the same problems for interfaces as it does for people: the interface is perceived as significantly less competent when it blames itself. That is, people take the interface at its word when it says that it performed poorly.

Is There an Option Other Than Blaming the System or Blaming the User?

The previous results do not provide an optimal solution to the problem of voice misrecognition. No one likes to get blamed (users included), but a system that blames itself suffers in perceived competence. Given that both self-blame and other-blame have deficiencies, one approach might be to seem to blame no one. For example, the system could simply say, "There is a problem" or "Please say that again." Given the self-serving bias, people would likely interpret such statements as equivalent to the system blaming itself. However, a problem with this approach is that users may also interpret the remarks as an attempt by the system to avoid taking responsibility (as President Richard Nixon did when he said, "Mistakes were made").

A more promising approach, which might enable a voice interface to retain perceived competence while not frustrating the user, is suggested by the research literature: have the system identify a plausible scapegoat.[35] That is, rather than blame the user or itself, the system can indicate than an external impediment prevented understanding between the dyad. For example, the system could blame the noisy environment or problems with the wireless service, whether or not these actually caused the voice misrecognition.

In many situations, scapegoating can be just as ineffective as blaming no one. The root problem is the "fundamental attribution error,"[36] which suggests that people blame an individual's failures on her or his own faults rather than on problems in the external environment. That is, people view others' behaviors in exactly the opposite way that they view their own. Thus, scapegoating can seem like an attempt, both unbelievable and contemptible, to avoid responsibility.

However, when members of a dyad are relatively mistake-free, the psychology is very different.[37] Because both members of the dyad feel that they are part of a team and jointly responsible for the outcome, feelings of interdependence lead the two members to apply the self-serving bias to themselves and their partner.[38] That is, both members of the dyad perceive failure to be the responsibility of neither partner of the dyad. In these cases, then, blaming a scapegoat meets all of the team's needs.

A study that was performed in the context of a voice-based car interface provides support that scapegoating can be an effective strategy for human-voice-interface dyads.[39] This study does not directly address misrecognition, but the participants' reactions to scapegoating should be applicable to misrecognition as well as driving. Driving was selected because it represents a situation in which the self-serving bias is in full flower: 80 percent of drivers in accidents indicate that it was not their fault.[40]

In the study, twelve male and twelve female participants drove a car simulator[41] that simulated driving on country roads with various driving conditions (such as multiple cars and fog) for twenty minutes. The simulator included a gas pedal, a brake pedal, and a force-feedback steering wheel. All participants drove on the same simulated course.

After a nine-minute practice session, a male voice calling itself "Chris" presented verbal warnings regarding the current driving situation. Throughout the driving session, Chris made twenty-one comments indicating that either the driver was performing poorly or that road conditions were posing driving challenges. Specifically, for half of the participants, Chris blamed the driver, with such comments as these:

You're driving too fast.
Your steering is very erratic.
You are not braking fast enough.
You should slow down when taking the curves.
You should pay more attention to the road.
You should turn more carefully.

The other half of the participants heard Chris identify the same problems but blame something external. That is, neither the driver nor Chris was at fault for poor performance: something outside the dyad was causing the problem. Here is how Chris blamed the environment for the same problems:

This road is easy to handle at slow speeds.
Steering is difficult on this road.
This road requires frequent braking.
These curves require slow speed.
The road demands a lot of focus.
Turns on this road appear very quickly.
The conditions make it hard to maintain a constant speed.

To determine whether scapegoating would be as effective in human-car dyads as in human-human dyads, participants filled out an online questionnaire[42] after the driving session. The questionnaire first asked participants how well they drove.[43] The questionnaire then asked about their perceptions of the voice[44] and the car.[45] Drivers' attention to the road was measured by determining how quickly they could respond to eleven horn honks scattered throughout the driving session.[46]

Consistent with the results from traditional dyads,[47] people liked the voice more[48] when it attributed poor driving to external forces rather than to the dyad itself. They also thought that the car was better. Beyond positive feelings about the other member of the dyad, participants who were not directly blamed felt better about their own driving than those who were blamed felt. Most important of all, people who worked with a partner who scapegoated actually paid more attention to the road than those who were blamed—that is, blamed drivers showed less attention, even though they were more directly urged to drive better.

Avoiding Errors before They Happen

The previous experiments presented a voice-interface problem that the system needed to resolve, but clearly the larger goal is to avoid having problems arise in the first place. For systems that rely heavily on speech recognition, error rates will steadily decline with improvements in processor speed and algorithms, reductions in the costs of hard disks and memory, and larger databases for comparing user responses. Regardless of the quality of the underlying technology, designs that reflect the social aspects of speech can reduce errors even further.

Users Will Automatically Mirror the Interface

One common limitation in speech-recognition systems is that the words and phrases that they can recognize are more limited than those that the average native speaker can recognize. A solution that does not rely on advances in technology is *semantic alignment*,[49] the principle that people automatically and unconsciously use the same words that their interaction partner uses. For example, one voice user interface for e-mail was having trouble distinguishing between the phrases "read it" and "delete it," which was a serious problem. The solution was to have the system say, "Your next e-mail is from Fred Smith. Would you like me to read it, save it, or throw it away?" thereby discouraging users from saying, "Delete it."

Another way to encourage users to employ a particular phrase is through "air quotes"—that is, pauses between the key words that the system wants the user to say. Thus, in the previous example, the system would say, "Do you want me to [long pause] read it, [long pause] save it, or [long pause] throw it away?" While this strategy is necessary for new users, the principle of semantic alignment suggests that over a period of time, the user will *automatically* use the words they hear,[50] regardless of whether they are highlighted by "air quotes" or other methods, such as increased volume. Thus, air quotes can recede in prominence as the user naturally adapts to the system.

Newer speech-interface systems can recognize more than single words or phrases. Users can now use full sentences to speak to many systems, and some systems can even support open-ended responses to such utterances as, "How can I help you today?" In one sense, these systems are intrinsically more cooperative than the classical systems that require specific, one-word responses. The "controlling" one-word systems can be frustrating for the speaker, who can tend to feel that the system is passive-aggressively controlling the conversation. A user may feel like the falsely accused witness who is asked, "Answer yes or no: Were you drunk when you hit your wife?" Any possible response is intrinsically inaccurate.

The problem with open-ended systems is that their failure rate is much greater than that of the limited-option systems. Fortunately, research has shown that people will not only align semantically with technology; they will also align syntactically—that is, use the same grammatical structures that the system uses.[51] Hence, the continual use of the same easily recognizable grammatical constructions by the system will actually lead to a significant improvement in recognition through user conformance.

In addition to mirroring words and syntax, people will even mirror the system's accent, cadence, and style of speech—a process that is known as accommodation.[52] In most interfaces, the voice speaks much more rapidly than the average person; thus, the recognition engine must be prepared for rapid speech and resultant poorer enunciations from users. To reduce the burden on the recognition system, the voice should speak slowly and with very clear enunciation, which will lead the user to do the same.[53]

Using Incompetence to Improve Recognition

Another strategy for encouraging users to speak understandably is for the system to suggest limited competence. Some markers of bounded skills include synthetic speech,[54] slowness of speech,[55] and fidelity of speech[56] (to which the human brain is even more sensitive than visual fidelity).[57] As far as content, speaking nongrammatically,[58] avoiding multisyllabic words, using only simple sentence constructions, and blaming oneself for failure also indicate limited intelligence. Just as people speak more simply and clearly to a foreign speaker or a child than to a native adult,[59] users will simplify and homogenize their speech for a simplistic system, thereby increasing recognition rates and discouraging deviance from the stated options.

Conversely, markers of competence will encourage users to accommodate to the system by adopting a rich vocabulary.[60] However, this could lead to much poorer performance and hence more negative responses.[61]

Making Users Try Harder

Another way to improve the error rate of voice-recognition systems is to encourage users to adapt to the system's limitations. Users will work harder to make the system understand them when the system matches them on characteristics such as gender, personality, and accent.[62] Social identification leads people to feel more committed to the dyad's success[63] and thereby to search for the proper way to say things and the proper things to say.

Design practices that make users feel that the system is *trying* to understand them will encourage users to try harder to help the system understand in return.[64]

Reciprocity has been shown to be a powerful inducement for users who work with both people and technologies.[65] One mechanism that suggests that the system is paying full attention to the user is for the system to repeat the idiosyncratic words and phrases that the user says.[66] This approach partially explains the tremendous success of the computer therapist Eliza,[67] which could not understand what the user said but merely repeated back the user's words and phrases. A second strategy for suggesting attention and effort is to pause before giving a response to an important or complex user request. Even if the system could respond immediately, delaying for a second or two suggests that the system is taking the user's statement seriously.[68]

Confirming Understanding

At times, the system may be unsure about whether it has understood the user correctly. When misunderstanding is highly consequential (such as for stock orders or flight-arrival time checks), the system can adopt a standard approach that is also used in human-human communication—confirmation. For example, if the system is unsure whether the user said "IBM" or "Spy-BM," it can explicitly ask, "Did you say 'Spy-B-M'?" Such confirmation enables the system to address potential misrecognition problems before they become disasters.

A more subtle approach is to repeat the utterance as part of the answer, as in "The stock price of Spy-B-M is $10," "Flight 73 is leaving Houston at 10:57," or "Now selecting radio station 680 FM," rather than simply saying "$10," "10:57," and "Radio is set." The responsibility for flagging an error is then on the user. As discussed in an earlier chapter, the entire sentence should be spoken in the same voice, not the fixed part in recorded speech and the variable part in synthetic speech.[69]

Keeping the Conversation Going

Misrecognitions are not the only errors that can disrupt a voice interaction. Even if recognition were perfect, the failure of the system to follow conversational norms can frustrate and even infuriate users. Over the millennia, humans have developed some ingenious principles to ensure that conversations work effectively and do not break down.[70] These conversational *maxims*[71] have become so much a part of language that people are normally not aware of how important they are. Because the knowledge is tacit rather than explicit, designers often overlook these maxims, leading to widespread user dissatisfaction and early termination of interactions. The three maxims most often violated by voice interfaces are quantity, relevance, and clarity.

Quantity

One of the fundamental unspoken rules in conversation is that conversants should provide no more or less information than the conversation demands. This is known as the maxim of quantity.[72] Voice interfaces are notoriously bad at following this convention. For example, imagine a voice user interface that asks ten yes or no questions. The first question might ask, "Are you female? Please answer yes or no." The second question would then follow, "Are you a U.S. citizen? Please answer yes or no." By the time the third question, "Are you over twenty-one years of age?" is asked, it would be a violation of the maxim of quantity to once again say, "Please answer yes or no." Because voice activates the (social) human-computer relationship, users would interpret a third request to "Please answer yes or no" in one of two ways: either "The system does not care enough about me to think about what it is asking," or "The system is trying to make me feel stupid," even if they also viewed the interface as "machinelike."

The problem of too much quantity also often occurs when porting a graphical user interface from the Web or a PC to voice. Because voices are very different than text,[73] large menus are extremely difficult to maneuver through in voice. The traditional strategy has been to create multiple levels of hierarchy to avoid an overwhelming number of options. For example, a repair system may have to deal with four types of televisions, VCRs, and stereos each. To avoid listing twelve options at once, the system can say, "Do you need help with your TV, VCR, or stereo?" If the user says "stereo," the system can then say, "Which model of stereo: the 200, the 300, the 400, or the 500?" On the other hand, if the hierarchy is created arbitrarily simply to reduce the number of options that are presented at any one time, these groupings increase cognitive load and user errors. The better alternative is to say a small number of options, no more than seven,[74] with the last option being "Something else." If only a few options represent the majority of requests, the system should not provide even seven possibilities: it should simply state the critical ones and finish with "Other options."

Sometimes, designers cannot gauge, before the interaction begins, how much information is appropriate. *Barge-in* is a technique for solving the overspeaking problem. Under barge-in, users may speak at any time, which causes the system to stop speaking and begin to interpret their utterances. Allowing users to speak as soon as they know what to say allows the interaction to move along quickly and leads users to feel that the system is cooperating by not saying more than necessary. In car contexts, barge-in is not effective because of the noisy environment. *Push-to-talk* addresses this constraint: when the user pushes a button, the system stops speaking and listens to the user. If users barge in a great deal, the system should assume that it is saying too much: solutions include curtailing the lists of options and shortening utterances.

Too little quantity can also be a problem in voice interfaces. For example, systems sometimes fail to describe the options in enough detail for users to know what they should say. For example, if a computer repair company's interface says, "Please indicate whether you have a problem with your motherboard or not," many users might think, "If I knew what a motherboard was, I probably wouldn't have to call you!" When users simply pick an option in desperation, the call center incurs high expenses as an expert, paid to work on a problem within her or his scope of expertise, must explain to users that they have the wrong person.

Another example of an underuse of quantity is the simple question, "How can I help you?" Questions like this provide too little information unless the system has a recognition capacity that is sufficient to accept virtually any utterance. The alternative need not be as crude as "Please say one of these three options: A, B, or C." Instead, the user can be asked, "Do you need help with A, B, or C?"

Relevance

Relevance is a second maxim requirement for successful conversation. Conversants are expected to make comments and ask questions that advance the conversation.[75] Users become frustrated when they cannot figure out why voice interfaces request information before it seems relevant. For example, credit-card information should be requested only when the transaction is completed, much as in a bricks-and-mortar interaction: early requests seem like bullying by or nosiness of the system.

Relevance should not be interpreted strictly as "task specificity." As noted earlier, humor,[76] an occasional flattering remark ("You have shown excellent judgment in your selections"),[77] and polite comments (such as "Thank you")[78] are not directly relevant to the task, but they support the social expectations activated by all voice interfaces and so are "relevant" to making users feel more comfortable.

Just as text-based designers have discovered the value of hiding infrequently used menu options, the best voice-interface systems should adapt to their users by detecting the most commonly used options of individuals and bringing them to the front of the menus. Although highly experienced users can simply barge in before any of the options are stated, users who want a quick reminder will greatly appreciate that options are thoughtfully presented. The user should not be constantly reminded that the system is recording their responses (in order to adapt) because this would make the user feel uncomfortable.[79]

Clarity

Clarity, the final conversational maxim, is greatly facilitated when the designer conforms with the domain knowledge of users by establishing "common ground."[80] This goes beyond the user's knowledge of how to use the interface to include the frequently more important question of how the system should provide answers. For example, consider a voice interface that allows customers to configure and buy computers. For a novice user, stating that "This will make graphics appear more rapidly on your screen" is probably the right level of complexity. Conversely, this is not the right level of clarity for an expert user, who might wonder, "Is this happening on the motherboard, the graphics card, or the accelerator board? Is it leveraging RAM or processing power?," and so on.

The principle of clarity states that a speaker must adopt words and concepts that the listener can understand. Hence, both permitting users to specify their expertise and adapting to users by monitoring their use of the interface and the questions they ask can be very effective strategies to maintain clarity.

When questioning and monitoring are not possible, an understanding of a typical user's background can be sufficient. For example, a site that sells do-it-yourself items can assume that users have a greater knowledge of tools than can a site that sells prebuilt goods.

Conversation as Cooperation

Conversing is more than spewing words at one another in turn: it is an agreement between participants to work toward mutual understanding. Partners in conversation must make a concerted effort to speak understandably, to listen with attention and sensitivity,[81] and to respond appropriately to what the other conversant is saying and thinking.[82] Humans are not simply wired to be talkers and listeners; they are members of a cooperative species[83] that is built to integrate talking and listening into a smooth, joint interaction, much like a ballroom dance.[84]

When things go wrong, cooperation can fall apart, or partners can work together to overcome the problem as a team. Blaming your partner for mistakes—or even attempting to avoid the placement of blame altogether—can have disastrous consequences. An awareness of conversational principles can thus help systems to minimize errors and deliver the most effective responses to errors.

15 Conclusion: From *Listening to* and *Talking at* to *Speaking with*

Speaking is intrinsically social. Whether it comes from a person or a machine, speech activates a powerful and varied cognitive apparatus that is designed to express and recognize who a person is and what she or he is thinking and feeling. Although people have separate parts of the brain that are devoted to each social judgment and each aspect of speech production and understanding, people do not have separate parts of the brain for human speech and technology-generated speech. Even when voice interfaces exhibit all of the limitations associated with machines—including bizarre pronunciations, emotional ignorance, and chronic inconsistencies—they are not exempted from the social expectations that are activated by talking and listening. When technologies, regardless of quality, fail to conform to social norms, users experience confusion, frustration, and cognitive exhaustion and question the competence, utility, and enjoyability of the system. Socially inept interfaces suffer the same fate as socially inept individuals: they are ineffective, criticized, and shunned.[1]

Fortunately, careful design that is grounded in the social and cognitive sciences can dramatically improve a voice interface's social success. An understanding of the wiring of the human brain can enable voice interfaces to be as compelling, competent, and supportive as the most successful friends, teachers, and salespeople. For example, creating a feeling of similarity between the user and the interface through matching gender, personality, or accent fosters feelings of liking and trust, two fundamental ingredients for cooperation and success. At the same time, interfaces should present a consistent social "face" to users: voices that talk, behave, and look like they sound are much more desirable, intelligent, and comfortable interaction partners.

Sensitivity to the emotional aspects of social life is also critical for both people and speaking technologies, as emotion influences every perception and conclusion that the human brain makes. Although voice interfaces cannot truly experience emotion, a voice that appropriately matches the emotional state of the user and the emotional tone of what it says communicates empathy, support, and sincerity. Conversely, voice interfaces that fail to express the appropriate emotion risk being labeled uncooperative, cognitively burdensome, or hypocritical.

The brain is wired to treat each voice in an interface as a separate individual, even when the person knows that the same technology is producing all of the voices. Thus, multiple voices enable designers to create a rich social landscape that can facilitate communication through the creation of community or overwhelm users through the complexity of too many interpersonal relationships.

Social rules also dictate that an interface should not be a "show off." This principle discourages the mix of nonhuman and human interface characteristics. It also suggests that interfaces do better when they speak uniformly in synthetic speech, even if the speech is of poor quality, rather than shifting back and forth between synthetic and higher-quality recorded speech.

Through thoughtful consideration of social factors, voice interfaces can even overcome situations that are highly stressful. The right microphone selection can limit speakers' feeling of being monitored, thereby enabling people to be more relaxed, creative, and disclosive. Similarly, when things go wrong, the strategic placement of blame can reassure users and improve system-user cooperation.

Successful voice interfaces require more than sophisticated algorithms and advanced hardware. They demand an appreciation of speech as a rich, mutually supportive, and inherently social interaction. When voice interfaces fully leverage how humans are wired for speech, users will not simply talk *at* and listen *to* computers, nor will computers simply talk *at* and listen *to* users. Instead, people and computers will cooperatively *speak with* one another.

Notes

Chapter 1

1. See, e.g., S. Pinker, *The language instinct* (New York: Morrow, 1994).

2. D. I. Slobin, *Psycholinguistics,* 2nd ed. (Glenview, Ill.: Scott, Foresman, 1979).

3. One can compare N. Chomsky, *Language and mind* (New York: Harcourt, Brace, & World, 1968), and Pinker, *The language instinct*, to C. Holden, How the brain understands music, *Science* 292 (2001): 623, and D. W. Massaro, *Perceiving talking faces: From speech perception to a behavioral principle* (Cambridge, Mass.: MIT Press, 1998).

4. Massaro, *Perceiving talking faces*; Slobin, *Psycholinguistics.*

5. Pinker, *The language instinct.*

6. Slobin, *Psycholinguistics.*

7. Y. S. Sininger and B. Cone-Wesson, Asymmetric cochlear processing mimics hemispheric specialization, *Science* 305, no. 5960 (2000): 1581.

8. C. Moon, P. Cooper, and W. P. Fifer, Two-day-olds prefer their native language, *Infant Behavior and Development* 16 (1993): 495–500. R. Naatanen, The perception of speech sounds by the human brain as reflected by the mismatch negativity (MMN) and its magnetic equivalent (MMNm), *Psychophysiology* 38 (2001): 1–21; Pinker, *The language instinct.*

9. M. Pena, A. Maki, D. Kovacic, G. Dehaene-Lambertz, H. Koizumi, F. Bouquet, and J. Mehler, Sounds and silence: An optical topography study of language recognition at birth, *Proceedings of the National Academy of Sciences*, 100 (2003): 11702–11705.

10. Slobin, *Psycholinguistics.*

11. Although the psychological literature frequently fails to distinguish between an "addressee" (a person to whom a comment is directed) and a "listener" (anyone who can hear the comment), there are important psychological differences between the two. H. H. Clark, *Using language* (New York: Cambridge University Press, 1996). Because the listeners who are discussed in this book are

addressees of the interface, no confusion should arise. The term *listener* was chosen because it is more commonplace and more euphonious.

12. C. Nass and L. Gong, Social aspects of speech interfaces from an evolutionary perspective: Experimental research and design implications, *Communications of the ACM* 43, no. 9 (2000): 36–43; S. Romaine, *Language in society: An introduction to sociolinguistics* (New York: Oxford University Press, 2000); R. Wardhaugh, *An introduction to sociolinguistics*, 3rd ed. (Malden, Mass.: Blackwell, 1998).

13. See, e.g., R. Dunbar, *Grooming, gossip, and the evolution of language* (Cambridge, Mass.: Harvard University Press, 1997).

14. There is significant disagreement in the literature concering when to use the term "gender" and when to use the term "sex." J. Roughgarden, *Evolution's rainbow: Diversity, gender, and sexuality in nature and people* (Berkeley, CA: University of California Press, 2004). To avoid confusion, we have opted to consistently use the word "gender."

15. J. W. Mullennix, K. Johnson, M. Topcu-Durgun, and L. W. Farnsworth, The perceptual representation of voice gender, *Journal of the Acoustical Society of America* 98, no. 6 (1995): 3080–3095. See chapters 2 and 3 for more information.

16. H. Giles, K. Henwood, N. Coupland, and J. Harriman, Language attitudes and cognitive mediation, *Human Communication Research* 18, no. 4 (1992): 500–527; T. Holtgraves, *Language as social action: Social psychology and language* (Mahwah, N.J.: Erlbaum, 2002); E. A. Strand, *Gender stereotype effects on speech processing*, unpublished doctoral dissertation, Ohio State University, Columbus, Ohio, 2001. See chapters 2 and 3 for more information; E. A. Strand, Uncovering the role of gender stereotypes in speech perception, *Journal of Language and Social Psychology* 18, no. 1 (1999): 86–99; D. Tannen, *Gender and discourse* (New York: Oxford University Press, 1996); D. Tannen, *You just don't understand: Men and women in conversation* (New York: Ballantine, 1990); P. Trudgill, *Sociolinguistics: An introduction to language and society* (London: Penguin Books, 2000).

17. C. D. Aronovitch, The voice of personality: Stereotyped judgments and their relation to voice quality and sex of speaker, *Journal of Social Psychology* 99 (1976): 207–220; D. B. Buller and J. K. Burgoon, The effects of vocalics and nonverbal sensitivity on compliance: A replication and extension, *Human Communication Research* 14 (1986): 548–568; K. J. Tusing and J. P. Dillard, The sounds of dominance: Vocal precursors of perceived dominance during interpersonal influence, *Human Communication Research* 26, no. 1 (2000): 148–171. See chapter 4 for more information.

18. G. Ball and J. Breese, Emotion and personality in conversational agents, in J. Cassell, J. Sullivan, S. Prevost, and E. Churchill, eds., *Embodied conversational agents* (Cambridge, Mass.: MIT Press, 2000), pp. 189–219; S. Brave and C. Nass, Emotion in human-computer interaction, in J. Jacko and A. Sears, eds., *Handbook of human-computer interaction* (New York: Erlbaum, 2002), pp. 251–271; K. R. Scherer, Speech and emotional states, in J. K. Darby, ed., *Speech evaluation in psychiatry* (New York: Grune and Stratton, 1981), pp. 189–220. See chapter 8 for more information.

19. M. Kaplan, New York City: Capital of the world, *CIO Magazine*, November 1, 2000.

20. D. R. Van Lancker and J. Kreiman, Voice discrimination and recognition are separate abilities, *Neuropsychologia* 25, no. 5 (1987): 829–834. See chapter 9 for more information.

21. J. Kess, *Psycholinguistics: Psychology, linguistics and the study of natural language* (Philadelphia: Benjamin, 1992); B. S. Kisilevsky, S. M. J. Hains, K. Lee, Xie, X., H. Huang, H. H. Ye, et al., Effects of experience on fetal voice recognition, *Psychological Science* 14, no. 3 (2003): 220–224.

22. A. J. deCasper and W. P. Fifer, Of human bonding: Newborns prefer their mothers' voices, *Science* 208 (1980): 174–1176.

23. C. Floccia, T. Nazzi, and J. Bertoncini, Unfamiliar voice discrimination for short stimuli in newborns, *Developmental Science* 3, no. 3 (2000): 333–343.

24. E. C. Cherry, Some experiments on the recognition of speech, with one and with two ears, *Journal of the Acoustical Society of America* 25 (1953): 975–979; R. S. Newman and P. W. Jusczyk, The cocktail party effect in infants, *Perception and Psychophysics* 58, no. 8 (1996): 1145–1156.

25. G. Lakoff and M. Johnson, *Metaphors we live by* (Chicago: University of Chicago Press, 1983). See chapter 10 for more information.

26. See chapter 14 for an extended discussion of this point.

27. C. Nass and K. M. Lee, Does computer-synthesized speech manifest personality? Experimental tests of recognition, similarity-attraction, and consistency-attraction, *Journal of Experimental Psychology: Applied* 7, no. 3 (2001): 171–181. Also see, e.g., chapters 3, 5, and 8 for more information.

28. See chapter 5 for more details.

29. Holtgraves, *Language as social action*; Nass and Gong, Social aspects of speech interfaces from an evolutionary perspective.

30. Lakoff and Johnson, *Metaphors we live by*; Pinker, *The language instinct*; G. A. Miller and P. M. Gildea, How children learn words, *Scientific American* 257, no. 3 (1987): 94–99.

31. R. W. Gibbs and T. Matlock, Psycholinguistics and mental representations, *Cognitive Linguistics* 10, no. 3 (1999): 263–269.

32. J. Edwards, Refining our understanding of language attitudes, *Journal of Language and Social Psychology* 18, no. 1 (1999): 101–110; H. Hörmann, *Psycholinguistics: An introduction to theory and research* (New York: Springer, 1971); T. Parsons, *The evolution of societies* (Englewood Cliffs, N.J.: Prentice-Hall, 1970).

33. D. Goleman, *Emotional intelligence: Why it can matter more than IQ* (New York: Bantam Books, 1995).

34. Holtgraves, *Language as social action*; Hörmann, *Psycholinguistics*; Mullennix, Johnson, Topcu-Durgun, and Farnsworth, The perceptual representation of voice gender; Nass and Gong, Social aspects of speech interfaces from an evolutionary perspective.

35. B. Shneiderman and C. Plaisant, *Designing the user interface*, 4th ed. (Reading, Mass.: Addison-Wesley, 2003).

36. M. Weiser, The computer for the twenty-first century, *Scientific American* 265, no. 3 (1991): 94–104.

37. This approach was pioneered by Nass and colleagues. C. Nass and Y. Moon, Machines and mindlessness: Social responses to computers, *Journal of Social Issues* 56, no. 1 (2001): 81–103; C. Nass, Y. Moon, and P. Carney, Are people polite to computers? Responses to computer-based interviewing systems, *Journal of Applied Social Psychology* 29, no. 5 (1999): 1093–1110; C. Nass and J. Steuer, Voices, boxes, and sources of messages: Computers and social actors, *Human Communication Research* 19, no. 4 (1993): 504–527; B. Reeves and C. Nass, *The media equation: How people treat computers, television, and new media like real people and places* (New York: Cambridge University Press, 1996).

38. D. Byrne and D. Nelson, Attraction as a linear function of proportion of positive reinforcements, *Journal of Personality and Social Psychology Bulletin* 4 (1965): 240–243; C. Nass, Y. Moon, B. J. Fogg, B. Reeves, and D. C. Dryer, Can computer personalities be human personalities? *International Journal of Human-Computer Studies* 43, no. 2 (1995): 223–239.

39. D. J. Kiesler, The 1982 interpersonal circle: A taxonomy for complementarity in human transactions, *Psychological Review* 90 (1983): 185–214.

40. See chapters 4 and 5.

41. B. L. Brown, H. Giles, and J. N. Thakerar, Speaker evaluations as a function of speech rate, accent, and context, *Language and Communication* 5, no. 3 (1985): 207–220; H. Giles, Ethnocentrism and the evaluation of accented speech, *British Journal of Social and Clinical Psychology* 10 (1971): 187–188; R. Lippi-Green, *English with an accent: Language, ideology, and discrimination in the United States* (London: Routledge, 1997); M. J. Munro and T. M. Derwing, Processing time, accent, and comprehensibility in the perception of native and foreign-accented speech, *Language and Speech* 38, no. 3 (1995): 289–306.

Chapter 2

1. This question is reminiscent of Kuhn and McPartland's twenty-questions test, which simply asks "Who am I?" followed by twenty blank lines. M. H. Kuhn and T. S. McPartland, An empirical investigation of self-attitudes, *American Sociological Review* 19 (1954): 68–76.

2. C. Shannon and W. Weaver, *The mathematical theory of communication* (Urbana: University of Illinois Press, 1962).

3. A. E. Beall and R. J. Sternberg, *The psychology of gender* (New York: Guilford Press, 1993); J. P. Butler, *Gender trouble (tenth anniversary edition)* (New York: Routledge, 1999); M. Foucault, *The history of sexuality: an introduction* (London: Vintage, 1990); C. Gilligan, *In a different voice: Psychological theory and women's development* (Cambridge, Mass.: Harvard University Press, 1993); J. A. Howard and J. A. Hollander, *Gendered situations, gendered selves: A gender lens on social psy-*

chology (Lanham, Md.: Rowman & Littlefield, 1996); R. C. Monk, *Taking sides: Clashing views on controversial issues in sex and gender*, 4th ed. (New York: McGraw-Hill, 2001); C. M. Renzetti and D. J. Curran, *Women, men, and society*, 5th ed. (Upper Saddle River, N.J.: Pearson, Allyn & Bacon, 2002); W. S. Rogers and R. S. Rogers, *The psychology of gender and sexuality*. (Maidenhead, UK: Open University Press, 2001); D. Tannen, *You just don't understand: Men and women in conversation* (New York: Ballantine, 1990).

4. C. L. Martin and D. N. Ruble, Children's search for gender cues: Cognitive perspectives on gender development, *Current Directions in Psychological Science* 13, no. 2 (2004): 67–70.

5. J. Coates and D. Cameron, eds., *Women in their speech communities* (London: Longman, 1989); E. Durkheim, *The division of labor in society*, trans. G. Simpson (New York: Free Press, 1947).

6. E. E. Maccoby, *The two sexes: Growing up apart, coming together* (Cambridge, Mass.: Harvard University Press, 1998); Martin and Ruble, Children's search for gender cues.

7. Beall and Sternberg, *The psychology of gender*; Butler, *Gender trouble*; Foucault, *The history of sexuality*; Renzetti and Curran, *Women, men, and society*; Gilligan, *In a different voice*; Howard and Hollander, *Gendered situations, gendered selves*; Monk, *Taking sides*; Rogers and Rogers, *The psychology of gender and sexuality*; Tannen, *You just don't understand*.

8. H. Giles, K. Henwood, N. Coupland, and J. Harriman, Language attitudes and cognitive mediation, *Human Communication Research* 18, no. 4 (1992): 500–527; E. A. Strand, *Gender stereotype effects on speech processing*, unpublished doctoral dissertation, Ohio State University, Columbus, 2001; Tannen, *You just don't understand*.

9. S. Turkle, *The second self: Computers and the human spirit* (New York: Simon & Schuster, 1984).

10. D. I. Slobin, *Psycholinguistics*, 2nd ed. (Glenview, Ill.: Scott, Foresman, 1979); P. M. Smith, Sex markers in speech, in K. R. Scherer and H. Giles, eds., *Social markers in speech* (New York: Cambridge University Press, 1979), pp. 109–146.

11. Martin and Ruble, Children's search for gender cues; C. L. Miller, Developmental changes in male/female classification by infants, *Infant Behavior and Development* 6 (1983): 313–330; C. L. Miller, B. A. Younger, and P. A. Morse, The categorization of male and female voices in infancy, *Infant behavior and development* 5 (1982): 143–159.

12. Martin and Ruble, Children's search for gender clues.

13. R. O. Coleman, A comparison of the contributions of two voice quality characteristics to the perception of maleness and femaleness in the voice, *Journal of Speech and Hearing Research* 19 (1976): 168–180; D. Gunzburger, A. Bresser, and M. T. Keurs, Voice identification of prepubertal boys and girls by normally sighted and visually handicapped subjects, *Language and Speech* 30 (1987): 47–58; T. L. Perry, R. N. Ohde, and D. H. Ashmead, The acoustic bases for gender identification from children's voices, *Journal of the Acoustical Society of America* 109, no. 6 (2001): 2988–2998; B. Reeves and C. Nass, *The media equation: How people treat computers, television, and new media like real people and places* (New York: Cambridge University Press, 1996).

14. Females do, in fact, have higher pitch on average than males. Perry, Ohde, and Ashmead, The acoustic bases for gender identification from children's voices; Slobin, *Psycholinguistics*; Smith, Sex markers in speech.

15. These other factors include breathiness and formant frequency (a characteristic of the resonance of a voice). D. H. Klatt and D. C. Klatt, Analysis, synthesis, and perception of voice-quality variations among female and male talkers, *Journal of the Acoustical Society of America* 87 (1990): 820–857; Perry, Ohde, and Ashmead, The acoustic bases for gender identification from children's voices.

16. D. Drayna, A. Manichaikul, M. Lange, H. Sneider, and T. Spector, Genetic correlates of musical pitch recognition in humans. *Science* 291 (2001): 1969–1972.

17. S. Singh and T. Murry, Multidimensional classification of normal voice qualities, *Journal of the Acoustical Society of America* 64 (1978): 81–87.

18. Singh and Murry, Multidimensional classification of normal voice qualities; Smith, Sex markers in speech.

19. Smith, Sex markers in speech.

20. J. Gray, *Men are from Mars, women are from Venus: A practical guide for improving communication and getting what you want in your relationships* (New York: HarperCollins, 1993); Tannen, *You just don't understand.*

21. H. Tajfel, *Differentiation between social groups: Studies in the social psychology of intergroup relations* (London: Academic Press, 1978); H. Tajfel, *Human groups and social categories: Studies in social psychology* (Cambridge: Cambridge University Press, 1981); H. Tajfel, ed., *Social identity and intergroup behavior* (Cambridge: Cambridge University Press, 1982); H. Tajfel and J. C. Turner, *The social identity of intergroup relations*, 2nd ed. (Chicago: Nelson-Hall, 1986).

22. D. N. Ruble, J. Alvarez, M. H. Bachman, J. Cameron, A. Fuligni, C. Cargia-Coll, et al., The development and implications of children's social self or the "we," in M. Bennett and F. Sani, eds., *The development of the social self* (East Sussex, UK: Psychological Press, 2004); Tajfel, *Differentiation between social groups*; Tajfel, *Human groups and social categories*; Tajfel, *Social identity and intergroup behavior*; Tajfel and Turner, *The social identity of intergroup relations.*

23. H. Tajfel, Social identity and intergroup behavior. *Social Science Information/Sur les Sciences Social* 13, no. 2 (1974): 65–93.

24. N. Cantor and W. Mischel, Prototypes in person perception, *Advances in Experimental Social Psychology* 12 (1979): 3–52; S. T. Fiske and S. E. Taylor, *Social cognition* (New York: McGraw-Hill, 1991); Reeves and Nass, *The media equation.*

25. H. H. Kelley, Attribution theory in social psychology, in D. Levine, ed., *Nebraska symposium on motivation* (vol. 15) (Lincoln: University of Nebraska Press, 1967), pp. 192–240; H. H. Kelley, The processes of causal attribution, *American Psychologist* 28 (1973): 107–128; L. Z. McArthur, The how and what of why: Some determinants and consequences of causal attribution, *Journal of Personality and Social Psychology* 22 (1972): 171–193.

26. A. Newell, *Unified theories of cognition* (Cambridge, Mass.: Harvard University Press, 1990); H. A. Simon, *Sciences of the artificial*, 3rd ed. (Cambridge, Mass.: MIT Press, 1996).

27. E. Durkheim, *The division of labor in society*, trans. G. Simpson (New York: Free Press, 1947); E. Durkheim, *Elementary forms of the religious life*, trans. K. Fields (New York: Free Press, 1995).

28. Durkheim, *Elementary forms of the religious life*.

29. B. Monin, The warm glow heuristic: When liking leads to familiarity, *Journal of Personality and Social Psychology* 85, no. 6 (2003): 1035–1048; A. M. Colman, W. M. Best, and A. J. Austen, Familiarity and liking: Direct tests of the preference-feedback hypothesis, *Psychological Reports* 58, no. 3 (1986): 931–938; Fiske and Taylor, *Social cognition*; K. W. Kerber and R. Singleton, Trait and situational attributions in a naturalistic setting: Familiarity, liking, and attribution validity, *Journal of Personality* 52, no. 3 (1984): 205–219.

30. R. Dawkins, *The selfish gene*, 2nd ed. (Oxford: Oxford University Press, 1989).

31. Ruble, Alvarez, Bachman, Cameron, Fuligni, Cargia-Coll, et al., The development and implications of children's social self or the "we."

32. Maccoby, *The two sexes*.

33. J. P. Olive, The talking computer: Text to speech synthesis, in D. Stork, ed., *HAL's legacy: 2001's computer as dream and reality* (Cambridge, Mass.: MIT Press, 1997), pp. 101–130.

34. While word intelligibility scores for the best text-to-speech systems are close to 97 percent, approaching that of real human speech, even the best TTS systems do not match the quality and prosody of natural human speech. C. Kamm, M. Walker, and L. Rabiner, The role of speech processing in human-computer intelligent communication, Paper presented at the National Science Foundation Workshop on human-centered systems: Information, interactivity, and intelligence, 1997.

35. See chapter 1 for an extended discussion.

36. Slobin, *Psycholinguistics*.

37. H. P. Grice, Logic and conversation, in P. Cole and J. Morgan, eds., *Syntax and semantics* (vol. 3) (New York: Academic Press, 1975), pp. 41–58; H. P. Grice, Meaning, in P. F. Strawson, ed., *Philosophical logic* (Oxford: Oxford University Press, 1967), pp. 39–48.

38. This study is described in more detail in E.-J. Lee, C. Nass, and S. Brave, *Can computer-generated speech have gender? An experimental test of gender stereotypes*, paper presented at CHI 2000, the International Conference of the Association for Computing Machinery's (ACM) Special-Interest Group (SIG) on Computer-Human Interaction (CHI). The Hague, The Netherlands, 2000.

39. N. Kogan and M. A. Wallach, *Risk taking: A study in cognition and personality* (New York: Holt, Rinehart, and Winston, 1964).

40. Scales that range from "Definitely choose A" to "Definitely choose B" can be treated as Likert scales that can be averaged and analyzed using standard techniques. Two-choice A or B options

can also be averaged and analyzed using standard techniques. J. H. Watt and S. van den Berg, *Research methods for communication science* (Upper Saddle River, N.J.: Pearson, Allyn, & Bacon, 1995).

41. The voices were created by the Festival engine of the CSLU Toolkit. Center for Spoken Language Understanding, *CSLU Toolkit*, retrieved from <http://www.cslu.ogi.edu/toolkit/> (2004). The female voice was (F0 = 220 Hz; "tll" or "mwm2tll"). The male voice was (F0 = 115 Hz; "mwm" or "mwm2jph").

42. World Wide Web Consortium, *Cascading style sheets, level 2*, retrieved from <http://www.w3.org/TR/REC-CSS2/aural.html> (1998).

43. See chapters 4 through 8.

44. This is part of the reasoning behind the Solomon four-group design, which controls for the effects of a pretest. R. Rosenthal and R. L. Rosnow, eds., *Essentials of behavioral research: Methods and data analysis*, 2nd ed. (New York: McGraw-Hill, 1991); V. L. Willson and R. R. Putnam, A meta-analysis of pretest sensitization effects in experimental design, *American Educational Research Journal* 19 (1982): 249–258.

45. Kogan and Wallach, *Risk taking*; B. Reeves and S. Geiger, Designing experiments that assess psychological responses to media messages, in A. Lang, ed., *Measuring psychological responses to media messages* (Hillsdale, N.J.: Lawrence Erlbaum, 1994).

46. The questionnaire was organized around the question "How well do each of the following adjectives describes the voice you heard?" followed by a list of adjectives listed on ten-point scales ranging from "Describes very poorly" to "Describes very well."

47. Trustworthiness was an index of *trustworthy* and *reliable* (Cronbach's $\alpha = .68$).

48. Likeability was an index of *likable*, *pleasant*, and *friendly* ($\alpha = .86$).

49. Masculinity or femininity is an index of *masculine* and *feminine* (reverse-coded) ($\alpha = .96$).

50. The results table is presented below. The statistical analyses were based on a 2 (gender of voice) by 2 (gender of participant) between-participants ANOVA.

	Female Voice		Male Voice	
Dependent Variables	Females	Males	Females	Males
Masculinity or femininity of voice	2.08 (0.97)	2.54 (2.25)	8.67 (1.13)	8.83 (0.98)
Liking	5.31 (2.02)	3.00 (1.53)	4.25 (1.76)	4.56 (1.32)
Trustworthiness of voice	6.13 (1.40)	3.96 (1.30)	5.63 (1.4)	5.75 (1.18)
Conformity	4.40 (0.48)	3.61 (0.71)	4.84 (0.75)	5.29 (0.33)

Note: Standard deviations are in parentheses.

51. $F(1,44) = 239.2$, $p < .001$. There were no effects for participant gender and no interaction.

52. There was a significant crossover interaction with respect to conformity, such that participants conformed more when the voice's gender matched their own, $F(1,44) = 13.2$, $p < .001$. There was no main effect for participant gender.

53. There was a significant crossover interaction with respect to trustworthiness, such that participants perceived the voice to be more trustworthy when the voice's gender matched their own, $F(1,44) = 7.38$, $p < .01$. There was no main effect for participant gender.

54. There was a significant crossover interaction for liking, $F(1,44) = 6.6$, $p < .01$. There were no main effects.

55. All of the women in the audience nodded at the comment, while the men appeared surprised that such a thing could happen.

56. People conformed much more with the male voice than the female voice, $F(1,44) = 38.4$, $p < .001$. There was no main effect for participant gender.

57. Listeners also found the male voice to be more trustworthy, $F(1,44) = 3.58$, $p < .06$. Females found the voices to be more trustworthy overall than did males, $F(1,44) = 8.1$, $p < .01$.

58. C. West and D. H. Zimmerman, Doing gender, *Gender and Society* 1, no. 2 (1987): 125–151. Also see chapter 3.

59. See chapters 4 and 5.

60. S. L. Bem, *The lenses of gender: Transforming the debate on sexual inequality* (New Haven: Yale University Press, 1973); S. L. Bem, The measure of psychological androgyny, *Journal of Consulting and Clinical Psychology* 42, no. 2 (1974): 155–162.

61. C. Nass, Y. Moon, B. J. Fogg, B. Reeves, and D. C. Dryer, Can computer personalities be human personalities?, *International Journal of Human-Computer Studies* 43, no. 2 (1995): 223–239.

62. Reeves and Nass, *The media equation*; D. Voelker, *The effects of image size and voice volume on the evaluation of represented faces*, unpublished doctoral dissertation, Stanford University, Stanford, Calif., 1994.

63. Coleman, A comparison of the contributions of two voice quality characteristics to the perception of maleness and femaleness in the voice; R. O. Coleman, Male and female voice quality and its relationship to vowel formant frequencies, *Journal of Speech and Hearing Research* 14 (1971): 565–577; Gunzburger, Bresser, and Keurs, Voice identification of prepubertal boys and girls by normally sighted and visually handicapped subjects.

64. The Necker cube is described in R. Shepard, *Mind sights: Original visual illusions, ambiguities, and other anomalies, with a commentary on the play of mind in perception and art* (New York: Freeman, 1990).

65. Cantor and Mischel, Prototypes in person perception; Fiske and Taylor, *Social cognition*; Reeves and Nass, *The media equation*.

66. Cantor and Mischel, Prototypes in person perception; N. Cantor and W. Mischel, Prototypicality and personality: Effects on free recall and personality impressions, *Journal of Research in Personality* 13 (1979): 187–205; L. Gong, *The psychology of consistency in human-computer interaction*, unpublished doctoral dissertation, Stanford University, Stanford, Calif., 2000; Reeves and Nass, *The media equation*.

Chapter 3

1. L. A. Kohlberg, *Child psychology and childhood education: A cognitive developmental view*. Essex, UK: Longman Group, 1987); L. A. Kohlberg, A cognitive-developmental analysis of children's sex role concepts and attitudes, in E. E. Maccoby, ed., *The development of sex differences* (Stanford, Calif.: Stanford University Press, 1966), pp. 82–173; C. L. Martin and D. N. Ruble, Children's search for gender cues: Cognitive perspectives on gender development, *Current Directions in Psychological Science* 13, no. 2 (2004): 67–70.

2. Martin and Ruble, Children's search for gender cues.

3. Martin and Ruble, Children's search for gender cues.

4. Martin and Ruble, Children's search for gender cues; D. N. Ruble, J. Alvarez, M. H. Bachman, J. Cameron, A. Fuligni, C. Cargia-Coll, et al., The development and implications of children's social self or the "we," in M. Bennett and F. Sani, eds., *The development of the social self* (East Sussex, UK: Psychological Press, 2004).

5. Martin and Ruble, Children's search for gender cues.

6. Martin and Ruble, Children's search for gender cues.

7. M. R. Bradbard, C. L. Martin, R. C. Endsley, and C. F. Halverson, Influence of sex stereotypes on children's exploration and memory: A competence versus performance distinction, *Developmental Psychology* 22 (1986): 481–486; Martin and Ruble, Children's search for gender cues.

8. Bradbard, Martin, Endsley, and Halverson, Influence of sex stereotypes on children's exploration and memory; Martin and Ruble, Children's search for gender cues.

9. Martin and Ruble, Children's search for gender cues.

10. J. Gray, *Men are from Mars, women are from Venus: A practical guide for improving communication and getting what you want in your relationships* (New York: HarperCollins, 1993); D. Tannen, *You just don't understand: Men and women in conversation* (New York: Ballantine, 1990).

11. Tannen, *You just don't understand*.

12. Gray, *Men are from Mars, women are from Venus*.

13. American Film Institute, *AFI's 100 years . . . 100 movies*, retrieved from <http://www.afi.com/tvevents/100years/movies.aspx>, 2004.

14. N. Costrich, J. Feinstein, L. Kidder, J. Maracek, and L. Pascale, When stereotypes hurt: Three studies of penalties in sex-role reversals, *Journal of Experimental Social Psychology* 11 (1975): 520–530; C. J. Deutsch and L. A. Gilbert, Sex role stereotypes: Effect on perceptions of self and others and on personal adjustment, *Journal of Counseling Psychology* 23 (1976): 373–379; A. H. Eagly and W. Wood, Inferred sex differences in status as a determinant of gender stereotypes about social influence, *Journal of Personality and Social Psychology* 43 (1982): 915–928; P. A. Goldberg, Are women prejudiced against women?, *Trans-Action* 5 (1986): 28–80; J. Robinson and L. Z. McArthur, Impact of salient vocal qualities on causal attribution for a speaker's behavior, *Journal of Personality and Social Psychology* 43 (1982): 236–247; J. T. R. Spence, R. Helmreich, and J. Stapp, The Personal Attributes Questionnaire: A measure of sex-role stereotypes and masculinity-femininity, *JSAS Catalog of Selected Documents in Psychology* 4 (1974): 43.

15. A. Newell and H. A. Simon, *Human problem solving* (Englewood Cliffs, N.J.: Prentice-Hall, 1972).

16. C. Shannon and W. Weaver, *The mathematical theory of communication* (Urbana: University of Illinois Press, 1962).

17. Eagly and Wood, Inferred sex differences in status as a determinant of gender stereotypes about social influence; Robinson and McArthur, Impact of salient vocal qualities on causal attribution for a speaker's behavior.

18. See chapter 2.

19. For a discussion of experimental design considerations, see D. C. Montgomery, *Design and analysis of experiments,* 5th ed. (New York: Wiley, 2000).

20. For a discussion of experimental design considerations and a discussion of the advantages and disadvantages of within-participants designs, see Montgomery, *Design and analysis of experiments.*

21. L. H. Collings, J. C. Chrisler, and K. Quina, eds., *Career strategies for women in academe: Arming Athena* (Thousand Oaks, Calif.: Sage, 1998); P. M. Fandt and G. E. Stevens, Evaluation bias in the business classroom: Evidence relating to the effects of previous experiences, *Journal of Psychology* 125, no. 4 (1991): 469–477.

22. This study used NeXT computers, which were solid black cubes with black rectangular monitors. For advice on dress for female professors, see Collings, Chrisler, and Quina, *Career strategies for women in academe.*

23. This experiment is described in more detail in C. Nass, Y. Moon, and N. Green, Are computers gender-neutral? Gender-stereotypic responses to computers with voices, *Journal of Applied Social Psychology* 27, no. 10 (1997): 864–876.

24. Collings, Chrisler, and Quina, *Career strategies for women in academe.*

25. Collings, Chrisler, and Quina, *Career strategies for women in academe.*

26. J. St. Pierre, *Student evaluation of a teacher's use of student-disparaging versus self-disparaging humor,* unpublished doctoral dissertation, University of Alabama, Tuscaloosa, 2001.

27. J. Holmes, Paying compliments: A sex-preferential positive politeness strategy, *Journal of Pragmatics,* 12, no. 3 (1988): 445–465.

28. Collings, Chrisler, and Quina, *Career strategies for women in academe.*

29. Collings, Chrisler, and Quina, *Career strategies for women in academe;* Nass, Moon, and Green, Are computers gender-neutral?; N. Romer and D. Cherry, Ethnic and social class differences in children's sex-role concepts. *Sex Roles* 6 (1980): 246–263; T. L. Ruble, Sex stereotypes: Issues of change in the 1970s, *Sex Roles* 9 (1983): 397–402; Spence, Helmreich, and Stapp, The Personal Attributes Questionnaire.

30. Collings, Chrisler, and Quina, *Career strategies for women in academe;* M. E. Heilman, High school students' occupational interest as a function of projected sex ratios in male-dominated occupations, *Journal of Applied Psychology* 64 (1979): 275–279.

31. Because there was no hypothesis about the gender of the tester and because it was important to reduce complexity in the experiment, the second computer was not given a voice.

32. If the two computers had the same voice, the issue would have been identity effects rather than gender effects. See chapter 9 and C. Nass and J. Steuer, Voices, boxes, and sources of messages: Computers and social actors, *Human Communication Research* 19, no. 4 (1993): 504–527.

33. All of the items were measures on ten-point Likert scales.

34. Competence of the tutor computer was an index comprised of four items. Three of the items were of the form: "How [adjective] was the tutoring computer?" with the anchors as "Very un[adjective]" (= 1) and "Very [adjective]" (= 10); the three adjectives were *competent, informative,* and *knowledgeable.* The fourth item was "How well did the tutoring computer improve your final score?" with anchors "Not at all" (= 1) and "Very much" (= 10). The index was very reliable for both rounds (Cronbach's $\alpha = .78$)

35. Likeability of the tutor computer was an index comprised of four items of the form: "How [adjective] was the tutoring computer?" with the anchors as "Very un[adjective]" (= 1) and "Very [adjective]" (= 10). The four adjectives were *affectionate, likeable, sympathetic,* and *warm.* The index was very reliable ($\alpha = .82$).

36. Informativeness of the tutor computer was an index comprised of four items. Two of the items were of the form: "How [adjective] was the tutoring computer?" with the anchors as "Very un[adjective]" (= 1) and "Very [adjective]" (= 10); the two adjectives were *helpful* and *sophisticated.* The other items were "How well did the tutoring computer choose facts about [love and relationships/computers]?" with anchors "Very poorly" (= 1) and "Very well" (= 10). The index was reliable for both rounds ($\alpha = .68$ and .60 for the two topics).

37. Likeability of the evaluator computer was an index comprised of four items of the form: "How [adjective] was the evaluator computer?" with the anchors as "Very un[adjective]" (= 1) and "Very [adjective]" (= 10). The four adjectives were *affectionate, likeable, sympathetic,* and *warm.* The index was reliable ($\alpha = .67$).

38. Collings, Chrisler, and Quina, *Career strategies for women in academe*; Robinson and McArthur, Impact of salient vocal qualities on causal attribution for a speaker's behavior. This is similar to the finding in chapter 2 that suggestions from males are taken more seriously than suggestions from females.

39. Here is the results table for the overall evaluations.

Dependent Variable	Male Evaluator	Female Evaluator
Tutor competence	4.92	3.54
Tutor likeability	7.13	6.07
Evaluator likeability	4.06	2.89

Note: Standard deviations are not available.

40. This analysis was based on a 2 (sex of tutor) by 2 (sex of evaluator) by 2 (sex of participant) ANOVA, $F(1,32) = 5.74$, $p < .03$. There were no other significant effects.

41. This analysis was based on a 2 (sex of tutor) by 2 (sex of evaluator) by 2 (sex of participant) ANOVA, $F(1,32) = 5.10$, $p < .05$. There were no other significant effects.

42. This analysis was based on a 2 (sex of tutor) by 2 (sex of evaluator) by 2 (sex of participant) ANOVA, $F(1,32) = 6.03$, $p < .02$. There were no other significant effects.

43. Here is the results table:

Dependent Variable	Female Tutor	Male Tutor
Informativeness: love and relationships	3.66	3.36
Informativeness: computers	3.66	3.78

Note: Standard deviations are not available.

44. The analysis was based on a 2 (gender of tutor) by 2 (gender of evaluator) by 2 (sex of participant) by 2 (topic) mixed between and within ANOVA, with topic as the repeated factor. The sex of tutor by topic interaction was significant, $F(1,32) = 7.85$, $p < .01$. There was also a main effect for topic and a three-way interaction between topic, sex of tutor voice, and sex of evaluator voice.

45. To test this effect, the required statistic would be a three-way ANOVA. This would require a minimum of eighty participants.

46. This study is described in detail in Y. Morishima, C. Bennett, C. Nass, and K. M. Lee, *Effects of (synthetic) voice gender, user gender, and product gender on credibility in e-commerce* (Stanford, Calif.: Stanford University, 2002).

47. B. Feirstein, *Real men don't eat quiche: A guidebook to all that is truly masculine* (New York: Summit, 1982).

48. K. I. E. Debevec, The influence of spokespersons in altering a product's gender image: Implications for advertising effectiveness, *Journal of Advertising* 15, no. 4 (1986): 12–20; S. Feldman-Summers, D. E. Montano, D. Kasprzyk, and B. Wagner, Influence attempts when competing views are gender-related: Sex as credibility, *Psychology of Women Quarterly* 5, no. 2 (1980): 311–320; E. Iyer and K. Debevec, Gender stereotyping of products: Are products like people?, Paper presented at the Proceedings of the Annual Conference of the Academy of Marketing Science, 1986; J. R. Stuteville, Sexually polarized products and advertising strategy, *Journal of Retailing* 47, no. 2 (1971): 3–13.

49. See, e.g., M. A. Kamins, An investigation into the "match-up" hypothesis in celebrity advertising: When beauty may be only skin deep, *Journal of Advertising* 19, no. 1 (1990): 4–13.

50. Morishima, Bennett, Nass, and Lee, *Effects of (synthetic) voice gender, user gender, and product gender on credibility in e-commerce*.

51. See chapter 2.

52. To see the complete descriptions of all eight items, see Morishima, Bennett, Nass, and Lee, *Effects of (synthetic) voice gender, user gender, and product gender on credibility in e-commerce*.

53. Participants answered the questionnaire via the computer. All questions were based on seven-point semantic differential scales anchored by an adjective and its opposite.

54. The femininity or masculinity of the voice was a single item asking whether the voice was feminine or masculine.

55. The femininity or masculinity of the product was an index composed of two items: women (as opposed to men) like the product and femininity (as opposed to masculinity) of the product. The indices were reliable (r ranged from .58 to .80).

56. Credibility of the description was an index composed of four adjectives based on the question, "How well does each of the following adjectives describe the product description?" The four adjectives were *believable*, *informative*, *trustworthy*, and *sincere voice*. The indices were very reliable (α = .75 to .80).

57. Appropriateness of each particular voice-product combination was based on a single item: "How appropriate or inappropriate was the voice for this particular product?"

58. The complete results table is presented below. All analyses are based on a 2 (gender of voice) by 2 (gender of product) by 2 (gender of participant) full-factorial ANOVA.

Dependent Variable	Female Product/ Female Voice	Female Product/ Male Voice	Male Product/ Female Voice	Male Product/ Male Voice
Appropriateness of the voice	3.2 (1.6)	2.9 (1.6)	2.9 (1.3)	3.5 (1.6)
Femininity of the voice	5.6 (1.2)	2.3 (1.6)	5.5 (1.3)	2.0 (0.86)
Femininity of the product	3.9 (1.7)	2.8 (1.6)	4.1 (1.5)	2.1 (1.0)
Credibility of the description	3.7 (0.81)	3.7 (0.64)	3.6 (0.61)	4.3 (0.69)

Note: Standard deviation in parentheses.

59. Stereotypically female products were perceived as significantly more feminine than stereotypically male products, $F(1,86) = 225.6$, $p < .001$.

60. There was a significant interaction between gender of voice by gender of product, $F(1,86) = 22.2$, $p < .001$.

61. There was a significant interaction between gender of voice by gender of product, $F(1,86) = 16.8$, $p < .001$.

62. There was a significant interaction between gender of voice by gender of product, $F(1,86) = 225.6$, $p < .001$.

63. There was a significant interaction between gender of voice by gender of product, $F(1,86) = 6.96$, $p < .01$.

64. For females, the descriptions read by a female voice ($M = 3.78$) were perceived as more credible than those spoken by a male voice ($M = 3.63$), while males perceived the descriptions read by a male voice to be more credible ($M = 3.93$) than the descriptions read by a female voice ($M = 3.83$), a marginally significant difference, $F(1,86) = 3.11$, $p < .08$.

65. S. Argamon, M. Koppel, J. Fine, and A. Simoni, Gender, genre, and writing style in formal written texts, *Texts* 23, no. 3 (2003): 321–346; J. Holmes, Women's talk: The question of sociolinguistic universals, in J. Coates, ed., *Language and gender: A reader* (Oxford: Blackwell, 1998), 461–483; D. Tannen, *Gender and discourse* (New York: Oxford University Press, 1996).

66. Argamon, Koppel, Fine, and Simoni, Gender, genre, and writing style in formal written texts.

67. D. Biber, *Variation across speech and writing* (Cambridge, Cambridge University Press, 1988).

68. E. J. Aries and F. L. Johnson, Close friendship in adulthood: Conversational content between same-sex friends, *Sex Roles* 9, no. 12 (1983): 1183–1196.

69. R. Lakoff, *Language and woman's place* (New York: Harper & Row, 1975).

70. Holmes, Paying compliments: A sex-preferential positive politeness strategy.

71. J. Holmes, Sex differences and apologies: One aspect of communicative competence, *Applied Linguistics* 10, no. 2 (1989): 194–213.

72. Argamon, Koppel, Fine, and Simoni, Gender, genre, and writing style in formal written texts.

73. Johnstone, B., Community and contest: Midwestern men and women constructing their worlds in conversational storytelling, in D. Tannen, *Gender and conversational interaction* (Oxford, Oxford University Press, 1993), 62–80.

74. Argamon, Koppel, Fine, and Simoni, Gender, genre, and writing style in formal written texts.

75. Argamon, Koppel, Fine, and Simoni, Gender, genre, and writing style in formal written texts.

76. Argamon, Koppel, Fine, and Simoni, Gender, genre, and writing style in formal written texts.

77. V. Brescoll and M. LaFrance, The correlates and consequences of newspaper reports of research on sex differences, *Psychological Science* 15, no. 8 (2004): 515–520.

78. M. Gladwell, *The tipping point: How little things can make a big difference* (Boston: Back Bay Books, 2002); T. C. Schelling, *Micromotives and macrobehavior* (New York: Norton, 1978).

79. For a related argument, see G. Gerbner, L. Gross, M. Morgan, and N. Signorielli, Living with television: The dynamics of the cultivation process, in J. Bryant and D. Zillmann, eds., *Perspectives on media effects* (Hillsdale, N.J.: Lawrence Erlbaum, 1986), pp. 17–40.

80. R. M. Kantor, *Men and women of the corporation* (New York: Basic Books, 1977).

81. See also B. Reeves and C. Nass, *The media equation: How people treat computers, television, and new media like real people and places* (New York: Cambridge University Press, 1996).

82. Kantor, *Men and women of the corporation.*

83. Gray, *Men are from Mars, women are from Venus.*

84. Nass, Moon, and Green, Are computers gender-neutral?

85. For a lengthier discussion of the selection process for the voice of a car, see chapter 5.

86. For a discussion of how designers should consider a wide range of stakeholders, see B. Friedman, ed., *Human values and the design of computer technology,* vol. 72 (New York: Cambridge University Press/CSLI, 1999); B. Friedman and P. H. Kahn, Jr., Human agency and responsible computing: Implications for computer system design, in B. Friedman, ed., *Human values and the design of computer technology* (Stanford, Calif.: CSLI, 1999), pp. 221–235.

Chapter 4

1. D. C. Dryer, *Interpersonal goals and satisfaction with interactions,* unpublished dissertation, Stanford University, Stanford, Calif., 1993; S. T. Fiske and S. E. Taylor, *Social cognition* (New York: McGraw-Hill, 1991); R. R. McCrae and O. P. John, An introduction to the five-factor model and its implications, *Journal of Personality* 60 (1992): 175–215; M. L. Munick, J. L. Saiz, and D. L. Formy-Duval, Psychological importance of the "big five": Impression formation and context effects, *Personality and Social Psychology Bulletin* 21 (1995): 818–826; C. Nass, Y. Moon, B. J. Fogg,

B. Reeves, and D. C. Dryer, Can computer personalities be human personalities?, *International Journal of Human-Computer Studies* 43, no. 2 (1995): 223–239.

2. B. Reeves and C. Nass, *The media equation: How people treat computers, television, and new media like real people and places* (New York: Cambridge University Press, 1996).

3. G. Ball and J. Breese, Emotion and personality in conversational agents, in J. Cassell, J. Sullivan, S. Prevost and E. Churchill, eds., *Embodied conversational agents* (Cambridge, Mass.: MIT Press, 2000), pp. 189–219; McCrae and John, An introduction to the five-factor model and its implications; J. S. Wiggins, A psychological taxonomy of trait-descriptive terms: The interpersonal domain, *Journal of Personality and Social Psychology* 37, no. 3 (1979): 395–412.

4. K. Isbister and C. Nass, Personality in conversational characters: Building better digital interaction partners using knowledge about human personality preferences and perceptions, Paper presented at the First Workshop on Embodied Conversational Characters (WECC 98), Lake Tahoe, Calif., October 12–15, 1998; I. B. Myers and P. B. Myers, *Gifts differing: Understanding personality type* (Palo Alto, Calif.: Consulting Psychologist Press, 1995).

5. J. B. Murray, Review of research on the Myers-Briggs type indicator, *Perceptual and Motor Skills* 70 (1990): 1187–1202; Myers and Myers, *Gifts differing.*

6. C. Nass and K. M. Lee, Does computer-synthesized speech manifest personality? Experimental tests of recognition, similarity-attraction, and consistency-attraction, *Journal of Experimental Psychology: Applied* 7, no. 3 (2001): 171–181; Nass, Moon, Fogg, Reeves, and Dryer, Can computer personalities be human personalities?

7. K. Isbister and C. Nass, Consistency of personality in interactive characters: Verbal cues, nonverbal cues, and user characteristics, *International Journal of Human-Computer Interaction* 53, no. 1 (2000): 251–267; Isbister and Nass, *Personality in conversational characters.*

8. Reeves and Nass, *The media equation;* W. Sheldon, *Atlas of men: A guide for somatyping the adult image of all ages* (New York: Macmillan, 1970).

9. W. Apple, L. A. Streeter, and R. M. Krauss, Effects of pitch and speech rate on personal attributions, *Journal of Personality and Social Psychology* 37 (1979): 715–727; C. Nass and L. Gong, Social aspects of speech interfaces from an evolutionary perspective: Experimental research and design implications, *Communications of the ACM* 43, no. 9 (2000): 36–43; Nass and Lee, Does computer-synthesized speech manifest personality?; J. Pittam, *Voice in social interaction: An interdisciplinary approach* (Thousand Oaks, Calif.: Sage, 1994).

10. H. Giles and P. F. Powesland, *Speech style and social evaluation* (London: Academic Press, 1975).

11. Nass and Gong, Social aspects of speech interfaces from an evolutionary perspective.

12. Apple, Streeter, and Krauss, Effects of pitch and speech rate on personal attributions; Pittam, *Voice in social interaction;* K. R. Scherer, Personality inference from voice quality: The loud voice of extroversion, *European Journal of Social Psychology* 8 (1978): 467–487; K. R. Scherer,

Personality markers in speech, in K. R. Scherer and H. Giles, eds., *Social markers in speech* (New York: Cambridge University Press, 1979), pp. 147–209.

13. Volume, usually measured by mean amplitude, is positively associated with extroversion and dominance. D. B. Buller, and J. K. Burgoon, The effects of vocalics and nonverbal sensitivity on compliance: A replication and extension, *Human Communication Research* 14 (1986): 548–568; Pittam, *Voice in social interaction;* K. J. Tusing and J. P. Dillard, The sounds of dominance: Vocal precursors of perceived dominance during interpersonal influence, *Human Communication Research* 26, no. 1 (2000): 148–171.

14. Pitch is the number of vibrations per second that the vocal folds make when producing a sound. Nass and Lee, Does computer-synthesized speech manifest personality?

15. Extrovert or dominant people speak with higher pitch. Pittam, *Voice in social interaction;* K. R. Scherer, H. London, and J. J. Wolf, The voice of confidence: Paralinguistic cues and audience evaluation, *Journal of Research in Personality* 7 (1973): 31–44; Tusing and Dillard, The sounds of dominance.

16. Pitch range is the extent to which a vocalization varies around its mean F0 value: extrovert or dominant people speak with more pitch range than do introverts or submissive people. C. D. Aronovitch, The voice of personality: Stereotyped judgments and their relation to voice quality and sex of speaker, *Journal of Social Psychology* 99 (1976): 207–220; J. A. Hall, *Nonverbal sex differences: Communication accuracy and expressive style* (Baltimore: Johns Hopkins University Press, 1984); K. R. Scherer, Voice and speech correlates of perceived social influence in simulated juries, in H. Giles and R. N. St. Clair, eds., *Language and social psychology* (Oxford: Blackwell, 1979), pp. 88–120; Scherer, London, and Wolf, The voice of confidence.

17. R. Lakoff, *Language and woman's place* (New York: Harper and Row, 1975).

18. Speech rate refers to the number of words (or syllables) uttered in a given period of time: faster speech rate is associated with extroversion or dominance. Aronovitch, The voice of personality; Buller and Burgoon, The effects of vocalics and nonverbal sensitivity on compliance; Tusing and Dillard, The sounds of dominance; W. G. Woodall and J. K. Burgoon, Talking fast and changing attitudes: A critique and clarification, *Journal of Nonverbal Behavior* 8 (1983): 126–142.

19. Nass and Lee, Does computer-synthesized speech manifest personality?

20. Vocal cues interact in complex ways, so studying such cues in isolation may produce unrealistic results. Nass and Lee, Does computer-synthesized speech manifest personality?; R. L. Street, and R. M. Brady, Speech rate acceptance ranges as a function of evaluative domain, listener speech rate, and communication context, *Communication Monographs* 49 (1982): 290–308; Tusing and Dillard, The sounds of dominance.

21. W. A. Barry, Marriage research and conflict: An integrative review, *Psychological Bulletin* 73 (1970): 41–54; V. Blankenship, S. M. Hnat, T. G. Hess, and D. R. Brown, Reciprocal interaction and similarity of personality attributes, *Journal of Social and Personal Relationships* 1 (1984): 415–4432; D. Byrne, W. Griffitt, and D. Stefaniak, Attraction and similarity of personality

characteristics, *Journal of Personality and Social Psychology* 5 (1967): 82–90; S. W. Duck, Personality similarity and friendship choice: Similarity of what, when?, *Journal of Personality* 41 (1973): 543–558; J. M. Jellison and P. T. Zeisset, Attraction as a function of the commonality and desirability of a trait shared by others, *Journal of Personality and Social Psychology* 11 (1969): 115–120; D. W. Novak and M. J. Lerner, Rejection as a consequence of perceived similarity, *Journal of Personality and Social Psychology* 9 (1968): 147–152; P. A. Reagor and G. L. Clore, Attraction, test anxiety and similarity-dissimilarity of test performance, *Psychonomic Science* 18 (1970): 219–220; Street and Brady, Speech rate acceptance ranges as a function of evaluative domain, listener speech rate, and communication context; Tusing and Dillard, The sounds of dominance.

22. See chapter 2.

23. R. Dawkins, *The selfish gene*, 2nd ed. (Oxford: Oxford University Press, 1989).

24. For a discussion of this point, see Y. Moon and C. Nass, How "real" are computer personalities? Psychological responses to personality types in human-computer interaction, *Communication Research* 23, no. 6 (1996): 651–674.

25. B. J. Fogg and C. Nass, Silicon sycophants: The effects of computers that flatter, *International Journal of Human-Computer Studies* 46, no. 5 (1997): 551–561; Moon and Nass, How "real" are computer personalities?

26. See chapters 2 through 5, 8, and 9, and J. P. Olive, The talking computer: Text to speech synthesis, in D. Stork, ed., *HAL's legacy: 2001's computer as dream and reality* (Cambridge, Mass.: MIT Press, 1997), pp. 101–130.

27. See chapter 2.

28. This experiment is described in more detail in Nass and Lee, Does computer-synthesized speech manifest personality?

29. An example of the site can be found at K. M. Lee, *Synthetic voice personality experiment*, retrieved from <http://www.stanford.edu/class/comm169/Kwan/1–1.fft>, 2004.

30. To avoid possible influence from prior exposure to the books, the books and authors that were displayed did not have large sales. Fiction rather than nonfiction books were selected because people find it easier to form an opinion about fiction books based on reviews or descriptions.

31. Each question had a scale from one to ten asking for individuals' attitudes. For example, one question read, "How likely would you be to buy this book?" followed by ten dots anchored by "Definitely would not buy" and "Definitely would buy."

32. Participants used radio buttons to indicate their responses on independent, ten-point Likert scales. For a complete description of the questions asked, see Nass and Lee, Does computer-synthesized speech manifest personality?

33. The two Web-based standard personality questionnaires were the Myers-Briggs Type Indicator (Murray, Review of research on the Myers-Briggs type indicator; Myers and Myers, *Gifts*

differing) and the Wiggins Interpersonal Circumplex (Wiggins, A psychological taxonomy of trait-descriptive terms).

34. Native English speakers were chosen to avoid comprehension or other language difficulties.

35. The experiment was a 2 (computer-voice personality: extrovert versus introvert) by 2 (participant personality: extrovert versus introvert) balanced, between-subjects design, with the five book descriptions as a repeated factor.

36. The voices were created using the Festival engine of the CSLU Toolkit. Center for Spoken Language Understanding, CSLU Toolkit, obtained from <http://www.cslu.ogi.edu/toolkit>, 2004.

37. The extrovert voice had the maximum volume level possible within the CSLU Toolkit, a fundamental frequency of 140 Hz, a pitch range of 40 Hz, and a speech rate of 216 words per minute. The introvert voice had the volume level set at 15 percent of the maximum, a fundamental frequency of 84 Hz, a pitch range of 16 Hz, and a speech rate of 184 words per minute.

38. All indices were analytically distinct and reliable.

39. Voice personality was an index composed of ten Wiggins personality adjective items: *cheerful, enthusiastic, extroverted, introverted* (reverse coded), *inward* (reverse coded), *jovial, outgoing, perky, shy* (reverse coded), and *vivacious* (Cronbach's α = .89). The higher the score, the more extrovert the voice is. Wiggins, A psychological taxonomy of trait-descriptive terms.

40. Liking of the voice was an index composed of the items. "How much did you enjoy hearing the computer voice?" and "How likely would you be to have the voice read you other descriptions?" and the adjectives *enjoyable, likeable,* and *satisfying* (α = .89)

41. Quality of the review was an index composed of three items: "What was the quality of the review that you just heard?," "How much did you like the review?," and "How trustworthy was the review?" (α = .75 to .91, with a mean of .86).

42. Credibility of the review was an index composed of three adjectives: *credible, reliable,* and *trustworthy* (α = .89).

43. Users' buying intention was measured by a single item: "How likely would you be to buy this book?"

44. Liking of the reviewer was an index composed of three adjectives: *enjoyable, likable,* and *satisfying* (α = .92).

45. Credibility of the reviewer was measured by a standard trust scale (α = .88). L. R. Wheeless and J. Grotz, The measurement of trust and its relationship to self-disclosure, *Human Communication Research* 3, no. 3 (1977): 250–257.

46. Personality of the reviewer was an index composed of ten Wiggins personality adjective items: *cheerful, enthusiastic, extroverted, introverted* (reverse coded), *inward* (reverse coded), *jovial, outgoing, perky, shy* (reverse coded), and *vivacious* (α = .91). The higher the score, the more extrovert the reviewer. Wiggins, A psychological taxonomy of trait-descriptive terms.

47. The answers were combined across the reviews using a statistical technique called *repeated measures*. B. J. Winer and K. W. Michels, *Statistical principles in experimental design,* 3rd ed. (New York: McGraw-Hill, 1991). The analysis was based on a full-factorial repeated-measure ANCOVA with book as the repeated factor and computer-voice personality and subject personality as the between-subjects factors; sex was a covariate. For the items that were asked only once, the analysis was based on a full-factorial 2 × 2 ANCOVA.

48. Here is the entire results table.

	Introverted Participants		Extroverted Participants	
Dependent Variables	Introverted Voice	Extroverted Voice	Introverted Voice	Extroverted Voice
Voice extrovertedness	3.41 (1.02)	4.43 (1.73)	3.28 (.81)	5.30 (1.53)
Liking of the vocie	2.82 (1.26)	2.21 (.92)	1.69 (.96)	3.08 (1.32)
Quality of the review	5.44 (0.96)	4.96 (1.31)	4.06 (1.35)	4.79 (1.66)
Credibility of the review	6.43 (1.46)	5.06 (2.55)	4.18 (1.60)	5.46 (1.18)
Buying intention	3.68 (0.98)	3.10 (1.24)	2.93 (1.08)	3.59 (1.17)
Liking of the reviewer	5.06 (2.07)	4.74 (2.37)	2.89 (1.27)	5.24 (1.88)
Credibility of the reviewer	4.98 (0.55)	4.52 (0.89)	4.40 (0.70)	5.02 (0.57)
Reviewer extrovertedness	4.68 (1.39)	5.56 (1.37)	4.22 (1.66)	5.77 (1.42)

Note: Standard deviations are in parentheses.

49. $F(1, 67) = 23.71$, $p < .001$. Neither a main effect for subject personality nor an interaction effect was found.

50. $F(1, 67) = 14.6$, $p < .001$.

51. $F(1, 67) = 3.62$, $p < .06$.

52. $F(1, 67) = 7.86$, $p < .01$.

53. $F(1, 67) = 5.45$, $p < .05$.

54. $F(1, 67) = 8.35$, $p < .01$.

55. $F(1, 67) = 10.88$, $p < .01$.

56. $F(1, 67) = 12.47$, $p < .001$.

57. Reeves and Nass, *The media equation.*

58. That is, there were no significant main effects for voice personality (all $p > .10$).

59. Consistent with the literature, there was extremely high agreement between the two coders (intercoder reliability = .90; disagreements were resolved by discussion). Pittam, *Voice in social interaction;* R. W. Ramsay, Personality and speech, *Journal of Personality and Social Psychology* 4 (1996): 116–118. The raters were unaware of the speaker's actual personality.

60. $r = .24, p < .05$.

61. Because participants were approximately equally divided between extroverted and introverted participants, this was a viable strategy. There were no interactions for user-voice personality by text-to-speech (TTS) voice personality on any of the dependent measures.

62. Recent evidence does suggest that prosodic mirroring, that is, having the computer match the prosody of the user, can lead to similarity-attraction. N. Suzuki, K. Kakehi, Y. Takeuchi, and M. Okada, Social effects of the speech of hummed sounds on human-computer interaction, *International Journal of Human-Computer Studies* 60, no. 4 (2004): 455–468; N. Suzuki, Y. Takeuchi, K. Ishii, and M. Okada, Effects of echoic mimicry using hummed sounds on human-computer interaction, *Speech Communication* 40, no. 4 (2003): 559–573.

63. Olive, The talking computer.

64. J. Cassell, J. Sullivan, S. Prevost, and E. Churchill, eds., *Embodied conversational agents* (Cambridge, Mass.: MIT Press, 2000); B. Laurel, *Computers as theatre* (Reading, Mass.: Addison-Wesley, 1991).

65. For a similar argument with respect to textual personality, see Reeves, Nass, *The media equation.*

66. See chapters 10 through 12.

67. For a discussion of casting, see G. Goodell, *Independent feature film production: A complete guide from concept through distribution*, 2nd ed. (New York: St. Martin's Griffin, 1998).

68. Conversely, there are times when it is better to not have the system match the user. For examples, see chapters 3 and 5.

69. L. W. Harmon, J.-I. Hansen, F. Borgen, and A. Hammer, *Strong Interest Inventory: Applications and technical guide* (Palo Alto, Calif.: Consulting Psychologist Press, 1985).

70. See chapter 5.

71. Reeves and Nass, *The media equation.*

72. Reeves and Nass, *The media equation.*

73. B. M. DePaulo and H. S. Friedman, Nonverbal communication, in D. T. Gilbert, S. T. Fiske and G. Lindzey, eds., *Handbook of social psychology,* 4th ed. (Boston: McGraw Hill, 1998), 2:3–40; H. S. Friedman, R. E. Riggio, and D. F. Casella, Nonverbal skill, personal charisma, and initial attraction, *Personality and Social Psychology Bulletin* 14 (1988): 203–211.

74. E. S. Sullins, Perceptual salience as a function of nonverbal expressiveness, *Personality and Social Psychology Bulletin* 15 (1989): 584–595.

75. See chapter 2.

76. N. Cantor and W. Mischel, Prototypes in person perception, *Advances in Experimental Social Psychology* 12 (1979): 3–52; Reeves and Nass, *The media equation.*

77. Cantor and Mischel, Prototypes in person perception; Reeves and Nass, *The media equation.* For a similar argument concerning sex, see chapter 2.

78. See chapter 5.

79. K. M. Lee and C. Nass, The multiple source effect and synthesized speech: Doubly-disembodied language as a conceptual framework, *Human Communication Research*, 30, no. 2:182–207; Reeves and Nass, *The media equation*. See chapter 9 for more details.

80. For an extreme form of this problem, see chapter 11.

81. R. B. Cialdini, *Influence: Science and practice*, 3rd ed. (New York: Harper Collins, 1993); B. J. Fogg, *Persuasive computers: Using technology to change what we think and do* (San Francisco: Morgan Kaufman, 2002); Fogg and Nass, Silicon sycophants.

82. Wiggins's model is called the "interpersonal circumplex." Wiggins, A psychological taxonomy of trait-descriptive terms.

83. Apple, Streeter, and Krauss, Effects of pitch and speech rate on personal attributions; Scherer, Personality inference from voice quality; B. L. Smith, B. L. Brown, W. J. Strong, and A. C. Rencher, Effects of speech rate on personality perceptions, *Language and Speech* 18 (1975): 145–152.

84. Apple, Streeter, and Krauss, Effects of pitch and speech rate on personal attributions; Scherer, Personality inference from voice quality.

85. For an extended discussion of this point, see chapters 3 and 5.

Chapter 5

1. J. Kess, *Psycholinguistics: Psychology, linguistics and the study of natural language* (Philadelphia: Benjamin, 1992); B. S. Kisilevsky, S. M. J. Hains, K. Lee, Xie, X., H. Huang, H. H. Ye, et al., Effects of experience on fetal voice recognition, *Psychological Science* 14, no. 3 (2003): 220–224.

2. D. I. Slobin, *Psycholinguistics*, 2nd ed. (Glenview, Ill.: Scott, Foresman, 1979).

3. C. Floccia, T. Nazzi, and J. Bertoncini, Unfamiliar voice discrimination for short stimuli in newborns, *Developmental Science* 3, no. 3 (2000): 333–343.

4. S. Pinker, *The language instinct* (New York: Morrow, 1994).

5. C. L. Martin, and D. N. Ruble, Children's search for gender cues: Cognitive perspectives on gender development, *Current Directions in Psychological Science* 13, no. 2 (2004): 67–70.

6. J. W. Heyman, *Sensory dominance in infant perception of dynamic expressions of emotion*, unpublished doctoral dissertation, George Washington University, Washington, D.C., 1996.

7. Pinker, *The language instinct*; but see M. M. Chouinard and E. V. Clark, Adult reformulations of child errors as negative evidence, *Journal of Child Language* 30, no. 3 (2003): 637–669; E. V. Clark, *First language acquisition* (New York: Cambridge University Press, 2003).

8. N. Chomsky, *Language and mind* (New York: Harcourt, Brace, & World, 1968); Pinker, *The language instinct.*

9. Chomsky, *Language and mind*; Pinker, *The language instinct.*

10. Chouinard and Clark, Adult reformulations of child errors as negative evidence.

11. Clark, *First language acquisition.*

12. Clark, *First language acquisition.*

13. Pinker, *The language instinct*; but see Chouinard and Clark, Adult reformulations of child errors as negative evidence.

14. For a detailed account of how children acquire their first language, see Clark, *First language acquisition.*

15. Chomsky, *Language and mind*; H. P. Grice, Logic and conversation, in P. Cole and J. Morgan, eds., *Syntax and semantics* (New York: Academic Press, 1975), 3:41–58; H. P. Grice, Meaning, in P. F. Strawson, ed., *Philosophical logic* (Oxford: Oxford University Press, 1967), pp. 39–48 (originally published in 1957); Pinker, *The language instinct*; J. R. Searle, Minds, brains, and programs, in D. R. Hofstadter and D. C. Dennett, eds., *The mind's I* (Toronto: Bantam, 1981), pp. 353–372; J. R. Searle, *Speech acts: An essay in the philosophy of language* (London: Cambridge University Press, 1969).

16. Chomsky, *Language and mind*; Grice, Logic and conversation; Grice, Meaning; Pinker, *The language instinct.*

17. E. V. Clark, Conceptual perspective and lexical choice in acquisition, *Cognition* 64 (1997): 1–37; E. V. Clark and J. B. Grossman, Pragmatic directions and children's word learning, *Journal of Child Language* 25 (1998): 1–18; E. V. Clark and T. A. Svaib, Speaker perspective and reference in young children, *First Language* 17 (1997): 57–74.

18. H. H. Clark, *Using language* (New York: Cambridge University Press); Grice, Logic and conversation; Grice, Meaning.

19. For a detailed explanation of "surface structure," see Chomsky, *Language and mind*; Pinker, *The language instinct.*

20. C. Nass and K. M. Lee, Does computer-synthesized speech manifest personality? Experimental tests of recognition, similarity-attraction, and consistency-attraction, *Journal of Experimental Psychology: Applied* 7, no. 3 (2001): 171–181.

21. K. Isbister and C. Nass, Consistency of personality in interactive characters: Verbal cues, non-verbal cues, and user characteristics, *International Journal of Human-Computer Interaction* 53, no. 1 (2000): 251–267; Y. Moon and C. Nass, Adaptive agents and personality change: Complimentary versus similarity as forms of adaption, *Proceedings of CHI 96,* 1996; Y. Moon and C. Nass, How "real" are computer personalities? Psychological responses to personality types in human-computer interaction, *Communication Research* 23, no. 6 (1996): 651–674; Nass and Lee, Does

computer-synthesized speech manifest personality?; C. Nass, Y. Moon, B. J. Fogg, B. Reeves, and D. C. Dryer, Can computer personalities be human personalities?, *International Journal of Human-Computer Studies* 43, no. 2 (1995): 223–239.

22. Isbister and Nass, Consistency of personality in interactive characters; Moon and Nass, Adaptive agents and personality change; Moon and Nass, How "real" are computer personalities?; Nass and Lee, Does computer-synthesized speech manifest personality?; Nass, Moon, Fogg, Reeves, and Dryer, Can computer personalities be human personalities?

23. D. Cameron, F. McAlinden, K. O'Leary, Lakoff in context: The social and linguistic function of tag questions, in J. Coates and D. Cameron, eds., *Women in their speech communities: New perspectives on language and sex* (London, Longman, 1988), 74–93.

24. Isbister and Nass, Consistency of personality in interactive characters; Moon and Nass, Adaptive agents and personality change; Moon and Nass, How "real" are computer personalities?; Nass and Lee, Does computer-synthesized speech manifest personality?; Nass, Moon, Fogg, Reeves, and Dryer, Can computer personalities be human personalities?

25. S. Johnson, *Interface culture: How new technology transforms the way we create and communication* (San Francisco: HarperEdge, 1999).

26. For the initial description of the "Turing test," see A. Turing, Computing machinery and intelligence, *Mind* 59 (1950): 433–460.

27. "Hello World" was the first program designed for teaching the C programming language. B. W. Kernighan and D. M. Ritchie, *The C programming language* (Indianapolis: Prentice Hall PTR, 1978).

28. Johnson, *Interface culture.*

29. Nass and Lee, Does computer-synthesized speech manifest personality?

30. C. Nass and Y. Moon, Machines and mindlessness: Social responses to computers, *Journal of Social Issues* 56, no. 1 (2000): 81–103.

31. Nass and Moon, Machines and mindlessness.

32. Nass, Moon, Fogg, Reeves, and Dryer, Can computer personalities be human personalities?

33. Y. Moon, When the computer is the "salesperson": Computer responses to computer "personalities" in interactive marketing situations, unpublished manuscript, Boston, Mass., 1998.

34. R. E. Nisbett and L. Ross, *Human inference: Strategies and shortcomings of social judgment* (Englewood Cliffs, N.J.: Prentice-Hall, 1980); M. Zuckerman, Attribution of success and failure revisited, or: The motivational bias is alive and well in attribution theory, *Journal of Personality* 47 (1979): 245–287. See chapter 14 for more details.

35. Y. Moon and C. Nass, Are computers scapegoats? Attributions of responsibility in human-computer interaction, *International Journal of Human-Computer Studies* 49, no. 1 (1998): 79–94.

36. Moon, *When the computer is the "salesperson."*

37. See chapters 1, 3, and 8 for a discussion.

38. See chapter 4.

39. See chapter 3.

40. Nass and Lee, Does computer-synthesized speech manifest personality?

41. Clark, Conceptual perspective and lexical choice in acquisition.

42. The following three paragraphs follow the approach of L. Gong, *The psychology of consistency in human-computer interaction*, unpublished doctoral dissertation, Stanford University, Stanford, Calif., 2000.

43. J. R. Stroop, Studies of interference in serial verbal reactions, *Journal of Experimental Psychology* 18 (1935): 643–663.

44. The Stroop effect is described in detail in C. M. MacLeod, Half a century of research on the Stroop effect: An integrative review, *Psychological Bulletin* 109 (1991): 163–203.

45. MacLeod; Half a century of research on the Stroop effect.

46. J. F. Hamers and W. E. Lambert, Bilingual interdependencies in auditory perception, *Journal of verbal learning and verbal behavior* 11 (1972): 303–310.

47. J. M. Pieters, Ear asymmetry in an auditory spatial Stroop task as a function of handedness, *Cortex* 17 (1981): 369–379.

48. E. J. Green and P. J. Barber, An auditory Stroop effect with judgments of speaker gender, *Perception and Psychophysics* 30, no. 5 (1981): 459–466.

49. S. T. Fiske and S. E. Taylor, *Social cognition* (New York: McGraw-Hill, 1991).

50. N. Cantor and W. Mischel, Prototypes in person perception. *Advances in Experimental Social Psychology* 12 (1979): 3–52; N. Cantor and W. Mischel, Prototypicality and personality: Effects on free recall and personality impressions, *Journal of Research in Personality* 13 (1979): 187–205.

51. Fiske and Taylor, *Social cognition.*

52. H. H. Kelley, Attribution theory in social psychology, in D. Levine, ed., *Nebraska symposium on motivation* (vol. 15, pp. 192–240) (Lincoln: University of Nebraska Press, 1967); H. H. Kelley, The processes of causal attribution, *American Psychologist* 28 (1973): 107–128.

53. Nass and Lee, Does computer-synthesized speech manifest personality?

54. S. E. Asch, Forming impressions of personality, *Journal of Abnormal and Social Psychology* 41 (1946): 1230–1240; R. Erber and S. T. Fiske, Outcome dependency and attention to inconsistent information, *Journal of Personality and Social Psychology* 47 (1984): 709–726.

55. J. Crocker, D. B. Hannah, and R. Weber, Person memory and causal attributions, *Journal of Personality and Social Psychology* 44 (1983): 55–66; L. A. Festinger, *A theory of cognitive dissonance* (Stanford, Calif.: Stanford University Press, 1957); J. A. Kulik, Confirmatory attribution and the perpetuation of social beliefs, *Journal of Personality and Social Psychology* 44 (1983): 1171–1181.

56. Asch, Forming impressions of personality; N. H. Anderson and A. Jacobson, Effect of stimulus inconsistency and discounting instructions in personality impression formation, *Journal of Personality and Social Psychology* 2 (1965): 531–539; R. S. Wyer, Information redundancy, inconsistency, and novelty and their role in impression formation, *Journal of Experimental Social Psychology* 6 (1970): 111–127.

57. The following experiment is described in detail in Nass and Lee, Does computer-synthesized speech manifest personality?

58. A book Web site also would have been another good venue. A book Web site was used in the previous study, and diversity is desirable whenever possible.

59. Participants used radio buttons to indicate their responses on independent, ten-point Likert scales.

60. Liking of the voice was an index composed of these items: "How much did you enjoy hearing the computer voice?," "How likely would you be to have the voice read you other descriptions?," and the following adjectives: *enjoyable*, *likeable*, and *satisfying*. The index was very reliable (Cronbach's $\alpha = .89$).

61. Liking of the content was an index comprised of the following three adjectives: *enjoyable*, *likeable*, and *satisfying* ($\alpha = .89$).

62. Liking of the writer was an index composed of three adjectives: *enjoyable*, *likeable*, and *satisfying* ($\alpha = .83$).

63. Credibility of the writer was measured by Wheeless and Grotz's trust scale ($\alpha = .92$). L. R. Wheeless and J. Grotz, The measurement of trust and its relationship to self-disclosure, *Human Communication Research* 3, no. 3 (1977): 250–257.

64. Extrovertedness of the content was an index composed of ten Wiggins personality adjective items: *cheerful*, *enthusiastic*, *extroverted*, *introverted* (reverse coded), *inward* (reverse coded), *jovial*, *outgoing*, *perky*, *shy* (reverse coded), and *vivacious* ($\alpha = .90$). J. S. Wiggins, A psychological taxonomy of trait-descriptive terms: The interpersonal domain, *Journal of Personality and Social Psychology* 37, no. 3 (1979): 395–412.

65. Extrovertedness of the voice was an index composed of ten Wiggins personality adjective items: *cheerful*, *enthusiastic*, *extroverted*, *introverted* (reverse coded), *inward* (reverse coded), *jovial*, *outgoing*, *perky*, *shy* (reverse coded), and *vivacious* ($\alpha = .92$). Wiggins, A psychological taxonomy of trait-descriptive terms.

66. Here is the entire results table:

Dependent Variables	Voice × Content Consistency		Voice × Participant Similarity		Content × Participant Similarity	
	Matched	Mismatched	Matched	Mismatched	Matched	Mismatched
Liking of the voice	3.90 (1.77)	2.94 (1.20)	3.78 (1.92)	3.06 (1.06)	3.80 (1.78)	3.04 (1.27)
Liking of the content	4.44 (1.42)	3.75 (1.49)	4.11 (1.50)	4.10 (1.49)	4.22 (1.59)	3.97 (1.38)
Liking of the writer	4.62 (1.40)	4.11 (1.45)	4.65 (1.80)	4.08 (.89)	4.63 (1.40)	4.10 (1.45)
Credibility of the writer	4.74 (0.94)	4.30 (0.86)	4.56 (0.91)	4.48 (0.95)	4.42 (0.87)	4.63 (0.97)

Note: Standard deviations are in parentheses.

Here is the analysis-of-variance table:

	Voice × Content Consistency	Voice × Participant Similarity	Content × Participant Similarity	Three-way Interaction	Voice Personality	Content Personality	Participant Personality
Liking of the voice	13.52* ($\eta 2$ = .16)	7.50** ($\eta 2$ = .09)	8.36** ($\eta 2$ = .10)	1.52 ($\eta 2$ = .02)	34.28*** ($\eta 2$ = .32)	7.26** ($\eta 2$ = .09)	0.82 ($\eta 2$ = .01)
Liking of the content	5.57* ($\eta 2$ = .07)	0.00 ($\eta 2$ = .00)	0.72 ($\eta 2$ = .01)	0.00 ($\eta 2$ = .00)	11.81** ($\eta 2$ = .14)	12.77** ($\eta 2$ = .15)	0.95 ($\eta 2$ = .01)
Liking of the writer	3.10+ ($\eta 2$ = .04)	4.00* ($\eta 2$ = .05)	3.39+ ($\eta 2$ = .04)	0.14 ($\eta 2$ = .00)	10.57** ($\eta 2$ = .13)	1.45 ($\eta 2$ = .02)	5.27* ($\eta 2$ = .07)
Credibility of the writer	9.01** ($\eta 2$ = .11)	0.24 ($\eta 2$ = .00)	2.06 ($\eta 2$ = .03)	0.32 ($\eta 2$ = .00)	1.01 ($\eta 2$ = .30)	12.40*** ($\eta 2$ = .50)	0.96 ($\eta 2$ = .01)

+p < .10, * p < .05, ** p < .01, *** p < .001.

67. M = 5.84 versus M = 5.09, $F(1,72) = 9.9$, $f < .01$.

68. A. Cooper and P. Saffo, *The inmates are running the asylum* (New York: Sams, 1999).

69. For a discussion of personality in portals, see Moon, *When the computer is the "salesperson."*

70. This phrase was initially coined by an editor for the PBS series, *Do You Speak American*?

71. For a description of *Knight Rider*, see <http://www.knightrideronline.com/>.

72. See chapter 14 for a discussion of errors in voice interfaces.

73. For a discussion of the use of "I" in voice interfaces, see chapter 10.

74. See chapter 3.

75. The current data are consistent with this prediction but are not definitive.

76. A detailed discussion of the four Myers-Briggs preferences is presented in J. B. Murray, Review of research on the Myers-Briggs type indicator, *Perceptual and Motor Skills* 70 (1990): 1187–1202.

77. J. S. Wiggins and R. Broughton, The interpersonal circle: A structural model for the integration of personality research, *Perspectives in Personality* 1 (1985): 1–47.

78. J. T. Cacioppo, R. E. Petty, J. Feinstein, and B. Jarvis, Dispositional differences in cognitive motivation: The life and times of individuals varying in need for cognition, *Psychological Bulletin* 119 (1996): 197–253.

79. H. M. Lefcourt, *Locus of control: Current trends in theory and research*, 2nd ed. (Mahwah, N.J.: Lea, 1982).

80. A. M. Colman, W. M. Best, and A. J. Austen, Familiarity and liking: Direct tests of the preference-feedback hypothesis, *Psychological Reports* 58 (1986): no. 3, 931–938; R. Kaplan and E. J. Herbert, Familiarity and preference: A cross-cultural analysis, in J. L. Nasar, ed., *Environmental aesthetics: Theory, research, and applications* (New York: Cambridge University Press, 1988), pp. 379–389.

81. Moon and Nass, Adaptive agents and personality change. Also see chapter 4.

82. For a discussion of embodied conversational agents, see J. Cassell, J. Sullivan, S. Prevost, E. and Churchill, eds., *Embodied conversational agents* (Cambridge, Mass.: MIT Press, 2000).

83. Isbister and Nass, Consistency of personality in interactive characters.

84. Ibid.

85. W. Sheldon, *Atlas of men: A guide for somatyping the adult image of all ages* (New York: Macmillan Publishing, 1970); T. Arraj and J. Arraj, *Tracking the elusive human, Volume I: A practical guide to C. G. Jung's psychological types, W. H. Sheldon's body and temperament types, and their Integration* (Vol. 1) (Chiloquin, Ore.: Inner Growth Books, 1988).

Chapter 6

1. H. H. Clark, *Using language* (New York: Cambridge University Press, 1996); R. Stalnaker, Assertion, in P. Cole, ed., *Syntax and semantics 9: Pragmatics* (New York: Academic Press, 1978), pp. 315–332.

2. Clark, *Using language*.

3. Clark, *Using language*; H. P. Grice, Logic and conversation, in P. Cole and J. Morgan, eds., *Syntax and semantics* (New York: Academic Press, 1975), 3: 41–58.

4. Clark, *Using language*.

5. K. Anderson, M. Domosh, N. Thrift, and S. Pile, eds., *Handbook of cultural geography* (Thousand Oaks, Calif.: Sage, 2002); W. A. D. Jackson, *The shaping of our world: A human and cultural geography* (Hoboken, N.J.: Wiley, 1985).

6. J. F. Hamers and M. H. A. Blanc, *Bilinguality and bilingualism* (New York: Cambridge University Press, 2000); R. Lippi-Green, English with an accent: Language, ideology, and discrimination in the United States (London, Routledge, 1997).

7. E. Newport, Maturational constraints on language learning, *Cognitive Science* 14 (1990): 11–28; S. Pinker, *The language instinct* (New York: Morrow, 1994).

8. K. R. Scherer and H. Giles, *Social markers in speech* (New York: Cambridge University Press, 1979).

9. Pinker, *The language instinct.*

10. Newport, Maturational constraints on language learning; Pinker, *The language instinct.*

11. Newport, Maturational constraints on language learning; Pinker, *The language instinct.*

12. R. Lippi-Green, *English with an accent: Language, ideology, and discrimination in the United States* (London: Routledge, 1997); Pinker, *The language instinct*; P. Trudgill, *Sociolinguistics: An introduction to language and society* (London: Penguin Books, 2000).

13. A. Cook, *American accent training,* 2nd ed. (Hauppauge, N.Y.: Barron's Educational Series, 2000).

14. Thanks to Teenie Matlock for this example.

15. Judges 12: 5–6; C. Nass and L. Gong, Social aspects of speech interfaces from an evolutionary perspective: Experimental research and design implications, *Communications of the ACM* 43, no. 9 (2000): 36–43.

16. E. B. Ryan and H. Giles, eds., *Attitudes towards language variation* (London: Edward Arnold, 1982).

17. C. A. Gallagher, ed., *Rethinking the color line: Readings in race and ethnicity* (New York: McGraw-Hill, 1999).

18. L. L. Cavalli-Sforza, *The great human diasporas: The history of diversity and evolution,* trans. S. Thorne (Boulder, Colo.: Perseus, 1996).

19. *Britannica concise encyclopedia* (Chicago: Encyclopaedia Britannica, 2002).

20. E. V. Clark, *First language acquisition* (New York: Cambridge University Press, 2003); Pinker, *The language instinct.*

21. Cavalli-Sforza, *The great human diaspora.*

22. D. Blumenthal, Race versus ethnicity, *Academic Medicine* 74, no. 12 (1999): 1259.

23. See chapters 2 through 5 for more discussion on this point.

24. See chapters 2 and 4.

25. See chapters 3, 5, and 8.

26. S. T. Fiske and S. E. Taylor, *Social cognition* (New York: McGraw-Hill, 1991); R. Kaplan and E. J. Herbert, Familiarity and preference: A cross-cultural analysis, in J. L. Nasar, ed., *Environmental aesthetics: Theory, research, and applications* (New York: Cambridge University Press, 1988), pp. 379–389.

27. See chapter 5.

28. See chapter 1.

29. S. McCloud, *Understanding comics* (New York: Kitchen Sink Press, 1994); R. Shepard, *Mind sights: Original visual illusions, ambiguities, and other anomalies, with a commentary on the play of mind in perception and art* (New York: Freeman, 1990).

30. D. W. Massaro, *Perceiving talking faces: From speech perception to a behavioral principle* (Cambridge, Mass.: MIT Press, 1998).

31. G. E. Moore, Cramming more components onto integrated circuits, *Electronics* 38, no. 8 (1965).

32. J. Cassell, J. Sullivan, S. Prevost, and E. Churchill, eds., *Embodied conversational agents* (Cambridge, Mass.: MIT Press, 2000).

33. K. Isbister, H. Nakanishi, T. Ishida, and C. Nass, *Helper agent*: Designing an assistant for human-human interaction in a virtual meeting space. Paper presented at the International Conference on Human Factors in Computing Systems (CHI-00), The Hague, Netherlands, 2000; H. Nakanishi, K. Isbister, T. Ishida, and C. Nass, Designing a social agent for a virtual meeting space, in R. Trappl and S. Payr, eds., *Agent culture: Designing virtual characters for a multi-cultural world* (New York: Erlbaum, 2004), 245–266; H. Nakanishi, S. Nakazawa, T. Ishida, K. Takanashi, and K. Isbister, Can software agents influence human relations? Balance theory in agent-mediated communities. Paper presented at the International Joint Conference on Autonomous Agents and Multiagent Systems (AAMAS-03), 2003.

34. Massaro, *Perceiving talking faces.*

35. Cassell, Sullivan, Prevost, and Churchill, *Embodied conversational agents.*

36. Cassell, Sullivan, Prevost, and Churchill, *Embodied conversational agents;* B. Hayes-Roth and R. van Gent, Story-making with improvisational puppets, Paper presented at the Proceedings of the First International Conference on Autonomous Agents, Marina del Rey, Calif., February 1997; R. Moreno, R. E. Mayer, H. Spires, and J. Lester, The case for social agency in computer-based teaching: Do students learn more deeply when they interact with animated pedagogical agents?, *Cognition and Instruction* 19 (2001): 177–213.

37. H. Maldonado and B. Hayes-Roth, Toward cross-cultural believability in character design, in S. Payr and R. Trappl, eds., *Agent culture: Designing virtual characters for a multi-cultural world* (Mahwah, N.J.: Lawrence Erlbaum, 2004), pp. 143–175.

38. Maldonado and Hayes-Roth, Toward cross-cultural believability in character design.

39. See chapters 2 and 4.

40. See chapters 3 and 5.

41. This experiment is described in more detail in C. Nass and S. Najmi, Race vs. culture in computer-based agents and users: Implications for internationalizing websites, manuscript, Stanford University, Stanford, Calif., 2003.

42. Because U.S. accents are not associated with particular races, it would not be unusual to see a Korean face with an American accent. Ideally, this study would have been done with Australian participants. As a compromise, we view Australian culture as *closer* to U.S. culture than to Korean culture and interpret the study accordingly.

43. Product likeability was an index composed of three adjectives, which asked about each of the four products. The question asked, "How well does each of the following adjectives describe the product?" Answers were based on ten-point Likert scales ranging from "Describes very poorly" (= 1) to "Describes very well" (= 10). The adjectives were *good, appealing,* and *likable.* The indices were very reliable (α-.90 to .96).

44. Description credibility was an index comprised of three adjectives, which asked about each of the four product descriptions. The question asked, "How well does each of the following adjectives describe the product description?" Answers were based on ten-point Likert scales ranging from "Describes very poorly" (= 1) to "Describes very well" (= 10). The adjectives were *trustworthy, accurate,* and *informative.* The indices were very reliable (Cronbach's α = .85 to .93).

45. Agent quality was an index created by averaging participants' responses to eleven adjectives under the question, "How well does each of these adjectives describe the agent?" Answers were based on ten-point Likert scales ranging from "Describes very poorly" (= 1) to "Describes very well" (= 10). The adjectives were *informative, trustworthy, intelligent, expert, honest, likeable, sincere, appropriate, credible, friendly,* and *easy-to-understand.* The index was very reliable (α = .93).

46. See chapters 2 and 3.

47. Here is the results table:

	User and Accent Matching		User and Race Matching		Accent and Race Consistency	
Dependent Variables	Matched	Mismatched	Matched	Mismatched	Matched	Mismatched
Product likeability	4.77 (1.30)	4.26 (1.06)	4.45 (1.24)	4.58 (1.19)	4.75 (1.14)	4.29 (1.23)
Description credibility	4.67 (0.93)	4.09 (0.85)	4.50 (1.01)	4.25 (0.85)	4.64 (1.05)	4.12 (0.73)
Agent quality	4.90 (1.13)	3.81 (1.14)	4.45 (1.47)	4.25 (1.00)	4.85 (1.26)	3.85 (1.04)

Note: Standard deviations are in parentheses.

All analyses are based on 2 (user ethnicity) by 2 (agent accent) by 2 (agent race) between-participants ANOVA. For product likeability and description credibility, averages were taken across the four products ($\alpha = .86$ and $\alpha = .90$, respectively). *F*-values and significance tests refer to the relevant two-way interaction.

48. $F(1, 88) = 32.63$, $p < .001$, $\eta 2 = .27$.

49. $F(1, 88) = 4.43$, $p < .05$, $\eta 2 = .05$.

50. $F(1, 88) = 12.86$, $p < .001$, $\eta 2 = .13$.

51. Spokesperson: $F(1, 88) = 1.11$, $p > .29$; product likeability: $F(1, 88) = 0.38$, $p > .54$; and description credibility: $F(1, 88) = 2.33$, $p > .13$. The clear results for accent identification and for the accent and race interactions indicate that these results are not a function of low reliability.

52. $F(1, 88) = 27.87$, $p < .001$, $\eta 2 = .24$.

53. $F(1, 88) = 4.17$, $p < .05$, $\eta 2 = .05$.

54. $F(1, 88) = 10.27$, $p < .01$, $\eta 2 = .11$.

55. For another example of this phenomenon, see chapter 11.

56. R. B. Rubin and M. P. McHugh, Development of parasocial interaction relationships, *Journal of Broadcasting and Electronic Media* 31 (1987): 279–292.

57. Trudgill, *Sociolinguistics*.

58. See chapter 3.

59. H. Giles, Ethnocentrism and the evaluation of accented speech, *British Journal of Social and Clinical Psychology* 10 (1971): 187–188; H. Giles, Evaluative reactions to accents, *Educational Review* 22 (1970): 211–227; H. Giles, A. Williams, D. M. Mackie, and F. Rosselli, Reactions to Anglo- and Hispanic-American-accented speakers: Affect, identity, persuasion, and the English-only controversy, *Language and Communication* 15, no. 2 (1995): 107–120; M. Hernandez, Perceived job suitability as a function of ethnicity. Poster presentation at the Proceedings of the 19th Annual Conference of the Society for Industrial and Organizational Psychology, Chicago, IL, 2004; R. Lippi-Green, *English with an accent*.

60. H. Giles, Evaluative reactions to accents.

61. See chapter 3.

62. R. Lippi-Green, *English with an accent*.

63. Fiske and Taylor, *Social cognition*; H. Tajfel, *Human groups and social categories: Studies in social psychology* (Cambridge: Cambridge University Press, 1981); H. Tajfel, Social identity and intergroup behavior, *Social science information/sur les sciences socials* 13, no. 2 (1974): 65–93.

64. Fiske and Taylor, *Social cognition*.

65. See chapters 4 and 5.

66. P. L. Berger and T. Luckmann, *The social construction of reality* (New York: Doubleday, 1967); C. H. Cooley, *Social process* (Carbondale: Southern Illinois University Press, 1966); G. H. Mead, *Mind, self, and society, from the standpoint of a social behaviorist* (Berkeley, Calif.: University of California Press, 1934).

67. Fiske and Taylor, *Social cognition.*

68. J. M. Montepare and L. A. Zebrowitz, Person perception comes of age: The salience and significance of age in social judgments, in M. P. Zanna, ed., *Advances in experimental social psychology* (San Diego, Calif.: Academic Press, 1998), 30: 93–161.

69. D. A. Matcha, *The sociology of aging: A social problems perspective* (New York: Pearson, Allyn & Bacon, 1996).

70. J. Keith, C. L. Fry, A. P. Glascock, C. Ikels, J. Dickerson-Putnam, H. C. Harpending, et al., *The aging experience: Diversity and commonality across cultures* (Thousand Oaks, Calif.: Sage, 1994).

71. Matcha, *The sociology of aging.*

72. H. Helfrich, Age markers in speech, in K. R. Scherer and H. Giles, eds., *Social markers in speech* (New York: Cambridge University, 1979), pp. 63–108.

73. Helfrich, Age markers in speech.

74. D. B. Grusky, ed., *Social stratification: Class, race, and gender in sociological perspective*, 2nd ed. (Boulder, Colo.: Westview Press, 2000).

75. McCloud, *Understanding comics*; Shepard, *Mind sights.*

76. S. Romaine, *Language in society: An introduction to sociolinguistics* (New York: Oxford University Press, 2000); Trudgill, *Sociolinguistics*; R. Wardhaugh, *An introduction to sociolinguistics*, 3rd ed. (Malden, Mass.: Blackwell, 1998).

77. Lippi-Green, *English with an accent* Romaine, *Language in society*; Trudgill, *Sociolinguistics*; Wardhaugh, *An introduction to sociolinguistics.*

78. Romaine, *Language in society*; Trudgill, *Sociolinguistics*; Wardhaugh, *An introduction to sociolinguistics.*

79. J. R. Beniger, Personalization of mass media and the growth of pseudo-community, *Communication Research* 14, no. 3 (1987): 352–371; R. Merton, *Mass persuasion: The social psychology of a war bond drive* (New York: Harper, 1946).

80. A Hobson's choice is no choice at all: "Hobson was a stable owner who rented out horses. His customers were obliged to take the horse nearest the door." Ironically, "Hobson's choice" is the Cockney rhyming slang for voice. Retrieved from http://phrases.shu.ac.uk/meanings/183300.html, 2004.

81. See chapters 3 and 5.

82. S. Brave and C. Nass, Emotion in human-computer interaction, in J. Jacko and A. Sears, eds., *Handbook of human-computer interaction* (New York: Lawrence Erlbaum, 2002), pp. 251–271.

83. For an exception, see chapters 10 and 12. For a striking example of the equivalence between responses to computers and responses to people, see L. Zadro, K. D. Williams, and R. Richardson, How low can you go? Ostracism by a computer lowers belonging, control, self-esteem, and meaningful existence, *Journal of Experimental Social Psychology* 40 (2004): 560–567.

84. Walt Whitman, "Song of Myself," 51, in *Walt Whitman: Selected poems* (New York: Gramercy, 2001).

85. This was a common refrain in the United States in the 1960s and was part of the introduction of the television series *The Prisoner*.

86. M. H. Cohen, J. P. Giangola, and J. Balogh, *Voice user interface design* (Boston: Addison-Wesley, 2004); B. Kotelly, *The art and business of speech recognition: Creating the noble voice* (Boston: Addison-Wesley, 2003).

87. D. I. Slobin, *Psycholinguistics*, 2nd ed. (Glenview, Ill.: Scott, Foresman, 1979).

Chapter 7

1. R. M. Ryckman, *Theories of personality*, 7th ed. (Belmont, Calif.: Wadsworth, 1999).

2. G. Simmel, *The sociology of Georg Simmel*, trans. K. H. Wolff (New York: Free Press, 1985).

3. S. Brave and C. Nass, Emotion in human-computer interaction, in J. Jacko and A. Sears, eds., *Handbook of human-computer interaction* (New York: Lawrence Erlbaum, 2002), pp. 251–271.

4. Brave and Nass, Emotion in human-computer interaction.

5. A. S. Heberlein and R. Adolphs, Impaired spontaneous anthropomorphizing despite intact perception and social knowledge, *Proceedings of the National Academy of Sciences* 101, no. 19 (2004): 7487–7491.

6. Brave and Nass, Emotion in human-computer interaction.

7. R. W. Picard, *Affective computing* (Cambridge, Mass.: MIT Press, 1997); R. W. Picard, Does HAL cry digital tears? Emotions and computers, in D. G. Stork, ed., *HAL's legacy: 2001's computer as dream and reality* (Cambridge, Mass.: MIT Press, 1997), pp. 279–303.

8. J. J. Gross, Emotion and emotion regulation, in L. A. Pervin and O. P. John, eds., *Handbook of personality: Theory and research*, 2nd ed. (New York: Guildford, 1999), pp. 525–552. Recently, however, there has been an explosion of research on the psychology of emotion. Brave and Nass, Emotion in human-computer interaction.

9. F. W. Taylor, *The principles of scientific management* (New York: Harper, 1911); F. W. Taylor, *Scientific management* (New York: Harper, 1947).

10. C. Breazeal, *Designing sociable robots* (Cambridge, Mass.: MIT Press, 2002); D. A. Norman, *The design of everyday things* (Garden City, N.J.: Doubleday, 1990); D. A. Norman, *Emotional design: Why we love (or hate) everyday things* (New York: Basic Books, 2003); D. A. Norman, *Things that make us smart: Defending human attributes in the age of the machine* (New York: Perseus, 1994); Picard, *Affective computing*; Picard, Does HAL cry digital tears?; B. Reeves and C. Nass, *The media equation: How people treat computers, television, and new media like real people and places* (New York: Cambridge University Press, 1996).

11. Brave and Nass, Emotion in human-computer interaction.

12. Brave and Nass, Emotion in human-computer interaction.

13. Brave and Nass, Emotion in human-computer interaction.

14. Brave and Nass, Emotion in human-computer interaction.

15. Brave and Nass, Emotion in human-computer interaction.

16. J. Tooby and L. Cosmides, The past explains the present: Emotional adaptations and the structure of ancestral environments, *Ethology and Sociobiology* 11 (1990): 407–424.

17. The model is based on LeDoux's work in neuropsychology. J. E. LeDoux, *The emotional brain* (New York: Simon & Schuster, 1996).

18. Brave and Nass, Emotion in human-computer interaction. The limbic system is often considered to include the hypothalamus, the hippocampus, and the amygdala. The amygdala is the only area that is critical for emotion. J. E. LeDoux and E. A. Phelps, Emotional networks in the brain, in M. Lewis and J. M. Haviland-Jones, eds., *Handbook of emotions* (New York: Guilford Press, 2000), pp. 157–172.

19. A. R. Damasio, *Descartes' error: Emotion, reason, and the human brain* (New York: Putnam, 1994).

20. "You've got mail," spoken in a male, middle-aged, upbeat voice is the way that America Online users are notified of incoming messages.

21. N. I. Eisenberger, M. D. Lieberman, and K. D. Williams, Does rejection hurt? An fMRI study of social exclusion, *Science* 302 (2003): 290–292; P. J. Lang, The emotion probe: Studies of motivation and attention, *American Psychologist* 50, no. 5 (1995): 372–385; N. Malamuth, Sexually explicit media, gender differences, and evolutionary theory, *Journal of Communication* 46 (1996): 8–31; Reeves and Nass, *The media equation.*

22. C. Darwin, *The expression of the emotions in man and animals* (London: HarperCollins, 1998) (originally published in 1872); P. Ekman, All emotions are basic, in P. Ekman and R. J. Davidson, eds., *The nature of emotion: Fundamental questions* (New York: Oxford University Press, 1994), pp. 7–19; C. E. Izard, Basic emotions, relations among emotions, and emotion-cognition relations, *Psychological Review* 99, no. 3 (1992): 561–565; Tooby and Cosmides, The past explains the present.

23. J. R. Averill, A constructionist view of emotion, in R. Plutchik and H. Kellerman, eds., *Emotion: Theory, research, and experience* (vol. 1, pp. 305–339) (New York: Academic Press, 1980); A. Ortony and T. J. Turner, What's basic about emotions?, *Psychological Review* 97, no. 3 (1990): 315–331; R. A. Shweder, "You're not sick, you're just in love": Emotions as an interpretive system, in P. Ekman and R. J. Davidson, eds., *The nature of emotions* (New York: Oxford University Press, 1994), pp. 32–44; A. Wierzbicka, Talking about emotions: Semantics, culture, and cognition, *Cognition and Emotion* 6, nos. 3/4 (1992): 285–319.

24. L. F. Barrett and J. A. Russell, The structure of current affect: Controversies and emerging consensus, *Current Directions in Psychological Science* 8, no. 1 (1999): 10–14; Lang, The emotion probe.

25. P. Ekman, An argument for basic emotions, *Cognition and Emotion* 6 (1992): 169–200; K. Oatley and P. N. Johnson-Laird, Towards a cognitive theory of emotions, *Cognition and Emotion* 1, no. 1 (1987): 29–50; J. Panksepp, A critical role for "affective neuroscience" in resolving what is basic about basic emotions, *Psychological Review* 99, no. 3 (1992): 554–560.

26. Brave and Nass, Emotion in human-computer interaction.

27. G. H. Bower, How might emotions affect learning?, in C. Sven-Åke, ed., *The Handbook of Emotion and Memory: Research and Theory* (Hillsdale, N. J.: Lawrence Erlbaum, 1992), pp. 3–31.

28. G. C. Clore and K. Gasper, Feeling is believing: Some affective influences on belief, in N. H. Frijda, A. S. R. Manstead, and S. Bem, eds., *Emotions and beliefs: How feelings influence thoughts* (Paris: Editions de la Maison des Sciences de l'Homme and Cambridge University Press, 2000), pp. 10–44.

29. G. H. Bower and J. P. Forgas, Affect, memory, and social cognition, in E. Eich, J. F. Kihlstrom, G. H. Bower, J. P. Forgas, and P. M. Niedenthal, eds., *Cognition and Emotion* (Oxford: Oxford University Press, 2000), pp. 87–168.

30. J. J. Gross, Antecedent- and response-focused emotion regulation: Divergent consequences for experience, expression, and physiology, *Journal of Personality and Social Psychology* 74 (1998): 224–237.

31. D. M. Wegner, Ironic processes of mental control, *Psychological Review* 101 (1994): 34–52.

32. E. R. Hirt, R. J. Melton, H. E. McDonald, and J. M. Harackiewicz, Processing goals, task interest, and the mood-performance relationship: A mediational analysis, *Journal of Personality and Social Psychology* 71 (1996): 245–261; A. M. Isen, Positive affect and decision making, in M. Lewis and J. M. Haviland-Jones, eds., *Handbook of emotions* (New York: Guilford Press, 2000); N. Murray, H. Sujan, E. R. Hirt, and M. Sujan, The influence of mood on categorization: A cognitive flexibility interpretation, *Journal of Personality and Social Psychology* 59 (1990): 411–425.

33. K. Duncker, On problem-solving, *Psychological Monographs* 58 (whole no. 5) (1945).

34. A. M. Isen, K. A. Daubman, and G. P. Nowicki, Positive affect facilitates creative problem solving, *Journal of Personality and Social Psychology* 52, no. 6 (1987): 1122–1131.

35. A. M. Isen, A. S. Rosenzweig, and M. J. Young, The influence of positive affect on clinical problem solving, *Medical Decision Making* 11, no. 3 (1991): 221–227.

36. Isen, Positive affect and decision making; Reeves and Nass, *The media equation*; N. Schwartz and H. Bless, Happy and mindless, but sad and smart? The impact of affective states on analytic reasoning, in J. P. Forgas, ed., *Emotion and Social Judgment* (Oxford: Pergamon, 1991), pp. 55–71.

37. G. C. Clore, R. S. Wyer, Jr., B. Diened, K. Gasper, C. Gohm, and L. Isbell, Affective feelings as feedback: Some cognitive consequences, in L. L. Martin and G. C. Clore, eds., *Theories of mood and cognition: A user's handbook* (Mahwah, N.J.: Lawrence Erlbaum, 2001), pp. 63–84; R. Erber and M. W. Erber, Mood and processing: A view from a self-regulation perspective, in Martin and Clore, *Theories of mood and cognition*, pp. 63–84; P. M. Niedenthal, M. B. Setterlund, and D. E. Jones, Emotional organization of perceptual memory, in P. M. Niedenthal and S. Kitayama, eds., *The heart's eye* (San Diego: Academic Press, 1994), pp. 87–113.

38. Isen, Positive affect and decision making.

39. T. E. Galovski and E. B. Blanchard, Road rage: A domain for psychological intervention?, *Aggression and Violent Behavior* 9, no. 2 (2004): 105–127.

40. J. A. Groeger, *Understanding driving: Applying cognitive psychology to a complex everyday task* (Philadelphia: Psychology Press, 2000).

41. This experiment is described in more detail in C. Nass, I.-M. Jonsson, B. Reaves, H. Harris, S. Brave, and L. Takayama, Increasing safety in cars by matching driver emotion and car voice emotion, Proceedings of the 2005 CHI Conference (Portland, OR, 2005).

42. The driving simulator was STISIM Drive System projected on a six-foot diagonal, rear-projection screen.

43. The driving conditions included highways, country roads, and city driving.

44. To establish an initial emotional state in the drivers, all participants were shown one of two five-minute movies, consisting of thirty-seven video clips each, before entering the driving simulator. These clips were selected from a wide variety of films and television programs and were a subset of those used previously by B. H. Detenber and B. Reeves, A bio-informational theory of emotion: Motion and image size effects on viewers, *Journal of Communication* 46, no. 3 (1996): 66–84.

45. To check the effectiveness of the emotion manipulation, participants were asked to self-evaluate their emotional state using a variant of Izard's Differential Emotion Scale after watching the clips but before beginning driving. C. E. Izard, *Patterns of emotions* (New York: Academic Press, 1972). The index was comprised of twelve adjectives: *ashamed, fear, sad, scared, shocked, afraid, dislike, unhappy, upset, frightened, guilt,* and *revulsion*, all measured on five-point scales. The index was very reliable (Cronbach's $\alpha = .95$). As expected, participants who saw the upsetting videotape were much more upset, $M = 3.4$, $SD = 1.3$, than were participants who saw the pleasant videotape, $M = 1.6$, $SD = 3.2$, based on a two-tailed t-test, $t(38) = 6.11$, $p < .001$.

46. Here are some examples of the remarks made by the virtual passenger: "How do you think that the car is performing?," "Do you generally like to drive at, below, or above the speed limit?," "Don't you think that these lanes are a little too narrow?," "One of my favorite parts of this drive is the lighthouse. Be sure to tell me what you think of it once you see it," and "What kinds of things do you think about when you're driving?"

47. The next chapter discusses how emotion can be manifested in voice. To ensure that the voices were perceived to be energetic or subdued as intended, after participants completed the driving simulation, they were asked to rate the emotional tone of the voice with which they interacted. A participant's perception of the voice of the virtual passenger was based on the question, "How well does each of the following adjectives describe the voice of the virtual passenger?" This was followed by a list of adjectives on ten-point Likert scale ranging from "Describes very Poorly" (= 1) to "Describes very well" (= 10). Voice energy was an index based on two adjectives: *aroused* and *calm* (reverse-coded). The index was very reliable ($\alpha = .76$). Consistent with the voice manipulation, the energetic voice was perceived to be much more energetic, $M = 7.3$, $SD = 2.1$, than was the subdued voice, $M = 3.4$, $SD = 1.2$, based on a two-tailed t-test, $t(38) = 5.1$, $p < .001$.

48. The questionnaire was based on the question, "How well does each of the following adjectives describe how you felt while driving with the virtual passenger?" This was followed by a list of adjectives on ten-point Likert scale ranging from "Describes very poorly" (=1) to "Describes very well" (=10). Attentiveness was an index created by averaging responses to four adjectives in the questionnaires: *alert*, *careful*, *safe*, and *confident*. The index was very reliable ($\alpha = .83$).

49. The complete results table is presented below:

	Happy Drivers		Upset Drivers	
Dependent Variables	Enthused Voice	Subdued Voice	Enthused Voice	Subdued Voice
Number of accidents	2.0 (2.8)	8.3 (9.2)	9.6 (10.57)	6.3 (7.1)
Perceived attentiveness	7.4 (0.84)	5.7 (0.51)	5.6 (1.1)	7.4 (0.63)
Amount of speaking (min.)	5.77 (2.28)	4.19 (1.79)	3.90 (1.02)	4.67 (1.82)

Note: Standard deviations are in parentheses. All statistical analyses are based on 2 (driver emotion) by 2 (voice emotion), between-participants ANOVA.

50. $M = 4.15$ versus $M = 8.95$, $F(1,36) = 4.10$, $p < .05$. The effect of voice was so strong that it eliminated the inevitably significant difference in accident rate between happy and upset drivers, although the former tended to be larger than the latter, $F(1,36) = 2.23$, $p > .14$. There was no main effect for voice emotion.

51. $F(1,36) = 4.29$, $p < .05$. There were no main effects for driver emotion or for voice emotion.

52. $F(1,36) = 4.50$, $p < .04$. There were no main effects for driver emotion or for voice emotion.

53. For a similar finding concerning persuasion, see D. T. Wegener, R. E. Petty, and S. M. Smith, Positive mood can increase or decrease message scrutiny: The hedonic contingency view of mood and message processing, *Journal of Personality and Social Psychology* 69, no. 1 (1995): 5–15.

54. L. Gong, *The psychology of consistency in human-computer interaction*, unpublished doctoral dissertation, Stanford University, Stanford, Calif., 2000.

55. P. Ekman and W. V. Friesen, *Unmasking the face: A guide to recognizing emotions from facial clues* (Englewood Cliffs, N.J.: Prentice-Hall, 1975).

56. Picard, *Affective computing.*

57. E. H. Hess, Pupilometrics, in N. Greenfield and R. Sternbach, eds., *Handbook of psychophysiology* (New York: Holt, Rinehart & Winston, 1972).

58. Picard, *Affective computing.*

59. Picard, *Affective computing.*

60. S. Brave, C. Nass, and K. Hutchinson, Computers that care: Investigating the effects of orientation of emotion exhibited by an embodied computer agent, *International Journal of Human-Computer Studies* 62, no. 2 (2005): 161–178.

61. Brave, Nass, and Hutchinson, Computers that care.

62. Picard, *Affective computing.*

63. C. Nass, Y. Moon, J. Morkes, E.-Y. Kim, and B. J. Fogg, Computers are social actors: A review of current research, in B. Friedman, ed., *Moral and ethical issues in human-computer interaction* (Stanford, CA: CSLI Press, 1997), 137–162; C. Nass and J. Steuer, Voices, boxes, and sources of messages: Computers and social actors, *Human Communication Research* 19, no. 4 (1993): 504–527; Reeves and Nass, *The media equation.*

64. R. J. Davidson, On emotion, mood, and related affective constructs, in P. Ekman and R. J. Davidson, eds., *The Nature of Emotion* (New York: Oxford University Press, 1994), pp. 51–55.

65. D. Bishop, H. Jacks, and S. B. Tandy, The Structure of Temperament Questionnaire (STQ): Results from a U.S. sample, *Personality and Individual Differences* 14, no. 3 (1993): 485–487; D. Watson and L. A. Clark, Emotions, moods, traits, and temperaments: Conceptual distinctions and empirical findings, in P. Ekman and R. J. Davidson, eds., *The nature of emotion: Fundamental questions* (New York: Oxford University Press, 1994), pp. 89–93.

66. Watson and Clark, Emotions, moods, traits, and temperaments.

67. A. Cooper and P. Saffo, *The inmates are running the asylum* (New York: Sams, 1999).

Chapter 8

1. B. Reeves and C. Nass, *The media equation: How people treat computers, television, and new media like real people and places* (New York: Cambridge University Press, 1996).

2. C. Z. Malatesta and J. M. Haviland, Learning display rules: The socialization of emotion expression in infancy, *Child Development* 53 (1982): 991–1003.

3. J. M. Smith, *The theory of evolution* (New York: Cambridge University Press, 1993).

4. C. Darwin, *The expression of the emotions in man and animals* (London: HarperCollins, 1998) (originally published in 1872).

5. R. W. Picard, *Affective computing* (Cambridge, Mass.: MIT Press, 1997).

6. P. Ekman, Facial expression and emotion. *American Psychologist* 48 (1993): no. 4, 384–392.

7. G. Ball and J. Breese, Emotion and personality in conversational agents, in J. Cassell, J. Sullivan, S. Prevost and E. Churchill, eds., *Embodied conversational agents* (Cambridge, Mass.: MIT Press, 2000), pp. 189–219; K. R. Scherer, Speech and emotional states, in J. K. Darby, ed., *Speech Evaluation in Psychiatry* (New York: Grune and Stratton, 1981), pp. 189–220; K. R. Scherer, Vocal affect expression: A review and a model for future research, *Psychological Bulletin* 99 (1986): 143–165; K. R. Scherer, Vocal measurement of emotion, in R. Plutchik and H. Kellerman, eds., *Emotion: Theory, research, and experience* (San Diego: Academic Press, 1989), 4:233–259.

8. I. R. Murray and J. L. Arnott, Toward the simulation of emotion in synthetic speech: A review of the literature on human vocal emotion, *Journal Acoustical Society of America* 93, no. 2 (1993): 1097–1108.

9. R. L. C. Mitchell, R. Elliot, B. Martin, A. Cruttenden, and P. W. R. Woodruff, The neural response to emotional prosody, as revealed by functional magnetic resonance imaging, *Neuropsychologia* 41, no. 10 (2003): 1410–1421.

10. F. C. Merewether and M. Alpert, The components and neuroanatomic bases of prosody, *Journal of Communication Disorders* 23, nos. 4–5 (1990): 325–336.

11. Picard, *Affective computing.*

12. Picard, *Affective computing.*

13. People are generally about 60 percent accurate in recognizing the basic emotions in human speech. Scherer, Speech and emotional states.

14. People are generally about 50 percent accurate in recognizing the basic emotions in clearly synthetic speech. J. E. Cahn, The generation of affect in synthesized speech, *Journal of the American Voice I/O Society* 8 (1990): 1–19.

15. Murray and Arnott, Toward the simulation of emotion in synthetic speech.

16. Picard, *Affective computing.*

17. D. E. Bugental, L. R. Love, J. W. Kaswan, and C. April, Verbal-nonverbal conflict in parental messages to normal and disturbed children, *Journal of Abnormal Psychology* 77 (1971): 6–10; L. Gong, *The psychology of consistency in human-computer interaction*, unpublished doctoral dissertation, Stanford University, Stanford, Calif., 2000.

18. Bugental, Love, Kaswan, and April, Verbal-nonverbal conflict in parental messages to normal and disturbed children.

19. M. Argyle, F. Alkema, and R. Gilmour, The communication of friendly and hostile attitudes by verbal and non-verbal signals, *European Journal of Social Psychology* 1 (1971): 385–402; Gong, *The psychology of consistency in human-computer interaction.*

20. Argyle, Alkema, and Gilmour, The communication of friendly and hostile attitudes by verbal and non-verbal signals; Gong, *The psychology of consistency in human-computer interaction.*

21. Gong, *The psychology of consistency in human-computer interaction*; A. Mehrabian, When are feelings communicated inconsistently?, *Journal of Experimental Research in Personality* 4, no. 3 (1971): 198–212.

22. Mitchell, Elliot, Martin, Cruttenden, and Woodruff, The neural response to emotional prosody, as revealed by functional magnetic resonance imaging.

23. S. Brave and C. Nass, Emotion in human-computer interaction, in J. Jacko and A. Sears, eds., *Handbook of human-computer interaction* (New York: Lawrence Erlbaum, 2002), pp. 251–271.

24. Brave and Nass, Emotion in human-computer interaction; C. Nass, M. Lombard, L. Henriksen, and J. Steuer, Anthropocentrism and computers, *Behaviour and Information Technology* 14, no. 4 (1995): 229–238; Picard, *Affective computing.*

25. This experiment is described in more detail in C. Nass, U. Foehr, S. Brave, and M. Somoza, The effects of emotion of voice in synthesized and recorded speech, Paper presented at the Proceedings of Emotional and Intelligent II: The Tangled Knot of Social Cognition, North Falmouth, Mass., November 2–4, 2001.

26. The experiment was controlled by the CSLU Toolkit running on a Windows NT machine. Center for Spoken Language Understanding, CSLU Toolkit, retrieved from <http://www.cslu.ogi.edu/toolkit/>, 2004). A Dialogics board answered the phone calls. The synthesized voices were based on the default male voice provided by the Toolkit.

27. Questions about perceptions of story content, liking of the content, and suitability of the stories for extroverts and introverts were asked for each story. The first set of questions (which included questions about perceptions of story content and suitability of the stories) asked, "Please indicate how well the following adjectives describe the story about . . ." followed by a ten-point Likert scale anchored by "Describes very poorly" (=1) and "Describes very well" (=10). The second set of questions (which included questions about liking) asked, "Please indicate how well the following adjectives describe your feelings about the story about . . ." followed by a ten-point Likert scale anchored by "Describes very poorly" (=1) and "Describes very well" (=10).

28. Perception of happiness of content was an index comprised of the adjectives *happy* and *sad* (reverse-coded). The index was very reliable (across the six stories, average $r = .86$).

29. Liking of the content was an index comprised of six adjectives: *boring* (reverse-coded), *engaging, enjoyable, interesting, informative,* and *likeable*. The indices were highly reliable (average Cronbach's $\alpha = .91$).

30. Interest in the content by extroverts and introverts was an index comprised of two adjectives: *interesting for extroverts* and *interesting for introverts* (reverse coded). The indices were highly reliable (average $\alpha = .82$).

31. $M = 6.9$ versus $M = 5.4$, $F(1,27) = 51.2$, $p < .001$. This ANOVA analysis used valence of voice emotion as the between-participants factor and content as the repeated factor.

32. $M = 3.9$ versus $M = 2.6$, $F(1,27) = 29.8$, $p < .001$. This ANOVA analysis used valence of voice emotion as the between-participants factor and content as the repeated factor.

33. $M = 4.9$ versus $M = 4.4$, $F(1,27) = 6.3$, $p < .02$. This analysis used the six stories as the repeated factor and the consistency of voice and content (matched or mismatched) as the between-participants factor.

34. See chapters 2 through 6.

35. J. P. Olive, The talking computer: Text to speech synthesis, in D. Stork, ed., *HAL's legacy: 2001's computer as dream and reality* (Cambridge, Mass.: MIT Press, 1997), pp. 101–130.

36. R. W. Picard, Does HAL cry digital tears? Emotions and computers, in D. G. Stork, *HAL's legacy*, pp. 279–303.

37. For a discussion of emoticons and the definitions of many emoticons, see D. W. Sanderson, *Smileys* (Sebastopol, Calif.: O'Reilly, 1993).

38. Sanderson, *Smileys*.

39. A. Marriott, *VHML: Virtual human markup language*, retrieved from <http://www.talkingheads.computing.edu.au/documents/workshops/TalkingHeadTechnologyWorkshop/workshop/marriott/vhml_workshop.pdf>, 2001.

40. This paragraph is based on L. Gong and C. Nass, *Emotional expressions on computer interfaces: Testing the hedonic preference principle* (Stanford, Calif.: Stanford University, 2003).

41. N. H. Frijda, The laws of emotion, *American Psychologist* 43 (1988): 349–358; D. G. Myers and E. Diener, Who is happy? *Psychological Science* 6 (1995): 10–19.

42. K. C. Berridge, Pleasure, pain, desire, and dread: Hidden core processes of emotion, in D. Kahneman, E. Diener, and N. Schwarz, eds., *Well-being: The foundations of hedonic psychology* (New York: Russell Sage, 1999), pp. 525–557.

43. P. A. Bell, Affective state, attraction, and affiliation: Misery loves happy company, too, *Personality and Social Psychology Bulletin* 4 (1978): 616–619.

44. S. Davis, *The role of discrete emotions in advertising context effects*, unpublished doctoral dissertation, University of Pennsylvania, Philadelphia, 2000; M. E. Goldberg and G. J. Gorn, Happy

and sad TV programs: How they affect reactions to commercials, *Journal of Consumer Research* 14 (1987): 387–403; M. A. Kamins, L. J. Marks, and D. Skinner, Television commercial evaluation in the context of program induced mood: Congruency versus consistency effects, *Journal of Advertising* 20, no. 2 (1991): 1–14.

45. Reeves and Nass, *The media equation.*

46. Reeves and Nass, *The media equation.*

47. H. S. Friedman, R. E. Riggio, and D. F. Casella, Nonverbal skill, personal charisma, and initial attraction, *Personality and Social Psychology Bulletin* 14 (1988): 203–211.

48. People reciprocate acts of disclosure with disclosure. Y. Moon, Intimate exchanges: Using computers to elicit self-disclosure from consumers, *Journal of Consumer Research* 26, no. 4 (2000): 323–339; Y. Moon, Intimate self-disclosure exchanges: Using computers to build reciprocal relationships with consumers, manuscript, Cambridge, Mass., 1998.

49. For a remarkable example of this, see Moon, *Intimate self-disclosure exchanges.*

50. A. H. Gregory, L. Worrall, and A. Sarge, The development of emotional responses to music in young children, *Motivation and Emotion* 20, no. 4 (1996): 341–348.

51. P. J. Lang, The emotion probe: Studies of motivation and attention, *American Psychologist* 50, no. 5 (1995): 372–385; Reeves and Nass, *The media equation.*

52. Lang, The emotion probe.

53. Lang, The emotion probe; Reeves and Nass, *The media equation.*

54. Reeves and Nass, *The media equation.*

55. Reeves and Nass, *The media equation*; H. A. Sackeim, M. S. Greenberg, A. L. Weiman, R. C. Gur, J. P. Honogerbuhler, and N. Geschwind, Hemispheric asymmetry in the expression of positive and negative emotion, *Archives of neurology* 39 (1982): 687–692.

56. Sackeim, Greenberg, Weiman, Gur, Honogerbuhler, and Geschwind, Hemispheric asymmetry in the expression of positive and negative emotion. For other evidence of hemispheric specialization in emotion, see R. J. Davidson, Hemispheric asymmetry and emotion, in K. R. Scherer and P. Ekman, eds., *Approaches to emotion* (Hillsdale, N.J.: Lawrence Erlbaum, 1984), pp. 39–58; D. M. Tucker, Lateral brain function, emotion, and conceptualization, *Psychological Bulletin* 89 (1981): 19–46.

57. Brave and Nass, Emotion in human-computer interaction; E. Hatfield, J. T. Cacioppo, and R. L. Rapson, *Emotional contagion* (Paris: Editions de la Maison des Sciences de l'Homme and Cambridge University Press, 1994).

58. Reeves and Nass, *The media equation*; D. Zillmann, Television viewing and physiological arousal, in J. Bryant and D. Zillmann, eds., *Responding to the screen: Reception and reaction processes* (Hillsdale, N.J.: Lawrence Erlbaum, 1991), pp. 103–133.

59. Nass, Foehr, Brave, and Somoza, *The effects of emotion of voice in synthesized and recorded speech.*

60. $M = 5.9$ versus $M = 5.1$, $F(1, 27) = 6.2$, $p < .02$.

61. $M = 6.0$ versus $M = 5.3$, $F(1, 27) = 6.3$, $p < .02$.

62. R. W. Levenson, L. L. Carstensen, W. V. Friesen, and P. Ekman, Emotion, physiology, and expression in old age, *Psychology and Aging* 6, no. 1 (1991): 28–35.

Chapter 9

1. J. Kreiman and D. R. van Lancker, Hemispheric specialization for voice recognition: Evidence from dichotic listening, *Brain and Language* 34 (1988): no. 2, 246–252; D. I. Slobin, *Psycholinguistics*, 2nd ed. (Glenview, Ill.: Scott, Foresman, 1979).

2. J. Kess, *Psycholinguistics: Psychology, linguistics and the study of natural language* (Philadelphia: John Benjamin, 1992); B. S. Kisilevsky, S. M. J. Hains, K. Lee, X. Xie, H. Huang, H. H. Ye, et al., Effects of experience on fetal voice recognition, *Psychological Science* 14, no. 3 (2003): 220–224.

3. I. W. R. Bushnell, Mother's face recognition in newborn infants: Learning and memory, *Infant and Child Development* 10, nos. 1–2 (2001): 67–74.

4. J. A. Mennella and G. K. Beauchamp, The ontogeny of human flavor perception, in G. K. Beauchamp and L. Bartoshuk, eds., *Tasting and smelling*, 2nd ed. (San Diego: Academic Press, 1997), pp. 199–221.

5. C. Floccia, T. Nazzi, and J. Bertoncini, Unfamiliar voice discrimination for short stimuli in newborns, *Developmental Science* 3, no. 3 (2000): 333–343.

6. C. D. Tsang and L. J. Trainor, Spectral scope discrimination in infancy: Sensitivity to socially important timbres, *Infant Behavior and Development* 25, no. 2 (2002): 183–194.

7. R. S. Newman and P. W. Jusczyk, The cocktail party effect in infants, *Perception and Psychophysics* 58, no. 8 (1996): 1145–1156.

8. M. Schueller, D. Fucci, and Z. S. Bond, Perceptual judgment of voice pitch during pitch-matching tasks, *Perceptual and Motor Skills* 94, no. 3 (2002): 967–974.

9. L. C. Nygaard and D. B. Pisoni, Talker-specific learning in speech perception, *Perception and Psychophysics* 60, no. 3 (1998): 355–376.

10. M. S. Vitetitch, Change deafness: The inability to detect changes between two voices, *Journal of Experimental Psychology: Human Perception and Performance* 29, no. 2 (2003): 333–342.

11. The basic pitch of the voice is used to identify gender (chapter 2), personality (chapter 4), and emotion (chapter 8).

12. See chapters 4 and 5.

13. S. Brave and C. Nass, Emotion in human-computer interaction, in J. Jacko and A. Sears, eds., *Handbook of human-computer interaction* (New York: Lawrence Erlbaum, 2002), pp. 251–271.

14. M. Matthews, Introduction to timbre, in P. R. Cook, ed., *Music, cognition, and computerized sound: An introduction to psychoacoustics* (Cambridge, Mass.: MIT Press, 1999).

15. W. R. Zemlin, *Speech and hearing science: Anatomy and physiology*, 4th ed. (New York: Pearson, Allyn & Bacon, 1997).

16. Zemlin, *Speech and hearing science*.

17. See chapter 6.

18. R. Dawkins, *The selfish gene*, 2nd ed. (Oxford: Oxford University Press, 1989).

19. R. Axelrod, *The evolution of cooperation* (New York: Basic Books, 1984); Dawkins, *The selfish gene*.

20. G. Dejong, *Earwitness characteristics and speaker identification accuracy*, unpublished doctoral dissertation, University of Florida, Gainesville, 1998.

21. Dejong, *Earwitness Characteristics*.

22. M. C. McDermott, T. Owen, and F. M. McDermott, *Voice identification: The aural/spectrographic method*, retrieved from <http://www.owlinvestigations.com/forensic_articles/aural_spectroographic/fulltext.html>, 1996.

23. *State v. Cary*, 230 A.2d 384 (New Jersey Supreme Court 1967).

24. McDermott, Owen, and McDermott, *Voice identification*.

25. Vocent Solutions, *Voice authentication: Datamonitor consumer survey results* (Mountain View, Calif.: Vocent Solutions, 2003).

26. J. P. Olive, The talking computer: Text to speech synthesis, in D. Stork, ed., *HAL's legacy: 2001's computer as dream and reality* (Cambridge, Mass.: MIT Press, 1997), pp. 101–130.

27. Olive, The talking computer.

28. S. G. Harkins and R. E. Petty, The effects of source magnification on cognitive effort and attitudes: An information processing view, *Journal of Personality and Social Psychology* 40 (1981): 401–413; S. G. Harkins and R. E. Petty, Information utility and the multiple source effect in persuasion, *Journal of personality and social psychology* 52 (1987): 260–268; S. G. Harkins and R. E. Petty, Social context effects in persuasion: The effects of multiple sources and multiple targets, in P. Paulus, ed., *Advances in group psychology* (New York: Springer/Verlag, 1983), pp. 149–175.

29. D. J. Moore, J. C. Mowen, and R. Reardon, Multiple sources in advertising appeals: When product endorsers are paid by the advertising sponsor, *Journal of the Academy of Marketing Sciences* 22, no. 3 (1994): 234–243; D. J. Moore and R. Reardon, Source magnification: The role of multiple sources in the processing of advertising appeals, *Journal of Marketing Research* 24 (1987): 412–417.

30. R. B. Cialdini, *Influence: Science and practice*, 3rd ed. (New York: Harper Collins, 1993); M. Deutsch and H. B. Gerard, A study of normative and informational social influences upon individual judgment, *Journal of Abnormal and Social Psychology* 51 (1955): 629–636.

31. S. E. Asch, Opinions and social pressure, in A. P. Hare, E. F. Borgatta, and R. Bales, eds., *Small groups: Studies in social interaction* (New York: Knopf, 1966), pp. 318–324; Cialdini, *Influence*; E. Noelle-Neumann, *The spiral of silence*, 2nd ed. (Chicago: University of Chicago Press, 1993).

32. Deutsch and Gerard, A study of normative and informational social influences upon individual judgment.

33. K. M. Lee, Presence, explicated, *Communication Theory* 14 (2004): 27–50; K. M. Lee, Why presence occurs: Evolutionary psychology, media equation, and presence, *Presence: Teleo-perators and Virtual Environments* 13, no. 4 (2004): 494–505; K. M. Lee and C. Nass, Social-psychological origins of feelings of presence: Creating social presence with machine-generated voices, *Media Psychology* 7 (2005): 31–45; M. Lombard and T. B. Ditton, At the heart of it all: The concept of presence, *Journal of Computer-Mediated-Communication* 3, no. 2 (1997), retrieved from <http://www.ascusc.org/jcmc/vol3/issue2/>, 2004.

34. This experiment is described in more detail in K. M. Lee and C. Nass, The multiple source effect and synthesized speech: Doubly disembodied language as a conceptual framework, *Human Communication Research* 30, no. 2 (2004): 182–207. This is not the same Web site as in chapter 4.

35. Three distinct voices were created by manipulating preset text-to-speech parameters provided by the Center for Spoken Language Understanding's CSLU Toolkit, retrieved from <http://www.cslu.ogi.edu/toolkit/>, 2004. The remaining two voices were the "big man" and "man" synthetic voices offered by Bell Lab's TTS engine demo Web site.

36. The order of the voices was balanced via Latin squares to control for possible order effects. The Latin-squares approach assumes that the position of the voices (e.g., which voice was heard first and which voice was heard last) might matter but that the order of voices does not matter. B. J. Winer and K. W. Michels, *Statistical principles in experimental design*, 3rd ed. (New York: McGraw-Hill, 1991).

37. See chapters 2 and 3.

38. Personal opinion of the reviewed book was an index of four items, all measured on ten-point Likert scales ranging from "Describes very poorly" (= 1) to "Describes very well" (= 10): "How likely would you be to recommend this book to your friends? How much would you enjoy reading this book? How would you judge the quality of this book? How likely would you be to buy this book if you were going to buy a novel?" The indices for each of the three books were very reliable (Cronbach's α = .93, .93, and .90).

39. Public opinion of the reviewed book was an index of four items, all measured on ten-point Likert scales ranging from "Describes very poorly" (= 1) to "Describes very well" (= 10): "How

likely would the typical reader be to recommend this book to their friends? How much would the typical reader enjoy reading this book? How would the typical reader judge the quality of this book? How likely would the typical reader be to buy this book if they were going to buy a novel?" The indices for each of the three books were very reliable (Cronbach's $\alpha = .93$, .93, and .91).

40. See Lombard and Ditton, At the heart of it all: The concept of presence.

41. Presence was an index of seven items, all measured on ten-point Likert scales ranging from "Describes very poorly" (= 1) to "Describes very well" (= 10): "While you were hearing each review, how much did you feel as if each reviewer was talking to you? While you were hearing each review, how vividly were you able to mentally imagine each reviewer? When moving from one review to another review, how easily were you able to distinguish one reviewer from another? After hearing all reviews for a book, how much did you feel as if two or more people had talked to you about the book? After hearing all reviews for a book, how vividly were you able to mentally imagine all reviewers? How much attention did you pay to the reviews? How much did you feel involved with the reviews?" The index was very reliable (Cronbach's $\alpha = .81$).

42. Here is the complete results table:

Dependent Variable	Single Voice (No Reminder)	Multiple Voices (No Reminder)	Single Voice (Reminder)	Multiple Voices (Reminder)
Personal opinion (average of three books)	4.51 (1.78)	5.63 (1.71)	4.66 (1.23)	5.64 (1.76)
Assessment of public opinion (average of three books)	4.99 (1.41)	5.93 (1.36)	5.30 (1.03)	6.08 (1.26)
Social presence	2.83 (1.42)	4.26 (1.54)	2.69 (1.16)	4.27 (1.43)

Note: Standard deviations are in parentheses. For participants' perceptions of the books and perceptions of public opinion, the statistical analysis was based on a repeated-measures ANOVA with number of voices as the between-participants factor and book as the repeated factor. For social presence, the analysis was based on a one-factor ANOVA with number of voices as the between-participants factor.

43. $F(1, 38) = 4.10$, $p < .05$.

44. $F(1, 38) = 4.65$, $p < .05$.

45. $F(1,38) = 9.24$, $p < .01$.

46. For a discussion of mindlessness, see E. Langer, *Mindfulness* (Reading, Mass.: Addison-Wesley, 1989).

47. Though it seemed likely that the warning would affect only the multiple-voice situation, *both* the single- and multiple-voice situations had to be done again, despite the cost of time for

the twenty participants. The basis of experimental inference is that making a valid comparison between two groups of randomly assigned people requires that *only one thing at a time* can be varied. If the initial one-voice participants were compared to the multiple-voice participants who were warned about computized speech and differences were noted between the two groups, then it wouldn't be clear whether the effect was caused by the number of voices, the warning, or a complex interaction between the warning and the number of voices. For a discussion of the logic of experimental design, see D. C. Montgomery, *Design and analysis of experiments*, 5th ed. (New York: Wiley, 2000).

48. $F(1, 38) = 4.14$, $p < .05$.

49. $F(1, 38) = 4.57$, $p < .05$.

50. $F(1, 38) = 14.9$, $p < .001$.

51. C. Nass, Y. Moon, and P. Carney, Are people polite to computers? Responses to computer-based interviewing systems, *Journal of Applied Social Psychology* 29, no. 5 (1999): 1093–1110.

52. S. E. Finkel, T. M. Guterbock, and M. J. Borg, Race-of-interviewer effects in a pre-election poll: Virginia 1989, *Public Opinion Quarterly* 55 (1991): 313–330; E. E. Kane, Interviewer gender and gender attitudes, *Public Opinion Quarterly* 57 (1993): 1–28; C. Nass, Etiquette equality: Exhibitions and expectations of computer politeness, *Communications of the ACM* 47, no. 4 (2004): 35–37; B. Reeves and C. Nass, *The media equation: How people treat computers, television, and new media like real people and places* (New York: Cambridge University Press, 1996).

53. Reeves and Nass, *The media equation*; Nass, Etiquette equality.

54. C. Nass and J. Steuer, Voices, boxes, and sources of messages: Computers and social actors, *Human Communication Research* 19, no. 4 (1993): 504–527; C. Nass, J. Steuer, L. Henriksen, and D. C. Dryer, Machines, social attributions, and ethopoeia: Performance assessments of computers subsequent to "self-" or "other-" evaluations, *International Journal of Human-Computer Studies* 40, no. 3 (1994): 543–559.

55. Reeves and Nass, *The media equation*; W. Wilson and W. Chambers, Effectiveness of praise of self versus praise of others, *Journal of Social Psychology* 129 (1989): 555–556.

56. Nass and Steuer, Voices, boxes, and sources of messages.

57. Nass and Steuer, Voices, boxes, and sources of messages.

58. This section draws heavily from Reeves and Nass, *The media equation*.

59. For an extended discussion and experimental evidence on this point, see K. M. Lee, *Social responses to synthesized speech: Theory and application*, unpublished doctoral dissertation, Stanford University, Stanford, Calif., 2002.

60. S. Bochner and C. A. Insko, Communication discrepancy, source credibility, and opinion change, *Journal of Personality and Social Psychology* 4 (1966): 614–621; Reeves and Nass, *The media equation*.

61. Reeves and Nass, *The media equation*; P. Zimbardo and M. R. Leippe, Shortcuts to acceptance: Using heuristics instead of systematic analysis, in P. Zimbardo and M. R. Leippe, eds., *The psychology of attitude change and social influence* (New York: McGraw-Hill, 1991).

62. See chapter 14 for a discussion of scapegoating.

63. See chapters 2 through 6.

64. E. L. Thorndike, A constant error on psychological rating, *Journal of Applied Psychology* 4 (1920): 25–29.

65. Nygaard and Pisoni, Talker-specific learning in speech perception.

66. P. P. Maglio, T. Matlock, S. J. Gould, D. Koons, and C. S. Campbell, On understanding discourse in human-computer interaction, Paper presented at the Twenty-fourth Annual Conference of the Cognitive Science Society, Fairfax, Va., 2002; T. Matlock, C. S. Campbell, P. P. Maglio, S. Zhai, and B. A. Smith, Designing feedback for an attentive office, Paper presented at the Eighth Conference on Human-Computer Interaction (Interact 2001), Tokyo, 2001.

67. Maglio, Matlock, Gould, Koons, and Campbell, On understanding discourse in human-computer interaction.

68. Matlock, Campbell, Maglio, Zhai, and Smith, Designing feedback for an attentive office.

69. This is a quotation from the movie *Star Wars*, in which James Earl Jones is the voice of Darth Vader.

70. This is a play by Athol Fugard in which James Earl Jones played a servant.

71. D. R. Van Lancker, J. L. Cummings, J. Kreiman, and B. H. Dobkin, Phonagnosia: A dissociation between familiar and unfamiliar voices, *Cortex* 24, no. 2 (1988): 195–209; D. R. Van Lancker and J. Kreiman, Voice discrimination and recognition are separate abilities, *Neuropsychologia* 25, no. 5 (1987): 829–834; D. R. Van Lancker, J. Kreiman, and J. L. Cummings, Voice perception deficits: Neuroanatomical correlates of phonagnosia, *Journal of Clinical and Experimental Neuropsychology* 11, no. 5 (1988): 665–674.

72. Van Lancker, Cummings, Kreiman, and Dobkin, Phonagnosia; Van Lancker and Kreiman, Voice discrimination and recognition are separate abilities; Van Lancker, Kreiman, and Cummings, Voice perception deficits.

73. Nass and Steuer, Voices, boxes, and sources of messages: Computers and social actors.

74. For a further discussion of branding, see chapter 5.

75. D. A. Norman, *The invisible computer: Why good products can fail, the personal computer is so complex, and information appliances are the solution* (Cambridge, Mass.: MIT Press, 1999); M. Weiser, The computer for the twenty-first-century, *Scientific American* 265, no. 3 (1991): 94–104.

76. H. F. Taylor, *Balance in small groups* (New York: Van Nostrand Reinhold, 1970).

77. See chapters 2 through 8.

78. D. S. Brungart, B. D. Simpson, M. A. Ericson, and K. R. Scott, Informational and energetic masking effects in the perception of multiple simultaneous talkers, *Journal of the Acoustical Society of America* 110, no. 5 (2001): 2527–2538.

79. R. Hammersley and J. D. Read, The effect of participation in a conversation on recognition and identification of the speakers' voices, *Law and Human Behavior* 9, no. 1 (1985): 71–81.

80. J. Kreiman and G. Papcun, Comparing discrimination and recognition of unfamiliar voice, *Speech Communication* 10, no. 3 (1991): 265–275.

81. H. von Restorff, Analyse von Vorgangen im Spurenfeld. I. Uber die Wirkung von Bereichsbildungen im Spurenfeld, *Psychologie Forschung* 21 (1933): 56–112.

82. B. Schwartz, *The paradox of choice: Why more is less* (Hopewell, N.J.: Ecco, 2004).

83. L. A. Festinger, *A theory of cognitive dissonance* (Stanford, Calif.: Stanford University Press, 1957).

84. Schwartz, *The paradox of choice.*

85. If the user interacts with the voice instead of merely listening to it, the voice will be more memorable and hence more likeable. Hammersley and Read, The effect of participation in a conversation on recognition and identification of the speakers' voices. See also A. M. Colman, W. M. Best, and A. J. Austen, Familiarity and liking: Direct tests of the preference-feedback hypothesis, *Psychological Reports* 58, no. 3 (1986): 931–938; S. T. Fiske and S. E. Taylor, *Social cognition* (New York: McGraw-Hill, 1991); K. W. Kerber and R. Singleton, Trait and situational attributions in a naturalistic setting: Familiarity, liking, and attribution validity, *Journal of Personality* 52, no. 3 (1984): 205–219.

86. Nass, Moon, and Carney, Are people polite to computers?; Reeves and Nass, *The media equation.*

87. S. S. Iyengar and M. R. Lepper, When choice is demotivating: Can one desire too much of a good thing?, *Journal of Personality and Social Psychology* 79, no. 6 (2000): 995–1006.

88. G. A. Miller, The magical number seven, plus or minus two: Some limits on our capacity for processing information, *Psychological Review* 63 (1956): 81–97.

89. C. Nass, E.-Y. Kim, and E.-J. Lee, When your face is the interface: An experimental comparison of interacting with one's own face or someone else's face, Paper presented at CHI 98, the International Conference of the Association for Computing Machinery's (ACM) Special-Interest group (SIG) on Computer-Human Intimation (CHI), Los Angeles, 1998.

90. See chapters 3 and 6 for an extended discussion of this point.

Chapter 10

1. See chapter 3.

2. See chapter 2.

3. See chapters 4 and 5.

4. See chapter 6.

5. See chapter 7.

6. See chapter 2.

7. See chapter 3.

8. See chapters 4 and 5.

9. See chapter 8.

10. See chapter 9.

11. N. Tinbergen, *The study of instinct* (Oxford: Clarendon Press, 1951).

12. Tinbergen, *The study of instinct.*

13. For a similar argument, see B. Reeves and C. Nass, *The media equation: How people treat computers, television, and new media like real people and places* (New York: Cambridge University Press, 1996).

14. For a discussion of mindlessness, see E. Langer, Matters of mind: Mindfulness/mindlessness in perspective, *Consciousness and Cognition* 1 (1992): 289–305; E. Langer, *Mindfulness* (Reading, Mass.: Addison-Wesley, 1989).

15. R. Descartes, *Meditations and other metaphysical writings*, trans. D. M. Clarke (New York: Penguin, 1999).

16. Descartes, *Meditations and other metaphysical writings.*

17. Descartes, *Meditations and other metaphysical writings.* Descartes then goes on to argue his way back to the real world, but that part of his argument is much weaker and not important to what follows.

18. *Guinness book of world records 2004* (New York: Time, 2003).

19. I. Asimov, *I, robot* (New York: Bantam, 1991).

20. These sentences come from interactions with the United Airlines system on May 24, 2004.

21. These sentences come from interactions with the Jet Blue Airlines system on May 24, 2004.

22. This is a foolish strategy. See this chapter and chapter 14.

23. This conclusion is based on interactions with toll-free information on May 24, 2004.

24. Orange Group, *Ananova*, retrieved from <http://www.ananova.com>, 2004.

25. Orange Group, *Ananova*.

26. These sentences are derived from the version available on May 24, 2004 on Orange Group, *Ananova*.

27. This experiment is described in more detail in A. Huang, F. Lee, C. Nass, Y. Paik, and L. Swartz, Can voice user interfaces say "I"? An experiment with recorded speech and TTS, unpublished manuscript, Stanford, Calif., 2001.

28. The experiment was controlled by the CSLU Toolkit running on a Windows NT machine. Center for Spoken Language Understanding, CSLU Toolkit, retrieved from <http://www.cslu.ogi.edu/toolkit/>, 2004. A Dialogics board answered the phone calls.

29. Gender was not expected to be an issue with the questions addressed in this research, but future research should explore any possible effects of gender, personality, or emotion.

30. The synthetic voices were produced using the Festival engine of the Center for Spoken Language Understanding (CSLU) Toolkit. The different voices were created by manipulating parameters that were provided by the synthetic engine.

31. Speech recognition was not used because it was important to ensure accuracy and to guarantee that people would not be asked to repeat their bids.

32. The questionnaire was organized around the question, "How well does each of the following adjectives describe your feelings about [the system, yourself]?" Each question was followed by a series of adjectives. Each adjective was addressed on an independent, ten-point Likert-type scale. The scales were anchored by "Describes very poorly" (= 1) and "Describes very well" (= 10). The indices were created based on theory and factor analysis.

33. Usefulness of the system was an index composed of four adjectives: *easy-to-use*, *useful*, *frustrating* (reverse-coded), and *complicated* (reverse-coded). The index was very reliable (α = .74).

34. Trustworthiness of the system was an index of trustworthy and fair. The index was reliable (r = .60).

35. Formality of the system was measured by a single adjective: *formal*.

36. Like a person was measured by a single questionnaire item that asked participants to indicate how much the auction system was "like a person."

37. Feeling relaxed was an index composed of four adjectives: *relax*, *calm*, *uneasy* (reverse-coded), and *comfortable*. The index was highly reliable (α = .92).

38. Enjoyment of the system was an index of *annoying* (reverse-coded), *boring* (reverse-coded), *engaging*, *enjoyable*, *fun*, *interesting*, and *likable*. The index was very reliable ($\alpha = .90$).

39. Here is the complete results table:

Dependent Variable	Recorded Voice "I"	Recorded Voice No "I"	Synthetic Voice "I"	Synthetic Voice No "I"
Like a person	6.2 (2.8)	4.6 (2.0)	4.06 (1.2)	3.4 (1.5)
Feeling relaxed	6.9 (1.4)	5.8 (1.1)	5.1 (1.76)	7.3 (1.6)
Usefulness of the system	7.7 (1.2)	7.2 (1.0)	6.0 (0.8)	7.15 (1.4)
Average bid price	24.4 (5.3)	21.3 (2.06)	23.9 (5.3)	25.4 (4.2)
Enjoyment of the system	5.8 (2.4)	6.2 (2.0)	4.3 (1.2)	5.2 (1.4)
Trustworthiness of the	5.1 (2.2)	5.8 (1.9)	4.9 (1.5)	6.7 (1.6)
Formality of the system	4.8 (2.2)	6.2 (2.3)	5.9 (2.3)	7.0 (1.7)

Note: Standard deviations are in parentheses. All statistical analyses were based on a full-factorial, 2 (type of voice) by 2 (used *I* or not) ANOVA.

40. $F(1,60) = 11.4$, $p < .001$.

41. $F(1,60) = 5.0$, $p < .03$. There was no significant interaction.

42. There was a significant interaction with respect to feeling relaxed, $F(1,60) = 19.9$, $p < .001$.

43. There was a significant interaction with respect to perceived usefulness of the system, $F(1,60) = 8.6$, $p < .01$.

44. $t(30) = 3.1$, $p < .01$.

45. $t(30) = 0.89$, $p > .35$. The interaction in the two-way ANOVA was not significant, $F(1,60) = 1.5$, $p > .20$.

46. There was a significant interaction with respect to the amount bid, $F(1,60) = 4.4$, $p < .05$. There were no main effects.

47. The word *evoked* was selected to echo the notion of "evocative object" developed by Turkle. S. Turkle, *The second self: Computers and the human spirit* (New York: Simon & Schuster, 1984).

48. There was a significant main effect with respect to recorded versus synthetic speech, $F(1,60) = 9.9$, $p < .001$. There was no main effect with respect to personal versus impersonal speech.

49. K. Isbister, How do we decide when a computer character is intelligent? Intelligence assessment and perceived intelligence in human-human interaction and how it relates to human-computer interaction, Paper presented at the Lifelike Computer Characters Conference, Snowbird, Utah, October 1995; C. Nass, E. Robles, and Q. Wang, "User as assessor" approach to embodied conversational agents (ECAs): The case of apparent attention in ECAs, in Z. Ruttkay and C. Pelachaud, eds., *Evaluating embodied conversational agents* (New York: Kluwer, 2004), pp. 164–187.

50. There was a significant main effect with respect to recorded versus synthetic speech, $F(1,60) = 7.2$, $p < .01$. There was no main effect with respect to personal versus impersonal speech and no interaction.

51. J. P. Olive, The talking computer: Text to speech synthesis, in D. Stork, ed., *HAL's legacy: 2001's computer as dream and reality* (Cambridge, Mass.: MIT Press, 1997), pp. 101–130.

52. There was a significant main effect with respect to recorded versus synthetic speech, $F(1,60) = 5.9$, $p < .01$.

53. See chapter 11 for further discussion.

54. For recorded speech participants, non-*I* participants perceived the system as more formal than *I* participants, $t(30) = 2.1$, $p < .01$.

55. See chapter 14 for more details.

56. D. O. Sears, The person-positivity bias, *Journal of Personality and Social Psychology* 44, no. 2 (1983): 233–250.

57. H. Maldonado and B. Hayes-Roth, Toward cross-cultural believability in character design, in S. Payr and R. Trappl, eds., *Agent culture: Designing virtual characters for a multi-cultural world* (Mahwah, N.J.: Lawrence Erlbaum, 2004), pp. 143–175; P. Miller, J. Kozu, and A. Davis, Social influence, empathy, and prosocial behavior in cross-cultural perspective, in W. Wosinska, D. Barrett, R. B. Cialdini and J. Reykowski, eds., *The practice of social influence in multiple cultures* (Mahwah, N.J.: Lawrence Erlbaum, 2001), pp. 63–77.

58. K. M. Lee, Presence, explicated, *Communication Theory* 14 (2004): 27–50.

59. W. Shakespeare, *The complete works of William Shakespeare* (New York: Gramercy, 1975).

60. C. Nass and Y. Moon, Machines and mindlessness: Social responses to computers, *Journal of Social Issues* 56, no. 1 (2000): 81–103; C. Nass, Y. Moon, J. Morkes, E.-Y. Kim, and B. J. Fogg, Computers are social actors: A review of current research, in B. Friedman, ed., *Moral and ethical issues in human-computer interaction* (Stanford, Calif.: CSLI Press, 1997), pp. 137–162; C. Nass and J. Steuer, Voices, boxes, and sources of messages: Computers and social actors, *Human Communication Research* 19, no. 4 (1993): 504–527; Reeves and Nass, *The media equation.*

Chapter 11

1. B. Laurel, *Computers as theatre* (Reading, Mass.: Addison-Wesley, 1991); B. Laurel, Interface agents: Metaphors with character, in B. Laurel, ed., *The art of human-computer interface design* (New York: Addison-Wesley, 1990); T. Oren, G. Salomon, K. Kreitman, and A. Don, Characterizing the interface, in B. Laurel, ed., *The art of human-computer interface design* (Reading, Mass.: Addison-Wesley, 1997); D. Stork, *HAL's legacy: 2001's computer as dream and reality* (Cambridge, Mass.: MIT Press, 1997).

2. J. Cassell, J. Sullivan, S. Prevost, and E. Churchill, eds., *Embodied conversational agents* (Cambridge, Mass.: MIT Press, 2000); Laurel, Interface agents; Laurel, *Computers as theatre*; L.

Sproull, M. Subramani, S. Kiesler, J. H. Walker, and K. Waters, When the interface is a face, *Human-Computer Interaction* 11 (1996): 97–124.

3. Cassell, Sullivan, Prevost, and Churchill, *Embodied conversational agents*; Laurel, *Computers as theatre*; Laurel, Interface agents.

4. D. Jurafsky, J. H. Martin, K. Van der Linden, and N. Ward, *Speech and language processing: An introduction to natural language processing, computational linguistics, and speech recognition* (Upper Saddle River, N.J.: Prentice Hall, 2000); J. Lai, Conversational interfaces, *Communications of the ACM* 43, no. 9 (2000): 24–27; R. C. Schank, "I'm sorry, Dave, I'm afraid I can't do that": How could HAL use language?, in Stork, *HAL's legacy*.

5. M. T. Maybury, *Intelligent multimedia interfaces* (Menlo Park, Calif.: AAAI Press, 1993); D. W. Patterson, *Introduction to artificial intelligence and expert systems* (Englewood Cliffs, N.J.: Prentice Hall, 1990).

6. R. W. Picard, *Affective computing* (Cambridge, Mass.: MIT Press, 1997).

7. E. Jettmar and C. Nass, Adaptive interfaces: Effects on user performance, Paper presented at CHI 2002, the International Conference of the Association for Computing Machinery's (ACM) Special-Interest Group (SIG) on Computer-Human Interaction (CHI), Minneapolis, Minn., 2002; Y. Moon and C. Nass, Adaptive agents and personality change: Complimentary versus similarity as forms of adaption, Paper presented at CHI 1996, the International Conference of the Association for Computing Machinery's (ACM) Special-Interest Group (SIG) on Computer- Human Interaction (CHI), Vancouver, Calif., 1996.

8. C. Nass, Y. Moon, B. J. Fogg, B. Reeves, and D. C. Dryer, Can computer personalities be human personalities?, *International Journal of Human-Computer Studies* 43, no. 2 (1995): 223–239.

9. A. Rosenfeld, Eyes for computers: How HAL could "see," in Stork, *HAL's legacy*, pp. 211–235.

10. J. Lai, When computers speak, hear, and understand, *Communications of the ACM* 44, no. 3 (2001): 66–68; C. Nass and K. M. Lee, Does computer-synthesized speech manifest personality? Experimental tests of recognition, similarity-attraction, and consistency-attraction, *Journal of Experimental Psychology: Applied* 7, no. 3 (2001): 171–181; J. P. Olive, The talking computer: Text to speech synthesis, in Stork, *HAL's legacy*, pp. 101–130.

11. Cassell, Sullivan, Prevost, and Churchill, *Embodied conversational agents*; Sproull, Subramani, Kiesler, Walker, and Waters, When the interface is a face.

12. J. Cassell, Nudge nudge wink wink: Elements of face-to-face conversation for embodied conversational agents, in Cassell, Sullivan, Prevost, and Churchill, *Embodied conversational agents*, pp. 1–27.

13. V. M. Cassia, C. Turati, and F. Simion, Can a nonspecific bias toward top-heavy patterns explain newborn's face preferences?, *Psychological Science* 15, no. 6 (2004): 379–383.

14. C. A. Nelson, The development and neural bases of face recognition, *Infant and Child Development* 10 (2001): 3–18.

15. S. McCloud, *Understanding comics* (New York: Kitchen Sink Press, 1994); B. Reeves and C. Nass, *The media equation: How people treat computers, television, and new media like real people and places* (New York: Cambridge University Press, 1996).

16. D. W. Massaro, *Perceiving talking faces: From speech perception to a behavioral principle* (Cambridge, Mass.: MIT Press, 1998).

17. H. McGurk and J. MacDonald, Hearing lips and seeing voices, *Nature* 264 (1976): 746–748.

18. McGurk and MacDonald, Hearing lips and seeing voices.

19. Massaro, *Perceiving talking faces.*

20. L. D. Rosenblum, M. A. Schmuckler, and J. A. Johnson, The McGurk effect in infants, *Perception and Psychophysics* 59, no. 3 (1997): 347–357.

21. M. Pare, R. C. Richler, M. ten Hove, and K. G. Munhall, Gaze behavior in audiovisual speech perception: The influence of ocular fixations on the McGurk effect, *Perception and Psychophysics* 65, no. 4 (2003): 553–567.

22. J. MacDonald, S. Anderson, and T. Bachmann, Hearing by eye: How much spatial degradation can be tolerated?, *Perception* 29, no. 10 (2000): 1155–1168.

23. J. A. Jones and D. E. Callan, Brain activity during audiovisual speech perception: An fMRI study of the McGurk effect, *Neuroreport* 14, no. 8 (2003): 1129–1133.

24. For a discussion of asynchrony and integration of voice and face, see D. W. Massaro, Integrating multiple sources of information in listening and reading, in A. Allport, D. Mackay, W. Prinz, and E. Scheerer, eds., *Language perception and production: Shared mechanisms in listening, speaking, reading, and writing* (San Diego: Academic Press, 1987), 111–129; D. W. Massaro, Language processing and information processing, in N. H. Anderson, ed., *Contributions to information integration theory* (Hillsdale, NJ: Erlbaum, 1991), 259–292.

25. Reeves and Nass, *The media equation*; B. Reeves and D. H. Voelker, *Effects of audio-video asynchrony on viewer's memory, evaluation of content, and detection ability* (Stanford, Calif.: Stanford University, 1993).

26. A summary of the literature suggests that adding a face to audio improves understanding relative to audio alone until the asynchrony is larger than between 200 and 500 ms. D. W. Massaro, *Perceiving talking faces: From speech perception to a behavioral principle* (Cambridge, MA: MIT Press, 1998).

27. F. R. Volkmar and A. E. Siegel, Young children's responses to discrepant social communications, *Journal of Child Psychology and Psychiatry and Allied Disciplines* 20, no. 2 (1979): 139–149.

28. B. B. Domangue, Decoding effects of cognitive complexity, tolerance of ambiguity, and verbal-nonverbal inconsistency, *Journal of Personality* 46, no. 3 (1978): 519–535.

29. P. Noller, Channel consistency and inconsistency in the communications of married couples, *Journal of Personality and Social Psychology* 43 (1982): 732–741.

30. D. E. Bugental, L. R. Love, J. W. Kaswan, and C. April, Verbal-nonverbal conflict in parental messages to normal and disturbed children, *Journal of Abnormal Psychology* 77 (1971): 6–10; L. Gong, *The psychology of consistency in human-computer interaction,* unpublished doctoral dissertation, Stanford University, Stanford, Calif., 2000.

31. P. Ekman and W. V. Friesen, Detecting deception from the body or face, *Journal of Personality and Social Psychology* 29, no. 3 (1974): 288–298; P. Ekman, and W. V. Friesen, Nonverbal leakage and clues to deception, *Psychiatry* 32 (1969): 88–95; M. Zuckerman, R. Driver, and R. Koestner, Discrepancy as a cue to actual and perceived deception, *Journal of Nonverbal Behavior* 7, no. 2 (1982): 95–100.

32. T. Allison, G. McCarthy, A. B. Nobre, A. Puce, and A. Belger, Human extrastriate visual cortex and the perception of faces, words, numbers, and colors, *Cerebral Cover* 5 (1994): 544–554; V. P. Clark, K. Keil, J. M. Maisog, S. M. Courtney, L. G. Ungerleider, and J. V. Haxby, Functional magnetic resonance imaging of human visual cortex during face matching: A comparison with positron emission tomography, *NeuroImage* 4 (1996): 1–15; E. E. Cooper and T. J. Wojan, Differences in the coding of spatial relations in face identification and basic-level object recognition, *Journal of Experimental Psychology: Learning, Memory, and Cognition* 26, no. 2 (2000): 470–488; A. Puce, T. Allison, M. Asgari, J. C. Gore, and G. McCarthy, Differential sensitivity of human visual cortex to faces, letter strings, and textures: A functional magnetic resonance imaging study, *Journal of Neuroscience* 16 (1996): 5205–5215; J. Sergent, S. Ohta, and B. MacDonald, Functional neuroanatomy of face and object processing: A positron emission tomography study, *Brain* 115 (1992): 15–36.

33. McCloud, *Understanding comics.*

34. McCloud, *Understanding comics.*

35. Reeves and Nass, *The media equation.*

36. Reeves and Nass, *The media equation.*

37. C. F. Keating, A. Mazur, and M. H. Segall, Facial gestures which influence the perception of status, *Social Psychology Quarterly* 40, no. 4 (1977): 374–378; Reeves and Nass, *The media equation;* F. Tong, *Cognitive and neural mechanisms in face perception,* unpublished doctoral dissertation, Harvard University, Cambridge, Mass., 2000.

38. D. Evans, *Herbie the Love Bug fan club,* retrieved from <http://hometown.aol.com/vwdude1957>, 2004; Walt Disney Studios, *Walt Disney's the Love Bug, Herbie's special friends* (Chicago: Goldencraft, 1976).

39. Herbie also communicated by revving his engine and moving back and forth.

40. D. A. Norman, *Turn signals are the facial expression of automobiles* (Upper Saddle River, N.J.: Addison Wesley, 1993).

41. E. Rubin, Figure and ground, in S. Yantis, ed., *Visual perception: Essential readings* (Philadelphia: Psychology Press/Taylor & Francis, 2000), pp. 225–229 (originally published in 1921).

42. K. Isbister and C. Nass, Consistency of personality in interactive characters: Verbal cues, non-verbal cues, and user characteristics, *International Journal of Human-Computer Interaction* 53, no. 1 (2000): 251–267.

43. F. Robert and J. Robert, *Faces* (San Francisco: Chronicle Books, 2000). See also R. Shepard, *Mind sights: Original visual illusions, ambiguities, and other anomalies, with a commentary on the play of mind in perception and art* (New York: Freeman, 1990).

44. For an evocative presentation of the power of adding eyes and a mouth to vegetables, see S. Freymann and J. Elffers, *How are you peeling?* (New York: Levine, 1999).

45. See chapter 10 for a detailed description of Ananova.

46. Massaro, *Perceiving talking faces*.

47. D. W. Massaro and J. Light, Improving the vocabulary of children with hearing loss, *Volta Review* (in press).

48. A. Bosseler and D. W. Massaro, Development and evaluation of a computer-animated tutor for vocabulary and language learning for children with autism, *Journal of Autism and Developmental Disorders* 33, no. 6 (2003): 653–672; D. W. Massaro, Symbiotic value of an embodied agent in language learning, in R. H. Sprague, Jr., ed., *Proceedings of the 37th Annual Hawaii International Conference on System Sciences (HICCS'04)* (Gig Island, Hawaii: IEEE Computer Society Press, 2004).

49. D. W. Massaro and J. Light, Read my tongue movements: Bimodal learning to perceive and produce non-native speech /r/ and /l/, in *Proceedings of the 8th European Conference on Speech Communication and Technology* (*Eurospeech'03/Interspeech'03*), Geneva, Switzerland, 2003; D. W. Massaro and J. Light, Using visible speech for training perception and production of speech for hard of hearing individuals, *Journal of Speech, Language, and Hearing Research* 47, no. 2 (2004): 304–320.

50. D. Ferber, The man who mistook his girlfriend for a robot, *Popular Science*, September 2003.

51. The difficulty is that lip and facial movements are best controlled by phonemes and phonemes are easier to derive from text (which is converted into speech) than from spoken words.

52. Massaro, *Perceiving talking faces*.

53. For the best example of current technology in this domain, see T. Ezzat, G. Geiger, and T. Poggio, *Mary101: Videorealistic facial animation*, retrieved from <http://cerboli.mit.edu:8000/research/mary101/>, 2003.

54. Gong, *The psychology of consistency in human-computer interaction*.

55. Massaro, *Perceiving talking faces*.

56. In the nonmediated case, Steven Hawking, the physicist, does combine a human face with a synthetic voice.

57. There is a technology called Veepers (See <http://www.pulse3d.com>) that starts with a still photograph of a person and allows the face to synchronize with a synthetic voice, but the moving faces look more humanoid than human.

58. This could be called the "Tinbergen's birds" approach to faces (see chapter 10).

59. N. Mazanec and G. J. McCall, Sex factors and allocation of attention in observing persons, *Journal of Psychology* 93 (1976): 175–180.

60. J. A. Hall, Gender effects in decoding nonverbal cues, *Psychological Bulletin* 85 (1987): 845–857.

61. J. A. Hall, *Nonverbal sex differences: Communication accuracy and expressive style* (Baltimore: Johns Hopkins University Press, 1984).

62. Gong, *The psychology of consistency in human-computer interaction*; E. Otta, F. F. E. Abrosio, and R. L. Hoshino, Reading a smiling face: Messages conveyed by various forms of smiling, *Perceptual and Motor Skills* 82, no. 3 (1996): 1111–1121; Q. Rahman, G. D. Wilson, and S. Abrahams, Sex, sexual orientation, and identification of positive and negative facial affect, *Brain and Cognition* 54, no. 3 (2004): 179–185.

63. M. Zuckerman, B. M. de Paulo, and R. Rosenthal, Verbal and nonverbal communication of deception, in L. Berkowitz, ed., *Advances in experimental social psychology* (vol. 14) (New York: Academic Press, 1981).

64. M. Biehl, D. Matsumoto, P. Ekman, V. Hearn, K. Heider, T. Kudoh, et al., Matsumoto's and Ekman's Japanese and Caucasian Facial Expressions of Emotions (JACFEE): Reliability data and cross-national differences, *Journal of Nonverbal Behavior* 21 (1997): 3–21; R. Rosenthal, J. A. Hall, M. R. DiMatteo, P. L. Rogers, and D. Archer, *Sensitivity to nonverbal communication: The PONS test* (Baltimore: Johns Hopkins University Press, 1979).

65. Gong, *The psychology of consistency in human-computer interaction.*

66. Hall, Gender effects in decoding nonverbal cues.

67. N. Eisenberg and R. Lennon, Sex differences in empathy and related capacities, *Psychological Bulletin* 94, no. 1 (1983): 100–131.

68. Hall, *Nonverbal sex differences.*

69. This experiment is described in more detail in Gong, *The psychology of consistency in human-computer interaction.*

70. Center for Spoken Language Understanding, *CSLU Toolkit,* retrieved from <http://www.cslu.ogi.edu/toolkit/>, 2004.

71. Massaro, *Perceiving talking faces.*

72. These items are derived from Y. Moon, Intimate exchanges: Using computers to elicit self-disclosure from consumers, *Journal of Consumer Research* 26, no. 4 (2000): 323–339.

73. Amount of disclosure was measured with the average word count of the responses. Answers such as "I don't know," "I don't want to tell you," or "You are so nosy" were counted as zero words. The index was very reliable (Cronbach's $\alpha = .80$).

74. The questionnaire was a paper-and-pencil form with three types of items. One set of items was organized around the question "How well do each of the following adjectives describe your feelings about [the agent, yourself, the voice of the agent, the face of the agent]?" The question was followed by a series of adjectives. Each adjective was addressed on an independent, ten-point Likert-type scale. The scales were anchored by "Describes very poorly" (= 1) and "Describes very well" (= 10).

The second set of items was organized around the question "Please indicate how you felt about [the agent, yourself, the voice of the agent, the face of the agent]?" The question was followed by a series of ten-point semantic differentials anchored by an adjective on each side.

The third set of items involved single questions with two or more response options.

75. Participants indicated, as a forced choice, whether the face and voice were "computer-synthesized" or "of a real person."

76. Consistency was an index based on two semantic differential questions that described the interface agent: *inconsistent-consistent* and *mismatched-matched*. These two items were highly correlated, $r(77) = .70$.

77. Trustworthiness was an index of six items that were derived from the Wheeless and Grotz individualized trust scale and applied to the talking head: *trustworthy-untrustworthy* (reverse-coded), *distrustful of the agent-trustful of the agent, confidential-divulging* (reverse-coded), *safe-dangerous* (reverse-coded), *respectful-disrespectful* (reverse-coded), and *unreliable-reliable*. L. R. Wheeless and J. Grotz, The measurement of trust and its relationship to self-disclosure, *Human Communication Research* 3, no. 3 (1977): 250–257. The index was very reliable ($\alpha = .87$).

78. Upsetting was an index of three adjectives that related to how people felt about the talking head: *disconcerting, disturbing,* and *frustrating*. The index was very reliable ($\alpha = .80$).

79. Strangeness of the agent was an index three adjectives that related to how people felt about the talking head: *strange, surprising,* and *unusual*. The index was very reliable ($\alpha = .75$).

80. Rudeness of the agent was an index three adjectives that related to how people felt about the talking head: *intrusive, offensive,* and *rude*. The index was very reliable ($\alpha = .84$).

81. Liking of the face was an index of five pairs of adjectives on semantic differential scales that were based on describing the talking head: *pleasant-unpleasant* (reverse-coded), *likeable-annoying* (reverse-coded), *cold-warm, disturbing-pleasing,* and *nice-awful* (reverse-coded). The index was very reliable ($\alpha = .81$).

82. Liking of the voice was an index of three pairs of adjectives on semantic differential scales that were based on describing the talking head's voice: *jarring-soothing, unpleasant-pleasant,* and *awful-nice*. The index was very reliable ($\alpha = .86$).

83. Time spent on judging the talking-head agent was logged by the computer server that was running the experiment when each computer screen loaded. The duration of the screens

containing the trustworthiness scale and other attitudinal measures about the talking-head agent in the posttask questionnaire was divided by the number of items to provide an average time per question for judging the agent.

84. J. F. Hamers and W. E. Lambert, Bilingual interdependencies in auditory perception, *Journal of verbal learning and verbal behavior* 11 (1972): 303–310; J. R. Stroop, Studies of interference in serial verbal reactions, *Journal of Experimental Psychology* 18 (1935): 643–663.

85. S. M. Belmore, Determinants of attention during impression formation, *Journal of Experimental Psychology: Learning, Memory, and Cognition* 13 (1987): 480–489; E. Burnstein and Y. Schul, The informational basis of social judgments: Operations in forming impressions of other persons, *Journal of Experimental Social Psychology* 18 (1982): 217–234.

86. Here is the results table:

	Human Face		Synthetic Face	
Dependent Variables	Human Voice	Synthetic Voice	Human Voice	Synthetic Voice
Consistency of face and voice	7.4	2.9	5.5	7.0
Level of disclosure	17.37	11.2	9.0	11.3
Trustworthiness	7.1	6.2	6.1	7.5
Level of disclosure	16.1	11.2	9.8	9.9
Trustworthiness	4.96	4.35	4.30	5.23
Upsetting agent	3.2	5.2	4.4	4.1
Strange agent	4.3	5.6	5.5	5.2
Rudeness of agent	3.4	5.1	4.1	3.8
Liking of face	3.9	3.2	3.2	3.6
Liking of voice	4.5	2.4	3.7	2.7
Time to evaluate agent	4.2	5.1	5.1	4.2

Notes: Standard deviations are not available.
All statistical analyses are based on 2 (modality of face) by 2 (modality of voice) by 2 (gender of participant), between-participants ANOVA.

87. Gong, *The psychology of consistency in human-computer interaction.*

88. Overall face modality by voice modality interaction: $F(1,72) = 33.1$, $p < .001$.

89. Overall face modality by voice modality interaction: $F(1, 72) = 17.0$, $p < .001$; females: $F(1, 36) = 5.48$, $p < .05$; males: $F(1,36) = 14.5$, $p < .001$.

90. Overall face modality by voice modality interaction: $F(1, 72) = 13.27$, $p < .001$; females: $F(1, 36) = 4.45$, $p < .05$; males: $F(1, 36) = 11.05$, $p < .01$.

91. Overall face modality by voice modality interaction: $F(1, 72) = 10.71$, $p < .01$.

92. Overall face modality by voice modality interaction: $F(1, 72) = 6.96$, $p < .01$.

93. Overall face modality by voice modality interaction: $F(1, 72) = 5.52$, $p < .05$.

94. Overall face modality by voice modality interaction: $F(1, 72) = 7.13$, $p < .01$.

95. Overall voice modality effect: $F(1, 72) = 50.48$, $p < .001$.

96. Overall face modality by voice modality interaction: $F(1, 72) = 10.03$, $p < .01$.

97. Overall face modality by voice modality interaction: $F(1, 72) = 15.94$, $p < .001$.

98. Overall face modality by voice modality by gender of participant interaction: *upsetting* ($F(1, 72) = 7.93$, $p < .01$), *strange* ($F(1, 72) = 13.97$, $p < .001$), *rude* ($F(1, 72) = 6.41$, $p < .01$), *like face* ($F(1, 72) = 6.96$, $p < .01$), and *like voice* ($F(1, 72) = 2.96$, $p < .09$).

99. Reeves and Nass, *The media equation*. See also chapter 10.

100. For a delightful book on the importance of punctuation, see L. Truss, *Eats, shoots and leaves: The zero tolerance approach to punctuation* (New York: Gotham, 2004).

101. See chapter 8.

102. J. Allen, *Natural language understanding*, 2nd ed. (Upper Saddle River, N. J.: Addison Wesley, 1995); C. D. Manning and H. Schütze, *Foundations of statistical natural language processing* (Cambridge, Mass.: MIT Press, 1999).

103. For a discussion of mark-ups of text, see chapter 8.

104. R. Carpenter, *Jabberwacky.com*, retrieved from <http://www.jabberwacky.com/>, 2004.

105. J. Weizenbaum, Eliza: A computer program for the study of natural language communication between man and machine, *Communications of the ACM* 9, no. 1 (1966): 36–14.

106. A. Turing, Computing machinery and intelligence, *Mind* 59 (1950): 433–460.

107. Ivan Sag, personal communication.

108. W. A. Gamson, Hiroshima, the holocaust, and the politics of exclusion: 1994 presidential address, *American Sociological Review* 60, no. 1 (1995): 1–20; R. Lippi-Green, *English with an accent: Language, ideology, and discrimination in the United States* (London: Routledge, 1997).

109. S. L. Oviatt, G. Levow, E. Morenton, and M. MacEachern, Modeling global and focal hyperarticulation during human-computer error resolution, *Journal of the Acoustical Society of America* 104, no. 5 (1998): 1–19; S. L. Oviatt, M. MacEachern, and G.-A. Levow, Predicting hyperarticulate speech during human-computer error resolution, *Speech Communication* 24, no. 2 (1998): 87–110.

110. J. T. Cacioppo, J. C. Hager, and P. Ekman, The psychology and neuroanatomy of facial expression, in P. Ekman, T. S. Huang, T. J. Sejnowski and J. C. Hager, eds., *Final Report to NSF of the Planning Workshop on Facial Expression Understanding* (San Francisco: Human Interaction Lab, 1992); P. Ekman, Facial signs: Facts, fantasies, and possibilities, in T. Sebeok, ed., *Sight, sound and sense* (Bloomington: Indiana University Press, 1978). In contrast to these citations, we include "linguistic facial signals."

111. Cacioppo, Hager, and Ekman, The psychology and neuroanatomy of facial expression; Ekman, Facial signs.

112. Reeves and Nass, *The media equation*; Reeves and Voelker, *Effects of audio-video asynchrony on viewer's memory, evaluation of content, and detection ability*.

113. Cacioppo, Hager, and Ekman, The psychology and neuroanatomy of facial expression; Ekman, Facial signs.

114. Cacioppo, Hager, and Ekman, The psychology and neuroanatomy of facial expression.

115. Cacioppo, Hager, and Ekman, The psychology and neuroanatomy of facial expression.

116. Cacioppo, Hager, and Ekman, The psychology and neuroanatomy of facial expression.

117. Cacioppo, Hager, and Ekman, The psychology and neuroanatomy of facial expression; P. Ekman and W. V. Friesen, The repertoire of nonverbal behavior: Categories, origins, usage, and coding, *Semiotica* 1 (1969): 49–98.

118. Cacioppo, Hager, and Ekman, The psychology and neuroanatomy of facial expression.

119. Cassell, Nudge nudge wink wink.

120. Ekman and Friesen, The repertoire of nonverbal behavior.

121. Reeves and Nass, *The media equation*.

122. Tim Skelly, personal communication.

123. E. Brown and D. I. Perrett, What gives a face its gender?, *Perception* 22, no. 7 (1993): 829–840; R. Campbell, P. J. Benson, S. B. Wallace, S. Doesbergh, and M. Coleman, More about brows: How poses that change brow position affect perception of gender, *Perception* 28, no. 4 (1999): 489–594; C. Senior, J. Barnes, R. Jenkins, S. Landau, M. L. Phillips, and A. S. David, Attribution of social dominance and maleness to schematic faces, *Social Behavior and Personality* 27, no. 4 (1999): 331–338.

124. T. A. Ito and G. R. Urland, Race and gender on the brain: Electrocortical measures of attention to the race and gender of multiply categorizable individuals, *Journal of Personality and Social Psychology* 85, no. 4 (2003): 616–626.

125. M. D. Leinbach and B. I. Fagot, Categorical habituation to male and female faces: Gender schematic processing in infancy, *Infant Behavior and Development* 16, no. 3 (1993): 317–332; G. D. Levy and R. A. Haaf, Detection of gender-related categories by ten-month-old infants, *Infant Behavior and Development* 17, no. 4 (1994): 457–459.

126. R. Campbell, J. Walker, and S. Baron-Cohen, The development of differential use of inner and outer face features in familiar face identification, *Journal of Experimental Child Psychology* 59, no. 2 (1995): 196–210.

127. H. A. Wild, S. E. Barrett, M. J. Spence, A. J. O'Toole, Y. D. Cheng, and J. Brooke, Recognition and sex categorization of adults' and children's faces: Examining performance in the

absence of sex-stereotyped cues, *Journal of Experimental Child Psychology*, 77, no. 4 (2000): 269–291.

128. D. I. Perrett, K. J. Lee, I. Penton-Voak, D. Rowland, S. Yoshikawa, D. M. Burt, et al., Effects of sexual dimorphism on facial attractiveness, *Nature* 394 (6696) (1998): 884–887.

129. S. Campanella, A. Chrysochoos, and R. Bruyer, Categorical perception of facial gender information: Behavioural evidence and the face-space metaphor, *Visual Cognition* 8, no. 2 (2001): 237–262.

130. See chapter 2 and J. W. Mullennix, K. Johnson, M. Topcu-Durgun, and L. W. Farnsworth, The perceptual representation of voice gender, *Journal of the Acoustical Society of America* 98, no. 6 (1995): 3080–3095.

131. D. M. Burt and D. I. Perrett, Perceptual asymmetries in judgment of facial attractiveness, age, gender, speech, and expression, *Neuropsychologia* 35, no. 5 (1997): 685–693.

132. W. Sheldon, *Atlas of men: A guide for somatyping the adult image of all ages* (New York: Macmillan, 1970). See chapter 5 for a further discussion of somatotype theory.

133. A classic category of villain has a round face and a very round body—the classic endomorph, such as "The Fat Man" in the Spiderman comics and Sidney Greenstreet in *The Maltese Falcon.* Consistent with the endomorph personality, these villains are usually depicted as frequently laughing and jovial. The contrast between this friendly exterior and their evil deeds makes them particularly frightening characters (inconsistency is unsettling).

134. These descriptions of the three somatotypes are derived from T. Arraj and J. Arraj, *Tracking the elusive human, Vol. 1, A practical guide to C. G. Jung's psychological types, W. H. Sheldon's body and temperament types, and their Integration* (Chiloquin, Ore.: Inner Growth Books, 1988), and Sheldon, *Atlas of men.*

135. D. S. Berry and L. Z. McArthur, Perceiving character in faces: The impact of age-related craniofacial changes on social perception, *Psychological Bulletin* 100, no. 1 (1986): 3–18; L. A. Zebrowitz-McArthur and J. M. Montepare, Contributions of babyface and a childlike voice to impressions of moving and talking faces, *Journal of Nonverbal Behavior* 13, no. 3 (1989): 189–203.

136. Otta, Abrosio, and Hoshino, Reading a smiling face.

137. T. F. Pettijohn II and A. Tesser, Popularity in environment context: Facial feature assessment of American movie actresses, *Media Psychology* 1, no. 3 (1999): 229–247.

138. Arraj and Arraj, *Tracking the elusive human.*

139. Arraj and Arraj, *Tracking the elusive human.*

140. A. Mignault and A. Chaudhuri, The many faces of a neutral face: Head tilt and perception of dominance and emotion, *Journal of Nonverbal Behavior* 27, no. 2 (2003): 111–132.

141. Keating, Mazur, and Segall, Facial gestures which influence the perception of status.

142. Reeves and Nass, *The media equation.*

143. T. D. Brown, Jr., F. C. Dane, and M. D. Durham, Perception of race and ethnicity, *Journal of Social Behavior and Personality* 13, no. 2 (1998): 295–306.

144. J. M. Montepare and A. Opeyo, The relative salience of physiognomic cues in differentiating faces: A methodological tool, *Journal of Nonverbal Behavior* 26, no. 1 (2002): 43–59.

145. Ito and Urland, Race and gender on the brain.

146. See chapter 6.

147. Burt and Perrett, Perceptual asymmetries in judgment of facial attractiveness, age, gender, speech, and expression.

148. R. Behrents, *Atlas for growth in the aging craniofacial skeleton* (Ann Arbor: University of Michigan, 1986); C. S. Milner, R. A. Neave, and C. M. Wilkinson, Predicting growth in the aging craniofacial skeleton, *Forensic Science Communications* 3, no. 3 (2001).

149. Ekman and Friesen, The repertoire of nonverbal behavior.

150. M. D. Pell, Evaluation of nonverbal emotion in face and voice: Some preliminary findings on a new battery of tests, *Brain and Cognition* 48, nos. 2–3 (2002): 499–504.

151. M. H. Bornstein and M. E. Arteberry, Recognition, discrimination, and categorization of smiling by five-month-old infants, *Developmental Science* 6, no. 5 (2003): 585–599.

152. J. M. Leppanen and J. K. Hietanen, Affect and face perceptions: Odors modulate the recognition advantage of happy faces, *Emotion* 34, no. 4 (2003): 315–326.

153. Reeves and Nass, *The media equation.*

154. S. Brave and C. Nass, Emotion in human-computer interaction, in J. Jacko and A. Sears, eds., *Handbook of human-computer interaction* (New York: Lawrence Erlbaum, 2002), pp. 251–271.

155. P. Ekman and W. V. Friesen, *Facial Action Coding System* (Palo Alto, Calif.: Consulting Psychologist Press, 1977); P. Ekman and W. V. Friesen, *Unmasking the face: A guide to recognizing emotions from facial clues* (Englewood Cliffs, N.J.: Prentice-Hall, 1975); P. Ekman, W. V. Friesen, and P. Ellsworth, *Emotion in the human face: Guidelines for research and an integration of findings* (New York: Pergamon Press, 1972). For a wonderful description of Ekman's work, see M. Gladwell, The naked face, *New Yorker*, August 5, 2002.

156. Ekman and Friesen, *Facial Action Coding System.*

157. Brave and Nass, Emotion in human-computer interaction.

158. The table is derived from Ekman and Friesen, *Unmasking the face*, with permission, and Brave and Nass, Emotion in human-computer interaction, with permission.

159. P. Ekman and W. V. Friesen, Constants across cultures in the face and emotion, *Journal of Personality and Social Psychology* 17, no. 2 (1971): 124–129; Y.-L. Tian, T. Kanade, and J. F. Cohn,

Recognizing action units for facial expression analysis, *IEEE Transactions on Pattern Analysis and Machine Intelligence* 23, no. 2 (2001): 1–19.

160. M. Fallshore and L. Bartholow, Recognition of emotion from inverted schematic drawings of faces, *Perceptual and Motor Skills* 96, no. 1 (2003): 236–244.

161. Brave and Nass, Emotion in human-computer interaction.

162. J. T. Cacioppo, G. G. Bernston, D. J. Klein, and K. M. Poehlmann, Psychophysiology of emotion across the life span, *Annual Review of Gerontology and Geriatrics* 17 (1997): 27–74.

163. T. Indersmitten and R. C. Gur, Emotion processing in chimeric faces: Hemispheric asymmetries in expression and recognition of emotions, *Journal of Neuroscience* 23, no. 9 (2003): 3820–3825.

164. S. Berthoz, R. J. R. Brali, G. le Clec'h, and J.-L. Martino, Emotions: From neuropsychology to functional imaging, *International Journal of Psychology* 37, no. 4 (2002): 193–203.

165. See chapter 8.

166. B. De Gelder and J. Vroomen, The perception of emotion by ear and by eye, *Cognition and Emotion* 14, no. 3 (2000): 289–311; D. W. Massaro and P. B. Egan, Perceiving affect from the voice and the face, *Psychonomic Bulletin and Review* 3, no. 2 (1996): 215–221.

167. Campbell, Walker, and Baron-Cohen, The development of differential use of inner and outer face features in familiar face identification.

168. C. Vinette, F. Gosselin, and P. G. Schyns, Spatio-temporal dynamics of face recognition in a flash: It's in the eyes, *Cognitive Science* 28, no. 2 (2004): 289–301.

169. S. Bentin and L. Y. Deouell, Structural encoding and identification in face processing: ERP evidence for separate mechanisms, *Cognitive Neuropsychology* 17, nos. 1–3 (2000): 35–54; S. Campanella, C. Hanoteau, D. Depy, B. Rossion, R. Bruyer, M. Crommelinck et al., Right N170 modulation in a face discrimination task: An account for categorical perception of familiar faces, *Psychophysiology* 37 (2000): 796–806; H. D. Ellis, J. W. Shepherd, and G. M. Davies, Identification of familiar and unfamiliar faces from internal and external features: Some implications for theories of face recognition, *Perception* 8, no. 4 (1979): 431–439; L. Pizzamiglio, P. Zoccolotti, A. Mammucari, and R. Cesaroni, The independence of face identity and facial expression recognition mechanisms: Relationship to sex and cognitive style, *Brain and Cognition* 2, no. 2 (1983): 176–188; W. R. Uttal, Are reductive (explanatory) theories of face identification possible? Some speculations and some findings, in M. J. Wenger and J. T. Townsend, eds., *Computational, geometric, and process perspectives on facial cognition: Contexts and challenges* (Mahwah, N.J.: Lawrence Erlbaum, 2001), pp. 467–501; A. W. Young et al., Familiarity decisions for faces presented to the left and right cerebral hemispheres, *Brain and Cognition* 4, no. 4 (1985): 439–450.

170. T. S. Kuhn, *The Copernican revolution: Planetary astronomy in the development of Western thought* (Cambridge, Mass.: Harvard University Press, 1957).

171. M. Ruse, *The Darwinian revolution: Science red in tooth and claw* (Chicago: Chicago University Press, 1999).

172. J. D. Bolter, *Turing's man: Western culture in the computer age* (Chapel Hill: University of North Carolina Press, 1984).

Chapter 12

1. S. S. Iyengar and M. R. Lepper, When choice is demotivating: Can one desire too much of a good thing?, *Journal of Personality and Social Psychology* 79, no. 6 (2000): 995–1006.

2. G. A. Miller, The magical number seven, plus or minus two: Some limits on our capacity for processing information, *Psychological Review* 63 (1956): 81–97.

3. For the classic discussion of affordances in human-technology interaction, see D. A. Norman, *The design of everyday things* (Garden City, N.Y.: Doubleday, 1990).

4. B. J. Fogg, and C. Nass, Silicon sycophants: The effects of computers that flatter, *International Journal of Human-Computer Studies* 46, no. 5 (1997): 551–561.

5. For an extended discussion of this point, see B. Reeves and C. Nass, *The media equation: How people treat computers, television, and new media like real people and places* (New York: Cambridge University Press, 1996).

6. D. O. Sears, The person-positivity bias, *Journal of Personality and Social Psychology* 44, no. 2 (1983): 233–250.

7. For a similar argument, see S. E. Stern, J. W. Mullennix, and I. Yaroslavsky, *Human versus computers as source of persuasive appear: Are there ingroup-outgroup effects for computers?* Unpublished manuscript, University of Pittsburgh, Pittsburgh, PA.

8. See chapter 10.

9. See chapter 11.

10. A. R. Hochschild, *The managed heart: Commercialization of human feeling* (Berkeley: University of California Press, 1985).

11. I. Levin, *The Stepford wives: A novel* (New York: Random House, 1972).

12. D. Bryant, *The uncanny valley*, from <http://www.arclight.net/~pdb/glimpses/valley.html> (2004); M. Mori, *The Buddha in the robot* (Boston: Tuttle, 1982).

13. Bryant, *The uncanny valley*.

14. J. Nielsen, *Usability engineering* (Boston: Academic Press, 1993); B. Shneiderman and C. Plaisant, *Designing the user interface*, 4th ed. (Reading, Mass.: Addison-Wesley, 2003); T. Winograd, *Understanding natural language* (New York: Academic Press, 1972).

15. K. Binsted, *Machine humour: An implemented model of puns*, unpublished doctoral dissertation, University of Edinburgh, Edinburgh, 1996; D. L. F. Nilsen, A. P. Nilsen, and N. H. Combs, Teaching a computer to speculate, *Computers and the Humanities* 22 (1988): 193–201.

16. L. G. Bolman and T. E. Deal, What makes a team work?, *Organizational Dynamics* 21, no. 2 (1992): 34–44; C. M. Consalvo, Humor in management: No laughing matter, *Humor* 2, no. 3 (1989): 285–297.

17. R. W. Clouse and K. L. Spurgeon, Corporate analysis of humor, *Psychology: A Journal of Human Behavior* 32, nos. 3–4 (1995): 1–24.

18. J. Morkes, H. K. Kernal, and C. Nass, Effects of humor in task-oriented human-computer interaction and computer-mediated communication: A direct test of SRCT theory, *Human-Computer Interaction* 14, no. 4 (2000): 395–435.

19. J. C. Lafferty and P. M. Eady, *The desert survival problem* (Plymouth, Mich.: Experimental Learning Methods, 1974).

20. For examples, see Reeves and Nass, *The media equation.*

21. See chapter 8.

22. See chapters 6 and 11.

23. See chapter 9 and L. C. Nygaard and D. B. Pisoni, Talker-specific learning in speech perception, *Perception and Psychophysics* 60, no. 3 (1998): 355–376.

24. P. Luce, T. Feustel, and D. B. Pisoni, Capacity demands in short-term memory for synthetic and natural speech, *Human Factors* 25 (1983): 17–31; L. M. Manous, D. B. Pisoni, M. J. Dedina, and H. C. Nussbaum, *Comprehension of natural and synthetic speech using a sentence verification task* (No. 11) (Bloomington: Indiana University, 1985); D. B. Pisoni, Perception of speech: The human listener as a cognitive interface. *Speech Technology* 1 (1982): 10–23.

25. This experiment is described in more detail in L. Gong, C. Nass, C. Simard, and Y. Takhteyev, When non-human is better than semi-human: Consistency in speech interfaces, in M. J. Smith, G. Salvendy, D. Harris, and R. Koubek, eds., *Usability evaluation and interface design: Cognitive engineering, intelligent agents, and virtual reality* (Mahwah, N.J.: Lawrence Erlbaum, 2001), pp. 1558–1562; C. Nass, Simard, C., and Y. Takhteyev, *Should recorded and synthetic speech be mixed?*, manuscript, Stanford, Calif., 2001.

26. The experiment was controlled by the CSLU Toolkit running on a Windows NT machine. Center for Spoken Language Understanding, CSLU Toolkit, from <http://www.cslu.ogi.edu/toolkit/> (2004). A Dialogics board answered the phone calls.

27. The questionnaire was organized around the question "How well does each of the following adjectives describe your feelings about the housing information system?" Each question was followed by a series of adjectives; each adjective was addressed on an independent, ten-point Likert-type scale. The scales were anchored by "Describes very poorly" (= 1) and "Describes very well." (= 10). The factor scores were created based on theory and factor analysis.

28. Trust of the system was a factor score comprised of three items: *realistic, reliable,* and *trustworthy* ($\lambda = 2.3$; factor loadings ranged from .83 to .93).

29. Liking of the system was a factor score of five items: *enjoyable, entertaining, friendly, good,* and *likeable* ($\lambda = 2.9$; factor loadings ranged from .81 to .95).

30. Perceived competence of the system was a factor score comprised of four items: *clever, informative, useful,* and *well-designed* ($\lambda = 2.6$; factor loadings ranged from .82 to .96).

31. Here is the complete results table:

Dependent Variable	Synthetic First and Second	Recorded First Synthetic Second	Recorded First and Second
Trust in the system	0.14 (0.78)	–0.58 (0.52)	–0.10 (0.84)
Liking of the system	0.55 (1.14)	–0.61 (0.59)	0.06 (0.90)
Perceived competence of the system	0.30 (1.17)	–0.66 (0.66)	0.36 (0.82)

Note: Standard deviations are in parentheses. All statistical analyses were based on one-tailed t-tests.

32. $t(22) = 3.12$, $p < .01$.

33. $t(22) = 2.61$, $p < .01$.

34. $t(22) = 2.48$, $p < .01$. The task of presenting particular items from a large database is arguably simplistic and machinelike. Thus, the foregoing results might not be a result of a desire for consistency but rather discomfort with a recorded voice associated with a task better reserved for computers. However, when an all-recorded speech condition was added to the experiment, people clearly thought that it was more trustworthy ($t(22) = 2.2$, $p < .02$), more likeable ($t(22) = 2.61$, $p < .01$), and more competent ($t(22) = 1.99$, $p < .04$) than the mixed system, even though the content was identical.

35. Nass, Simard, and Takhteyev, Should recorded and synthetic speech be mixed?

36. C. P. Wilson, *Jokes: Form, content, use, and function* (London: Academic Press, 1979), pp. 159–160.

37. The questionnaire was organized around the question "How well does each of the following adjectives describe your feelings about the joke system?" Each question was followed by a series of adjectives; each adjective was addressed on an independent, ten-point Likert-type scale. The scales were anchored by "Describes very poorly" (= 1) and "Describes very well." (= 10). The factor scores were created based on theory and factor analysis.

38. Liking was a factor score of eight terms: *funny jokes, enjoyable system, entertaining system, good system, interesting system, likeable system,* and *well-designed system.* ($\lambda = 5.63$; factor loadings ranged from .87 to .95).

39. $M = 0.46$ vs. $M = -0.38$, $t(22) = 1.99$, $p < .03$.

40. E. Zerubavel, *The fine line: Making distinctions in everyday life* (Chicago: University of Chicago Press, 1993).

41. I. Borg and P. Groenen, *Modern multidimensional scaling: Theory and applications* (Berlin: Springer-Verlag, 1997).

42. H. Tajfel, *Human groups and social categories: Studies in social psychology* (Cambridge: Cambridge University Press, 1981).

43. H. Tajfel, Social identity and intergroup behavior, *Social science information/sur les sciences socials* 13, no. 2 (1974): 65–93; H. Tajfel and J. C. Turner, *The social identity of intergroup relations*, 2nd ed. (Chicago: Nelson-Hall, 1986).

44. L. A. Festinger, *A theory of cognitive dissonance* (Stanford, Calif.: Stanford University Press, 1957).

45. Reeves and Nass, *The media equation.*

46. H. H. Kelley, Attribution theory in social psychology, in D. Levine, ed., *Nebraska symposium on motivation* (Lincoln: University of Nebraska Press, 1967), 15: 192–240; H. H. Kelley, The processes of causal attribution, *American Psychologist* 28 (1973): 107–128; L. Z. McArthur, The how and what of why: Some determinants and consequences of causal attribution, *Journal of Personality and Social Psychology* 22 (1972): 171–193.

47. C. Nass, B. J. Fogg, and Y. Moon, Can computers be teammates?, *International Journal of Human-Computer Studies* 45, no. 6 (1996): 669–678.

48. E.-J. Lee and C. Nass, An experimental test of normative group influence and representation effects in computer-mediated communication, *Human Communication Research* 28, no. 3 (2002): 349–381.

49. See chapter 9 and C. Nass, B. Reeves, and G. Leshner, Technology and roles: A tale of two TVs, *Journal of Communication* 46, no. 2 (1996): 121–128.

50. See chapter 3.

51. Fogg and Nass, Silicon sycophants.

52. See chapter 4.

53. K. Isbister, How do we decide when a computer character is intelligent? Intelligence assessment and perceived intelligence in human-human interaction and how it relates to human-computer interaction, Paper presented at the Lifelike Computer Characters Conference, Snowbird, Utah, October 1995.

54. B. Friedman, ed., *Human values and the design of computer technology* (vol. 72) (New York: Cambridge University Press/CSLI, 1999); I. Kant, *The critique of pure reason* (London: Macmillan, 1929, originally published in 1781).

55. Hochschild, *The managed heart.*

56. Although see J. R. Beniger, Personalization of mass media and the growth of pseudo-community, *Communication Research* 14, no. 3 (1987): 352–371.

57. Reeves and Nass, *The media equation.*

58. D. Goleman, *Emotional intelligence: Why it can matter more than IQ* (New York: Bantam Books, 1995).

59. The discussion in this section draws heavily from Morkes, Kernal, and Nass, Effects of humor in task-oriented human-computer interaction and computer-mediated communication.

60. Morkes, Kernal, and Nass, Effects of humor in task-oriented human-computer interaction and computer-mediated communication; L. R. Smeltzer and T. L. Leap, An analysis of individual reactions to potentially offensive jokes in work settings, *Human Relations* 41, no. 4 (1988): 295–304; C. P. Wilson, *Jokes: Form, content, use and function* (London: Academic Press, 1979).

61. See chapter 3.

62. W. J. Duncan, L. R. Smeltzer, and T. L. Leap, Humor and work: Applications of joking behavior to management, *Journal of Management and Information Systems* 16, no. 2 (1990): 255–278.

63. See chapter 14.

64. B. D. Gelb and G. M. Zinkhan, The effect of repetition on humor in a radio advertising study, *Journal of Advertising* 14, no. 4 (1986): 13–20.

65. J. Morkes, *Effects of successful and unsuccessful attempts at humor in human-computer interaction and computer-mediated communication*, unpublished doctoral dissertation, Stanford University, Stanford, Calif., 1998.

66. L. Sproull and S. Kiesler, *Connections: New ways of working in the networked organization* (Cambridge, Mass.: MIT Press, 1992).

67. The first four guidelines come from V. Raskin, *Semantic mechanisms of humor* (Dordrecht, Holland: Reidel, 1985).

68. M. Ito and K. Nakakoji, Impact of culture on user interface design, in E. M. del Gado and J. Nielsen, eds., *International user interfaces* (New York: Wiley, 1996).

69. Morkes, Kernal, and Nass, Effects of humor in task-oriented human-computer interaction and computer-mediated communication.

70. Reeves and Nass, *The media equation.* D. Zillmann, Television viewing and physiological arousal, in J. Bryant and D. Zillmann, eds., *Responding to the screen: Reception and reaction processes* (Hillsdale, N.J.: Lawrence Erlbaum, 1991), pp. 103–133.

71. A. Pope, *Essay on man and other poems* (New York: Dover, 1994).

Chapter 13

1. J. Meyrowitz, *No sense of place: The impact of electronic media on social behavior* (New York: Oxford University Press, 1986).

2. H. H. Clark, *Using language* (New York: Cambridge University Press, 1996).

3. See chapter 11 and H. McGurk and J. MacDonald, Hearing lips and seeing voices, *Nature* 264 (1976): 746–748; D. W. Massaro, *Perceiving talking faces: From speech perception to a behavioral principle* (Cambridge, Mass.: MIT Press, 1998).

4. C. Nass, E. Robles, and Q. Wang, "User as assessor" approach to embodied conversational agents (ECAs): The case of apparent attention in ECAs, in Z. Ruttkay and C. Pelachaud, eds., *Evaluating embodied conversational agents* (New York: Kluwer, 2004), pp. 161–188.

5. Australian Broadcasting Company, *Whale dreams*, retrieved from <http://www.abc.net.au/oceans/whale/song.htm>, 2000.

6. P. B. Best, K. P. Findlay, K. Sekiguchi, V. M. Peddemors, B. Rakotonirina, A. Rossouw, et al., Winter distribution and possible migration routes of humpback whales *Megaptera novaeangliae* in the southwest Indian Ocean, *Marine Ecology Progress Series* 162 (1998): 287–299.

7. Australian Broadcasting Company, *Whale dreams.*

8. Australian Broadcasting Company, *Whale dreams.*

9. Australian Broadcasting Company, *Whale dreams.*

10. Australian Broadcasting Company, *Whale dreams.*

11. Massaro, *Perceiving talking faces.*

12. J. R. Beniger, *The control revolution* (Cambridge, Mass.: Harvard University Press, 1986).

13. C. Nass and L. Mason, On the study of technology and task: A variable-based approach, in J. F. C. Steinfeld, ed., *Organizations and communication technology* (Newbury Park, Calif.: Sage, 1990), pp. 46–67.

14. B. Steffens, *Phonograph: Sound on disk* (San Diego: Lucent Books, 1992).

15. Clark, *Using language.*

16. C. Nass and Y. Moon, Machines and mindlessness: Social responses to computers, *Journal of Social Issues* 56, no. 1 (2000): 81–103; B. Reeves and C. Nass, *The media equation: How people treat computers, television, and new media like real people and places* (New York: Cambridge University Press, 1996).

17. Microphone arrays filter individual microphone signals and combine them to enhance sound originating from a particular direction or location. M. Dahl and I. Claesson, Acoustic noise and echo canceling with microphone array, *IEEE Transactions on Vehicular Technology* 48, no. 9 (1999): 1518–1526. For more details, see D. Schreck and S. Nelson, *Directional microphone array processing unit* (1998), retrieved from <http://www.danschreck.com/microphone.pdf>, July 28, 2004.

18. All of the experiments in this chapter are described in more detail in Q. Wang and C. Nass, Less visible and wireless: Two experiments on the effects of microphone type on users' performance and perceptions, *Proceedings of the Computer-Human Interaction 2005 Conference* (Portland, Ore.: Association of Computing Machinery, 2005).

19. M. J. Grawitch, D. C. Munz, E. K. Elliott, and A. Mathis, Promoting creativity in temporary problem-solving groups: The effects of positive mood and autonomy in problem definition on idea-generating performance. *Group Dynamics* 7, no. 3 (2003): 200–213.

20. D. K. Simonton, Creative development as acquired expertise: Theoretical issues and an empirical test, *Developmental Review* 20, no. 2 (2000): 283–318.

21. E. Maisel and N. Maisel, *Sleep thinking: The revolutionary program that helps you solve problems, reduce stress, and increase creativity while you sleep* (Holbrook, Mass.: Adams Media, 2001).

22. Y. Senyshyn, Perspectives on performance and anxiety and their implications for creative teaching, *Canadian Journal of Education* 24, no. 1 (1999): 30–41.

23. N. Madjar, G. R. Oldham, and M. G. Pratt, There's no place like home? The contributions of work and nonwork creativity support to employees' creativity performance, *Academy of Management Journal* 4 (2002): 757–767.

24. J. M. McCoy and G. W. Evans, The potential role of the physical environment in fostering creativity, *Creativity Research Journal* 14, nos. 3–4 (2002): 409–426.

25. Grawitch, Munz, Elliott, and Mathis, Promoting creativity in temporary problem-solving groups.

26. J. L. Adams, *Conceptual blockbusting: A guide to better ideas*, 4th ed. (Boulder, Colo.: Perseus, 2001); T. Kelley, J. Littman, and T. Peters, *The art of innovation: Lessons in creativity from Ideo, America's leading design firm* (New York: Currency, 2001).

27. E. P. Torrance, *Norm-technical manual: Torrance Tests of Creative Thinking*. Lexington, Mass.: Personnel Press, 1974); E. P. Torrance and K. Goff, A quiet revolution, *Journal of Creative Behavior* 23, no. 2 (1989): 136–145.

28. One of two adult female voices (both age twenty-seven) was randomly selected for each participant.

29. D. C. Dryer, *Interpersonal goals and satisfaction with interactions*, unpublished doctoral dissertation, Stanford University, Stanford, Calif., 2003.

30. Torrance, *Norm-technical manual*. Each of the three metrics was ranked on a one (lowest) to five (highest) interval scale by two independent coders. For all three measures, agreement was very high ($r >= .70$). Disagreements were resolved by discussion.

31. Correlations between coders ranged from .81 to .93.

32. Number of words spoken was computed as the average number of words used in answering each creativity question.

33. The paper-and-pencil questionnaire presented a series of textual questions, beginning with "How well do these following words describe how you felt when completing the task?" followed by a list of adjectives. The response scales were anchored by "Describe very poorly" (= 1) and "Describe very well" (= 10).

34. Comfort was an index comprised of four adjectives: *comfortable, relaxed, stressed,* and *at ease.* The index was very reliable (α = .84).

35. B. Gerbert, A. Bronstone, S. Pantilat, S. McPhee, M. Allerton, and J. Moe, When asked, patients tell: Disclosure of sensitive health-risk behaviors, *Medical Care* 1 (1999): 104–111; C. Nass, E. Robles, H. Bienenstock, M. Treinen, and C. Heenan, Voice-based disclosure systems: Effects of modality, gender of prompt, and gender of user, *International Journal of Speech Technology* 6, no. 2 (2003): 113–121.

36. Nass, Robles, Bienenstock, Treinen, and Heenan, Voice-based disclosure systems.

37. P. Blau, *Exchange and power in social life* (New York: Transactions, 1986).

38. Nass, Robles, Bienenstock, Treinen, and Heenan, Voice-based disclosure systems.

39. See chapter 9.

40. The development of the disclosure questions began with twenty-two self-disclosure questions derived from Kroner and Weekes's balanced inventory of desirable responding and Moon's self-disclosure questionnaire. D. G. Kroner and J. R. Weekes, Balanced inventory of desirable responding: Factor structure, reliability, and validity with an offender sample, *Personality and Individual Differences* 21, no. 3 (1996): 323–333; Y. Moon, Intimate exchanges: Using computers to elicit self-disclosure from consumers, *Journal of Consumer Research* 26, no. 4 (2000): 323–339. Six judges (three male and three female), who were not participants in the study, rated the difficulty of answering these questions on a scale from one to ten. Ten questions were selected with medium levels of disclosure difficulty (scores of 4 through 7).

41. This coding strategy was developed by Moon (Moon, Intimate exchanges).

42. Inter-coder reliability was very high, r = .75.

43. "No comment" counted as zero words.

44. The measurement of comfort and the design of the posttest questionnaire were performed as in the first part of the experiment.

45. Here is the results table:

Dependent Variable	Voice Output: No Reminder	Voice Output: Reminder	Text Output: No Reminder	Text Output: Reminder
Number of ideas	3.19 (0.38)	2.40 (0.52)	4.44 (0.35)	3.48 (0.48)
Categories of ideas	3.46 (0.66)	2.77 (0.40)	3.34 (0.27)	2.51 (0.41)
Uniqueness of ideas	3.23 (0.66)	2.75 (0.69)	2.64 (0.63)	2.11 (0.61)
Number of words (creativity)	58.9 (30.0)	34.3 (19.4)	29.5 (27.2)	23.1 (24.8)
Comfort (creativity)	6.55 (1.13)	5.33 (1.45)	6.15 (1.09)	5.17 (0.69)
Breadth of disclosure	82.35 (47.67)	38.61 (22.2)	38.4 (18.4)	14.5 (7.60)
Depth of disclosure	3.83 (0.71)	3.17 (0.66)	4.13 (0.57)	2.83 (0.76)
Comfort (disclosure)	6.50 (1.19)	5.92 (1.61)	6.54 (0.90)	5.48 (1.29)

Note: Standard deviations are in parentheses.

46. Here are the statistical analyses:

Dependent Variable	Voice Output: Reminder vs. No Reminder *t*(22)	Text Output: Reminder vs. No Reminder *t*(22)	Voice Output vs. Text Output *F*(1,44)
Number of ideas	4.28***	5.56***	35.5***
Categories of ideas	4.43***	5.94***	2.25
Uniqueness of ideas	1.74*	2.09*	24.7***
Number of words (creativity)	2.36*	2.23*	0.39
Comfort (creativity)	2.26*	2.64**	10.5**
Breadth of disclosure	2.88**	3.46**	17.6***
Depth of disclosure	2.38*	4.74***	0.02
Comfort (disclosure)	1.00	2.34*	0.47

*$p < .05$.
**$p < .01$.
***$p < .001$.

47. For complete details on this condition, see Wang and Nass, Less visible and wireless.

48. Here is the results table:

Dependent Variable	Array Microphone Mean	Waist Microphone Mean	Comparison of Means $t(23)$
Number of ideas	3.19 (0.38)	3.21 (0.40)	–0.10
Categories of ideas	3.23 (0.66)	2.70 (0.73)	1.87*
Uniqueness of ideas	3.46 (0.36)	2.88 (0.40)	3.69***
Number of words (creativity)	46.4 (14.4)	33.00 (13.9)	2.31*
Comfort (creativity)	7.77 (1.55)	5.79 (1.94)	2.76**
Breadth of disclosure	82.35 (47.7)	42.23 (19.6)	2.70**
Depth of disclosure	3.83 (0.71)	3.09 (0.81)	2.39**
Comfort (disclosure)	8.17 (1.85)	5.58 (2.54)	2.85**

Notes: Standard deviations are in parentheses.
$^{*}p < .05$; $^{**}p < .01$; $^{***}p < .001$.

49. M. H. Cohen, J. P. Giangola, and J. Balogh, *Voice user interface design* (Boston: Addison-Wesley, 2004).

50. J. P. Olive, The talking computer: Text to speech synthesis, in D. Stork, ed., *HAL's legacy: 2001's computer as dream and reality* (Cambridge, Mass.: MIT Press, 1997), pp. 101–130.

51. For a detailed description of the experiment, see Wang, and Nass, Less visible and wireless.

52. The paper-and-pencil questionnaire presented a series of textual questions. The first question asked, "How well do the following words describe the software?" The second question asked, "How well do the following words describe how you felt when completing the task?" The response scales were anchored by "Describe very poorly" (= 1) and "Describe very well" (= 10).

53. Andrea Audio Test Labs, *Andrea superbeam array microphone speech recognition performance using Microsoft Office XP* (Melville, N.Y.: Andrea Electronics, 2002).

54. Quality of the interface was an index of seven items that described the software: *convenient, competent, easy to use, error-prone* (reverse-coded), *helpful, intelligent,* and *reliable.* The index was very reliable ($\alpha = .92$).

55. $M = 4.83$ (S.D. = 1.32) vs. $M = 2.51$ (S.D. = 1.32), $t(22) = 4.30$, $p < .001$.

56. Satisfaction with the interface was an index of four items that described the participant's feelings about the task: *enjoyed, pleasant, productive,* and *satisfied.* The index was very reliable ($\alpha = .91$).

57. $M = 4.60$ (S.D. = 1.29) vs. $M = 2.50$ (S.D. = 1.47), $t(22) = 3.73$, $p < .001$.

58. Wang and Nass, Less visible and wireless.

59. Similarly, psychiatrists try to take notes as inconspicuously as possible.

60. Online NewsHour, *TV jury: Have cameras in the courtroom undermined the U.S. justice system?,* retrieved from <http://www.pbs.org/newshour/forum/january98/tvcourts_1-19.html>, 1998.

61. Online NewsHour, *TV jury.*

62. M. J. Ananny, *Telling tales: A new way to encourage written literacy through oral language*, unpublished masters thesis, Massachusetts Institute of Technology, Cambridge, Mass., 2001.

63. M. P. Couper, R. P. Baker, J. Bethlehem, C. Z. F. Clark, J. Martin, W. L. Nicholis, et al., eds., *Computer-assisted survey information collection* (Hoboken, N.J.: Wiley-Interscience, 1998).

64. M. Diehl and W. Stroebe, Productivity loss in brainstorming groups: Towards the solution of a riddle, *Journal of Personality and Social Psychology* 53 (1987): 497–509; E.-J. Lee and C. Nass, An experimental test of normative group influence and representation effects in computer-mediated communication, *Human Communication Research* 28 (2002): no. 3, 349–381; C. J. Nemeth, Differential contributions of majority and minority influence, *Psychological Review* 93 (1986): 23–32.

65. E. Noelle-Neumann, *The spiral of silence*, 2nd ed. (Chicago: University of Chicago Press, 1993).

66. C. M. Christensen, *The innovator's dilemma* (New York: Harper Business, 2003).

67. M. McLuhan and L. H. Lapham (1994). *Understanding media: The extensions of man* (Cambridge, Mass.: MIT Press, 1994).

Chapter 14

1. J. D. Bransford, A. L. Brown, and R. R. Cocking, eds., *How people learn: Brain, mind, experience and school* (Washington, D.C.: National Research Council, National Academy Press, 1999); M. Goldman, A comparison of group and individual performance where subjects have varying tendencies to solve problems, *Journal of Personality and Social Psychology* 3, no. 5 (1966): 604–607; D. W. Johnson, R. T. Johnson, E. Johnson, and H. Holubec, *The new circles of learning: Cooperation in the classroom and school* (Alexandria, Va.: Association for Supervision and Curriculum Development, 1994).

2. For a contradictory perspective, see S. J. Karau and K. D. Williams, Social loafing: A meta-analytic review and theoretical integration, *Journal of Personality and Social Psychology* 65 (1993): 681–706; S. J. Karau and K. D. Williams, Social loafing: Research findings, implications, and future directions, *Current Directions in Psychological Science* 4 (1995): 134–139; K. D. Williams, S. G. Harkins, and S. J. Karau, Social performance, in M. A. Hogg and J. Cooper, eds., *Handbook of social psychology* (London: Sage, 2003), pp. 328–346.

3. M. Ross and G. J. O. Fletcher, Attribution and social perception, in G. Lindzey and E. Aronson, eds., *The handbook of social psychology*, 3rd ed., vol. 2 (New York: Random House, 1985).

4. A. G. Greenwald, The totalitarian ego: Fabrication and revision of personal history, *American Psychologist* 35 (1980): 603–618; R. E. Nisbett and L. Ross, *Human inference: Strategies and shortcomings of social judgment* (Englewood Cliffs, N.J.: Prentice-Hall, 1980); M. Zuckerman, Attribution of success and failure revisited, or: The motivational bias is alive and well in attribution theory, *Journal of Personality* 47 (1979): 245–287.

5. G. Keillor, *Lake Wobegon days* (New York: Penguin USA, 1985).

6. T. D. Green, R. B. Bailey, O. Zinser, and D. E. Williams, Causal attribution and affective response as mediated by task performance and self-acceptance, *Psychological Reports* 75 (1994): 1555–1562; S. Streufert and S. C. Streufert, Effects of conceptual structure, failure, and success on attribution of causality and interpersonal attitudes, *Journal of Personality and Social Psychology* 11 (1969): 138–147; R. J. Wolosin, S. J. Sherman, and A. Till, Effects of cooperation and competition on responsibility attribution after success and failure, *Journal of Experimental Social Psychology* 9 (1973): 220–235.

7. R. R. Lau and D. Russell, Attributions in the sports pages, *Journal of Personality and Social Psychology* 39 (1980): 29–38. For reviews, see Y. Moon, *Similarity effects in human-computer interaction: Effects of user personality, computer personality, and user control on attraction and attributions of responsibility*, unpublished doctoral dissertation, Stanford University, Stanford, Calif.; Y. Moon and C. Nass, Are computers scapegoats? Attributions of responsibility in human-computer interaction, *International Journal of Human-Computer Studies* 49, no. 1 (1998): 79–94.

8. Ross and Fletcher, Attribution and social perception.

9. T. Winograd and C. Flores, *Understanding computers and cognition: A new foundation for design* (Reading, Mass.: Addison-Wesley, 1987).

10. D. M. Tice, J. L. Butler, M. B. Muraven, and A. M. Stillwell, When modesty prevails: Differential favorability of self-presentation to friends and strangers, *Journal of Personality and Social Psychology* 69 (1995): 1120–1138.

11. J. Holmes, Sex differences and apologies: One aspect of communicative competence, *Applied Linguistics* 10, no. 2 (1989): 194–213.

12. H. P. Grice, Logic and conversation, in P. Cole and J. Morgan, eds., *Syntax and semantics* (New York: Academic Press, 1975), 3:41–58; H. P. Grice, Meaning, in P. F. Strawson, ed., *Philosophical logic* (Oxford: Oxford University Press, 1967, pp. 39–48 (originally published in 1957).

13. C. Nass and J. Steuer, Voices, boxes, and sources of messages: Computers and social actors, *Human Communication Research* 19, no. 4 (1993): 504–527; B. Reeves and C. Nass, *The media equation: How people treat computers, television, and new media like real people and places* (New York: Cambridge University Press, 1996).

14. Nass and Steuer, Voices, boxes, and sources of messages; Reeves and Nass, *The media equation*.

15. U.S. Federal Rules of Evidence, Rule 804(b)3 (2004).

16. Reeves and Nass, *The media equation*.

17. R. B. Cialdini, W. Wosinska, A. J. Dabul, R. Whetstone-Dion, and I. Heszen, When social role salience leads to social role rejection: Modest self-presentation among women and men in two cultures, *Personality and Social Psychology Bulletin* 24, no. 5 (1998): 473–481; R. Janoff-Bulman and

M. B. Wade, The dilemma of self-advocacy for women: Another case of blaming the victim?, *Journal of Social and Clinical Psychology* 15, no. 2 (1996): 445–446.

18. B. J. Fogg, *Persuasive computers: Using technology to change what we think and do* (San Francisco: Morgan Kaufman, 2002); B. J. Fogg and C. Nass, Silicon sycophants: The effects of computers that flatter, *International Journal of Human-Computer Studies* 46, no. 5 (1997): 551–561.

19. C. Nass, Etiquette equality: Exhibitions and expectations of computer politeness, *Communications of the ACM* 47, no. 4 (2004): 35–37; C. Nass, Y. Moon, and P. Carney, Are people polite to computers? Responses to computer-based interviewing systems, *Journal of Applied Social Psychology* 29, no. 5 (1999): 1093–1110; Reeves and Nass, *The media equation.*

20. See chapter 10 for a discussion of the advantages and disadvantages of using *we.*

21. Moon and Nass, Are computers scapegoats?

22. J. P. Olive, The talking computer: Text to speech synthesis, in D. Stork, ed., *HAL's legacy: 2001's computer as dream and reality* (Cambridge, Mass.: MIT Press, 1997), pp. 101–130.

23. Winograd and Flores, *Understanding computers and cognition.*

24. This experiment was designed and performed by C. Nass, A. Berjikly, and C. Yates in 2001.

25. The experiment was controlled by the *CSLU Toolkit* running on a Windows NT machine. Center for Spoken Language Understanding, *CSLU Toolkit,* retrieved from <http://www.cslu.ogi.edu/toolkit/>, 2004. A Dialogics board answered the phone calls.

26. With respect to modesty, there are fewer expectations for males.

27. See chapter 10 for a discussion of the use of *I.*

28. See chapter 10 for a discussion of this point.

29. The online questionnaire presented three sets of textual questions. The first set asked the question "How likely would you be to buy the [first/second/third/fourth] book?". The scale was anchored by "Definitely would not buy" (= 1) and "Definitely would buy" (= 10). The second set of questions asked, "How well do the following words describe the system?" followed by a list of adjectives. The third set asked, "How well do the following words describe the system?" The response scales for the second and third sets of questions were anchored by "Describes very poorly" (= 1) and "Describes very well" (= 10).

30. Likability of the interface was an index of three adjectives that describe the system: *friendly, likeable,* and *pleasant.* The index was very reliable ($\alpha = .89$).

31. Frustration with the interface was an index of two adjectives that describe the interface and the user: *frustrating* and *frustrated.* The index was reliable ($\alpha = .70$).

32. Likelihood of book buying was an index of how likely people were to buy each of the five books. The index was very reliable ($\alpha = .86$).

33. Competence of the interface is an index of four adjectives that describe the system: *expert, intelligent, competent,* and *knowledgeable*. The index was very reliable ($\alpha = .87$).

34. Here is the results table:

Dependent Variable	System Blame	User Blame	$t(34)$
Likability of the interface	8.83 (1.33)	7.69 (1.55)	2.35**
Frustration with the interface	9.21 (1.07)	7.89 (2.19)	2.29**
Likelihood of book buying	8.26 (2.19)	7.24 (1.78)	1.83*
Competence of the interface	5.55 (1.37)	8.10 (1.25)	3.78***

Note: Standard deviations are in parentheses.
*$p < .05$.
**$p < .01$.
***$p < .001$.

35. For reviews of the theory of scapegoating, see C. R. Shenassa, *The scapegoat mechanism in human group processes,* unpublished doctoral dissertation, Union Institute, Montpelier, Vt., 2001; E. Toker, The scapegoat as an essential group phenomenon, *International Journal of Group Psychotherapy* 22, no. 3 (1972): 320–332.

36. M. Hewstone, *Causal attribution: From cognitive processes to collective beliefs* (Malden, Mass.: Blackwell, 1990). There is evidence that the fundamental attribution error does not guide judgments in East Asia or India, where the external environment is given much more weight: J. G. Miller, Culture and development in everyday social explanation, *Journal of Personality and Social Psychology* 46 (1984): 961–978; M. W. Morris and K. Peng, Culture and cause: American and Chinese attributions for social and physical events, *Journal of Personality and Social Psychology* 67 (1994): 949–971.

37. M. H. Bond, C.-K. Chiu, and K.-C. Wan, When modesty fails: The social impact of group-effacing attributions following success or failure, *European Journal of Social Psychology* 14, no. 4 (1984): 335–338; Moon, *Similarity effects in human-computer interaction*; Moon and Nass, Are computers scapegoats?

38. B. J. Fogg, *Charismatic computers: Creating more likable and persuasive interactive technologies by leveraging principles from social psychology,* unpublished doctoral dissertation, Stanford University, Stanford, Calif., 1997; Fogg, *Persuasive computers*; Moon and Nass, Are computers scapegoats?; Moon, *Similarity effects in human-computer interaction*; C. Nass, B. J. Fogg, and Y. Moon, Can computers be teammates?, *International Journal of Human-Computer Studies* 45, no. 6 (1996): 669–678.

39. For a complete description of the experiment, see I.-M. Jonsson, C. Nass, J. Endo, B. Reaves, H. Harris, and J. L. Ta, Don't blame me, I'm only the driver: Impact of blame attribution on attitudes and attention to driving task, in *Extended abstracts of the 2004 Conference on Human Factors and Computing Systems* (New York: ACM Press, 2004), pp. 1219–1222.

40. R. Ho, G. Davidson, M. van Dyke, and M. Agar-Wilson, The impact of motor vehicle accidents on the psychological well-being of at-fault drivers and related passengers, *Journal of Health Psychology* 5 (2000): 33–51.

41. The simulator was a PlayStation2 running the game Gran Turismo 3 A-Spec projected onto a six-foot, rear-projection screen. The game was configured to run in Arcade Mode with a Free Run setup on the Trail Mountain Track. All subjects were driving a Mini Cooper that was selected from the slowest group of cars.

42. All attitudinal questions were based on a Web-based questionnaire. The first set of questions asked, "How well does each of the following adjectives describe how you felt while driving?" The second set of questions asked, "How well does each of the following adjectives describe the car?" The third set of questions asked, "How well does each of these following adjectives describe the virtual passenger?" The scales were all anchored by "Describes very poorly" (= 1) and "Describes very well" (= 10). The final set of questions was a standard scale asking about people's feelings of personal responsibility.

43. Driver's perceived safe driving was an index of five adjectives that describe the user: *safe, secure, steady, good driver*, and *safe driver*. The index was very reliable ($\alpha = .84$).

44. Quality of the virtual passenger was an index of six items that describe the virtual passenger: *well designed, intelligent, high quality, friendly, reliable*, and *fun*. The index was very reliable ($\alpha = .88$).

45. Likeability of the car was an index of six adjectives that describe the car: *like, use, buy, recommend, intelligent*, and *high quality*. The index was very reliable ($\alpha = .91$).

46. Attention to the road was measured by how quickly, on average, people responded to the sound of a honk during the driving session by saying the word *honk*. During the ten-minute driving session, there were eleven honks. The eleven honks were placed at the same temporal positions for all participants.

47. Bond, Chiu, and Wan, When modesty fails; Moon and Nass, Are computers scapegoats?

48. Here is the results table:

Dependent Variable	Scapegoating	User Blame	$t(23)$
Attention to the road (reaction time in secs.)	0.83 (0.2)	0.66 (0.10)	2.46*
Perceived safe driving	7.60 (1.16)	6.03 (2.07)	2.29*
Likeability of the car	8.48 (1.01)	6.32 (1.47)	2.25*
Quality of the virtual passenger	8.32 (0.88)	6.61 (1.81)	2.95**

Note: Standard deviations are in parentheses.
*$p < .05$.
**$p < .01$.
***$p < .001$.

49. H. P. Branigan, M. J. Pickering, J. Pearson, J. F. McLean, and C. Nass, Syntactic alignment between computers and people: The role of belief about mental states, Paper presented at the Twenty-fifth Annual Conference of the Cognitive Science Society, Boston, 2003; C. Nass and J. Hu, Linguistic alignment in HCI vs. CMC: Do users mimic interaction partners' grammar and word choices?, manuscript, Stanford University, Stanford, Calif., 2004; M. J. Pickering, and H. P. Branigan, Syntactic priming in language production, *Trends in Cognitive Sciences* 3 (1999): 136–141; M. J. Pickering and S. C. Garrod, Toward a mechanistic psychology of dialogue, *Behavioral and Brain Sciences,* in press. A similar argument can be derived from accommodation theory. H. Giles, N. Coupland, and J. Coupland, eds., *The contexts of accommodation: Developments in applied sociolinguistics* (New York: Cambridge University Press, 1991); H. Giles, A. Mulac, J. J. Bradac, and P. Johnson, Speech accommodation theory: The first decade and beyond, in E. M. McLaughlin, ed., *Communication yearbook 10* (Beverly Hills, Calif.: Sage, 1987), pp. 13–48.

50. H.-G. Bosshardt, C. Sappok, and C. Hoelscher, Spontaneous imitation of fundamental frequency and speech rate by nonstutterers and stutterers, *Journal of Psycholinguistic Research* 26, no. 4 (1997): 425–448; B. Guitar and L. Marchinkoski, Influence of mothers' slower speech on their children's speech rate, *Journal of Speech, Language, and Hearing Research* 44, no. 4 (2001): 853–861.

51. Branigan, Pickering, Pearson, McLean, and Nass, Syntactic alignment between computers and people; Nass and Hu, Linguistic alignment in HCI versus CMC.

52. C. Darves and S. L. Oviatt, Adaptation of users' spoken dialogue patterns in a conversational interface, in J. Hansen and B. Pellom, eds., *Proceedings of the Seventh International Conference on Spoken Language Processiong (ICSLP'200)* (Denver: Casual, 2002), 1:561–564; Giles, Coupland, and Coupland, *The contexts of accommodation*; Giles, Mulac, Bradac, and Johnson, Speech accommodation theory. People also prefer interfaces that accommodate: N. Suzuki, Y. Takeuchi, K. Ishii, and M. Okada, Effects of echoic mimicry using hummed sounds on human-computer interaction, *Speech Communication* 40, no. 4 (2003): 559–573.

53. J. Zheng, H. Franco, and A. Stolcke, Modeling word-level rate-of-speech variation in large vocabulary conversational speech recognition, *Speech Communication* 41, nos. 2–3 (2003): 273–285.

54. S. E. Stern, J. W. Mullennix, C. Dyson, and S. J. Wilson, The persuasiveness of synthetic speech versus human speech, *Human Factors* 41 (1999): 588–595; S. E. Stern, J. W. Mullennix, and S. J. Wilson, Effects of perceived disability on persuasiveness of computer synthesized speech, *Journal of Applied Psychology* 87 (2002): 411–417.

55. B. L. Brown, H. Giles, and J. N. Thakerar, Speaker evaluations as a function of speech rate, accent, and context, *Language and Communication* 5, no. 3 (1985): 207–220; H. Giles, K. Henwood, N. Coupland, J. Harriman, et al., Language attitudes and cognitive mediation, *Human Communication Research* 18, no. 4 (1992): 500–527; G. B. Ray, Vocally cued personality prototypes: An implicit personality theory approach, *Communication Monographs* 53, no. 3 (1986): 266–276.

56. Reeves and Nass, *The media equation.*

57. Reeves and Nass, *The media equation.*

58. K. Isbister, How do we decide when a computer character is intelligent? Intelligence assessment and perceived intelligence in human-human interaction and how it relates to human-computer interaction, Paper presented at the Lifelike Computer Characters Conference, Snowbird, Utah, October 1995.

59. Giles, Mulac, Bradac, and Johnson, Speech accommodation theory.

60. Giles, Coupland, and Coupland, *The contexts of accommodation*; Giles, Mulac, Bradac, and Johnson, Speech accommodation theory.

61. See chapter 12 for a similar claim.

62. D. B. Buller, and R. K. Aune, The effects of speech rate similarity on compliance: Application of communication accommodation theory, *Western Journal of Communication* 56, no. 1 (1992): 37–53; D. B. Buller, B. A. LePoire, R. K. Aune, and S. V. Eloy, Social perceptions as mediators of the effect of speech rate similarity on compliance, *Human Communication Research* 19 (1992): no. 2, 286–311; S. Feldstein, F.-A. Dohm, and C. L. Crown, Gender and speech rate in the perception of competence and social attractiveness, *Journal of Social Psychology* 141, no. 6 (2001): 785–806; Moon, *Similarity effects in human-computer interaction*; Y. Moon and C. Nass, Adaptive agents and personality change: Complimentary versus similarity as forms of adaption, *Proceedings of CHI 96* (1996).

63. Moon and Nass, Adaptive agents and personality change.

64. Winograd and Flores, *Understanding computers and cognition.*

65. Fogg, *Charismatic computers*; Y. Katagiri, C. Nass, and Y. Takeuchi, Cross-cultural studies of the computers are social actors paradigm: The case of reciprocity, in M. J. Smith, G. Salvendy, D. Harris and R. Koubek, eds., *Usability evaluation and interface design: Cognitive engineering, intelligent agents, and virtual reality* (Mahwah, N.J.: Lawrence Erlbaum, 2001), pp. 1558–1562; Y. Moon, Intimate self-disclosure exchanges: Using computers to build reciprocal relationships with consumers, manuscript, Cambridge, Mass., 1998.

66. C. Nass, E. Robles, and Q. Wang, "User as assessor" approach to embodied conversational agents (ECAs): The case of apparent attention in ECAs, in Z. Ruttkay and C. Pelachaud, eds., *From brows to trust: Evaluating embodied conversational agents* (Dordrecht: Kluwer, 2004), 161–188.

67. J. Weizenbaum, Eliza: A computer program for the study of natural language communication between man and machine, *Communications of the ACM* 9, no. 1 (1966): 36–14.

68. Nass, Robles, and Wang, "User as assessor" approach to embodied conversational agents (ECAs); Reeves and Nass, *The media equation.*

69. See chapter 12.

70. Winograd and Flores, *Understanding computers and cognition.*

71. These maxims were initially proposed by Grice, Logic and conversation; Grice, Meaning.

72. Grice, Logic and conversation; Grice, Meaning.

73. H. A. Innis, *The bias of communication* (Toronto: University of Torono Press, 1991); M. McLuhan, *Gutenberg galaxy: The making of typographic man* (Toronto: University of Toronto Press, 1962); M. McLuhan and L. H. Lapham, *Understanding media: The extensions of man* (Cambridge, Mass.: MIT Press, 1994); J. L. Singer, The power and limitations of television: A cognitive-affective analysis, in P. H. Tannenbaum and R. Abeles, eds., *The entertainment functions of television* (Hillsdale, N.J.: Lawrence Erlbaum, 1980).

74. G. A. Miller, The magical number seven, plus or minus two: Some limits on our capacity for processing information, *Psychology Review* 63 (1956): 81–97.

75. Grice, Logic and conversation; Grice, Meaning.

76. See chapter 12 and J. Morkes, H. K. Kernal, and C. Nass, Effects of humor in task-oriented human-computer interaction and computer-mediated communication: A direct test of SRCT theory, *Human-Computer Interaction* 14, no. 4 (2000): 395–435.

77. Fogg, and Nass, Silicon sycophants.

78. Nass, Etiquette equality.

79. See chapter 13.

80. H. H. Clark, *Arenas of language use* (Chicago: University of Chicago Press, 1993); H. H. Clark and S. E. Brennan, Grounding in communication, in L. B. Resnick, J. Levine, and S. D. Teasley, eds., *Perspectives on socially shared cognition* (Washington, D.C.: American Psychological Association, 1991), pp. 127–149.

81. Nass, Robles, and Wang, "User as assessor" approach to embodied conversational agents (ECAs).

82. Grice, Logic and conversation; Grice, Meaning.

83. R. Axelrod, *The evolution of cooperation* (New York: Basic Books, 1984).

84. H. H. Clark, *Using language* (New York: Cambridge University Press, 1996).

Chapter 15

1. D. Goleman, *Emotional intelligence: Why it can matter more than IQ* (New York: Bantam Books, 1995).

Author Index

Subject Index

Spiral Ancient Anew

The authors commissioned Tokyo-born, nationally acclaimed Sumi-e artist Drue Kataoka to paint the original brush painting *Spiral Ancient Anew* for the cover of *Wired for Speech*.

Brushed using an ancient technique from the 2,000-year-old Japanese art form Sumi-e, the ebony-inked spiral engages as a visual narrative of Nass and Brave's research. Suspended in white space, the textured stroke of the spiral's organic form juxtaposed against computer code immediately establishes the sophisticated relationship between human and computer. Inexorably linked in a dialogue, the spiral and the code influence and interact on all levels. The shared boundaries between black and white, between spiral and code represent not only the relationship between human and computer but also the evolution of human speech over 200,000 years.

Drue Kataoka